THE TASTE OF PORTUGAL

Edite Vieira

Grub Street • London

To Diana and Paul

This new edition published in 2013
by Grub Street
4 Rainham Close
London SW11 6SS
www.grubstreet.co.uk
email: food @grubstreet.co.uk
Twitter: @grub_street

Design: Sarah Driver
Photography: Michelle Garrett
Food Styling: Jayne Cross

A CIP record for this title is available from the British Library

ISBN 978-1-908117-40-3

Printed and bound by MPG Ltd, Bodmin, Cornwall on FSC (Forest Stewardship Council) paper

CONTENTS

PREFACE

This 5th edition of *The Taste of Portugal* sees its return to a hardback format, due to Grub Street's confidence in it – after its previous editions and many reprints. So thank you, Anne Dolamore. Acknowledgements, Foreword and Preface written previously, are still maintained, because they are relevant to this book's journey. In the same way, I make no apologies for my commitment to traditional examples of Portuguese food and products (although I did revise and update the text throughout), because they constitute the basis of all things Portuguese and are the hallmark of my country's – perhaps stubborn – individuality. You can deviate a little here and there, when you find it difficult to get hold of some specific ingredient. But do nag your suppliers. If there is enough demand, they will try to oblige.

Fortunately, Portuguese shops do exist in many countries. Keep looking. I have thought about this problem and offer a few ideas (see Useful Information), but remain convinced that, with just a bit of enterprise, it will be possible to eat Portuguese-style in most places. Or almost… Recreate typical, rustic combinations, such as my favourite one, made of garlic, coriander (cilantro), olive oil and some salt, well pounded together, and you'll be half-way there. These are basic, addictive, wonderful flavours that characterize Portugal. Enjoy them.

Edite Vieira
2012

PREFACE AND FOREWORD TO PREVIOUS EDITIONS

The Taste of Portugal is now in its 4th edition and I must first of all mention my Publishers, Grub Street, who very kindly took up the 3rd edition and, as much has happened in the years since the first edition, have invited me to revise it. To this end, I am indebted to the goodwill of Dr. António Silva, Dr. Mário Azevedo Ferreira, Luís Avides, Ruy Oliveira e Silva, José Aragão and Sue Glasgow, from the ICEP (Portuguese Trade and Tourism Office) and IVP (Port Wine Institute) as well as ICEP officials in Portugal, such as Mr. Francisco Morão Correia, who enabled me to visit some Portuguese regions in order to update myself and therefore the book. I am also grateful to Hotel Altis in Lisbon (through Sofia Nobre) and various other kind people who have assisted me along the way, now and in the past, such as (and especially) Maria Antónia de Vasconcelos, Chief Editor of Reader's Digest in Portugal, my Publishers Maria Rolim Ramos (from Colares Editora) and Francisco Espadinha (from Editorial Presença), Eugénio Lisboa, the Ambassador João Hall-Themido, Prof. Luís de Sousa Rebelo, Maria Adosinda Torgal Ferreira and many others, including my children Diana and Paul, and my late Mother.

However, I must not forget that without my first Publisher this particular book would simply not have happened. It was in fact Martin Kendall, one of the Directors of Hale Publishers, who first realised that a book on Portuguese gastronomy (which he relishes) had been long overdue and diligently set out to finding somebody to write one. It took him some doing and a bit of lateral thinking but in the end he found me and eventually the book was published, in 1988. To set the record straight, this is really how it all started. So I take this opportunity to acknowledge my first Publisher, as well as my latest, and to thank everybody for trusting me.

And now, thanks aside (with apologies to those who have not been mentioned) let us all celebrate – by eating Portuguese style!

Author's Preface to the 4th Edition

It is most rewarding that this book is now entering its 4th edition. After all, it concerns a cuisine which is not very influential in Britain, like the French, Italian or Oriental cuisines are.

When the book was first published, in 1988, the now popular phrase 'Mediterranean diet' had yet to be coined and cooking with lots of garlic, olive oil, wine, fresh coriander and – heavens! – salt cod, was still a bit frowned upon. Of course such ingredients did exist on sale, even then, if one cared to look for them in ethnic shops. However, they have now come out of the closet for good and their flavours are becoming more and more acceptable to British palates.

At the time, I was quite worried about the effect chemicals might have on agriculture and also about the many laws emanating from the EU, which, at a certain point, seemed to threaten the very existence of small holdings and the variety of traditional products such as cheeses like goat's and ewe's, which are such a blessing in Portugal and other countries. I am so glad that, meanwhile, these trends are receding, thanks to brave people who have and are tackling them. What a marvel it is to witness the return to organic methods and farmer's markets and see products such as cheese, wine and olive oil actually being developed as never before.

I include in the book some background information on Portugal (some customs, a few snippets of history and so on) to enhance and, as it were, frame the subject, so that the reader may have some idea of the setting in which the dishes were created. So even if you do not dash immediately into the kitchen to cook Portuguese style, I hope the book will provide a good read.

Until quite recently I thought that reading cookery books was just a mania of mine, but I have now discovered that many people use them even as bed-time reading matter. I would, however, prefer that you use this book not so much as a sleeping-pill as a guide for cooking.

When preparing Portuguese dishes I am, mainly, *matando saudades* of Portuguese food. Those who understand Portuguese will know that *saudade* is something like nostalgia, but somehow not quite the same and very difficult to define, and that the Portuguese are forever referring to *saudades*, meaning they miss this or that, or someone, most desperately. To relieve this painful feeling they must *matar saudades* (*matar* means to kill, hence to kill that deep nostalgia) by doing whatever is needed for the purpose. In this case . . . cooking.

I remember that when my children were small (after we came to live in London) they were always eager for their meals. For a while I wasn't working and had plenty of time for the kitchen, and they were delighted with my cooking. In their innocence they said once that surely the Queen of England did not have on her table such good food as we did. It is always a pleasure to prepare them such typical dishes as *caldo verde* (green broth), *fatias douradas* (golden slices), rice pudding and other delicious everyday Portuguese dishes. And they beg me to prepare 'my soups', each time they come home for a visit.

I used to take for granted the food I grew up with. It was only when I left Portugal, first to live in Africa, then in Spain and afterwards in Britain, that I began to realize how wonderful my childhood meals really had been and how much effort and care my mother lavished on the food she prepared for the family, day in and day out. Christmas, especially, was always something I longed for, as a child, partly because of the magnificent fried turnovers (*azevias*) she made, filled with a *compôte* of sweet potato spiced with cinnamon – my favourite flavouring. I shall always remember them as something unique and, alas, quite lost in the past, for I do not think I could ever again taste sweet-potato turnovers as good as those.

My mother used to have a very dab hand for soups and stews as well. Stews are much favoured by the Portuguese, and you will find exquisite ones made with fish, beef, chicken, lamb or almost anything. The basic preparation for the stew consists of the *refogado*, which I explain on p.22, and it is good to eat even by itself, especially if you have a piece of homemade bread at hand.

I have been 'commuting' quite a lot between London and Lisbon for the last few years, and find it fascinating to observe how Portuguese customs regarding food have been evolving. People are now much more open to international cuisine but, at the same time, are also more aware of the authentic fare still offered at many restaurants, particularly in rural areas.

Much basic Portuguese fare is simple, wholesome food, using straightforward ingredients. There are so many national and regional specialities in Portugal (not all of them available at restaurants, by any means) that it would be out of the question to cover in one single book more than a fraction of them, so I have had to pick some of the most popular or representative. Some dishes demand an acquired taste, perhaps, but I am sure you will be adventurous and try them. And, when you are eating, don't forget to ask others, as the Portuguese do: *É servido?*' ('Would you like some?'), to which they will say: '*Não obrigado, bom proveito*' ('No, thanks, enjoy it'). And so I hope you do.

Foreword (to the 1st edition)

As the author of this excellent and comprehensive book on traditional Portuguese cuisine states right at the beginning, there are not many books on the subject in English, and even less of sufficiently high quality. This in itself would justify the present publication, all the more so since the Portuguese art of cooking has been widely recognized as one of the most valued for its variety, richness and quite distinct character among the cuisines that the Western world may be proud of.

Eating is not similarly important in different countries. To the Portuguese *it is* important. Not only eating but eating well and speaking about it. There is nothing to be ashamed of in this love for one of the great pleasures of life. A notable French philosopher, Michel de Montaigne, once stated that 'the art of dining well is no slight art, the pleasure not a slight pleasure'. No Portuguese, I am sure, would disagree with the author of the famous *Essays*.

Eating well helps shape a better and happier view of life. No one and certainly no Portuguese sees the world quite in the same colours *before* and *after* a good meal. In this we are probably not vastly different from other peoples. Aldous Huxley, who is widely translated and appreciated in Portugal, once stated that 'a man may be a pessimistic determinist before lunch and an optimistic believer in the will's freedom after it'.

In different but not less striking words, the great gourmet and connoisseur Brillat-Savarin used to say that the discovery of a new dish does more for the happiness of mankind than the discovery of a star. Having read with unmitigated pleasure and profit Ms Vieira's book, I was left in no doubt that this useful and vivacious contribution to a better knowledge of the Portuguese art of cooking will do more than a little for the happiness of mankind – at least the mankind of the English-speaking kind.

João Hall-Themido
Former Ambassador of Portugal to Great Britain

INTRODUCTION

A Flavour of the Country

The remarkable thing about Portugal is that despite being so small –only 340 miles (561 km) long and 130 miles (218 km) wide – it embraces so much variety, both in climate, geography, people, food, crafts and so on.

Many races have amalgamated to produce strikingly different types of people, some tall, blondish, sometimes blue-eyed; others rather short, stocky, almost olive-skinned with dark eyes and hair. This is the legacy of so many invaders and settlers in the territory (Greeks, Phoenicians, Carthaginians, Iberians, Celts, Swabians, Visigoths, Romans, Moors from North Africa) before it finally became a nation in 1143 AD.

While being generally considered a Mediterranean country and sharing some of its characteristics, Portugal is quite a separate entity, set out into the Atlantic and, as it were, turning its back to Europe and opening itself to the sea. This, of course, brought the Portuguese to their great adventure of discovery and expansion, right back in the fifteenth century, when Prince Henry 'the Navigator' surrounded himself with sailors and scholars and planned the first expeditions to the unknown worlds only heard of in fantastic tales and legends. It was the start of an empire which lasted five hundred years and spread the Portuguese language throughout the world. It is at present one of the most widely-spoken languages and the official one of seven different countries.

Continental Portugal can be roughly divided into two main and contrasting regions: one to the north of the River Tagus (where highlands and the central range of mountains dominate) and the other to the south of the river, where the land never reaches great altitudes except when the plains of the Alentejo give way to the Algarve. Between the coast and the inland provinces there is a similar contrast, where the coastal lowlands, mainly sandy beaches, are followed by a steady increase in altitude, towards the interior, especially in the north. These characteristics, allied to the wind system and the influence of the Gulf Stream, give Portugal a temperate climate, though again the north is more rainy and colder. It bears more Atlantic features, while south of the Tagus a Mediterranean-type climate is more prevalent, with less rain and much higher temperatures in summer.

Although agriculture occupies about a quarter of the active population and almost half of the land, production far from covers the needs of the people. The main crops are wheat, maize, rice, potatoes, wine and olive oil.

In the lush and picturesque Minho and Douro Litoral provinces every inch is cultivated or covered by forests. The region is densely populated by vivacious and industrious people, much given to folk-religious festivities. Here originated many dishes later adopted by the whole country. Oporto is its proud and beautiful main city – the *Invicta* (Invincible) – resenting the attentions given to Lisbon, the capital. The region is dotted with old palaces and manor houses still lived in or converted into inns, lending an air of dignified elegance with their simple white façades where doors and windows stand out as frames of granite.

In the north-east lie the most remote and sparsely populated provinces – Trás-os-Montes (behind the mountains) and the Beiras – a rugged, spectacular and austere landscape becoming more colourful along the deep Douro river valley which crosses the region and looks up to the vines from which the port wine is made. These are planted in almost inaccessible terraces. Here all is sobriety and tradition, underlined by the warmth of the people.

The Beira Litoral province is noted for its sparkling wines, spas, suckling pig, and marvellous beaches. At its centre, the fascinating city of Coimbra, home to one of the oldest Universities in Europe. Nearby, Conimbriga is one of the most important Roman sites in the Iberian Peninsula.

We come now to the heart of the country – a land of rolling hills and vast plains. The Ribatejo and the two Alentejo provinces cling to an intensely rural life, where pure-bred horses are reared and great spaces offer an abundance of vines and olive trees, while wheat and cork forests tinge the land with yellow and ochre.

The Estremadura province and the majestic Setúbal peninsula are bustling regions, geared to serving the capital. Like Rome, Lisbon is built on seven hills. Its immense port at the estuary of the Tagus once attracted all the European merchants and the Romans, for over six centuries, under the name Olissipum Felicitas Julia.

Around Lisbon, there is a cluster of intriguing towns: Sintra, cherished by the Moors and all the peoples that once held the territory, is a unique World Heritage Site, enveloped by forests and dotted with old and unexpectedly exotic palaces – Regaleira topping them all. Cascais – with its lively fish market – was once just a small fishing village, but it has grown, keeping its charm. And, of course, all towns along the water-front (river estuary first, then sea), from Lisbon itself up to Guincho, with Estoril in the middle: there lived exiled kings, artists and famous spies (especially during World War II, as Portugal remained neutral). It was in fact the flamboyant ambience of Estoril's Casino that inspired Ian Fleming to start his James Bond series.

Down south is the Algarve, which is renowned the world over for its glorious beaches. Less well-known, I am sure, are its important nature reserves and beautiful inland villages. Winters are practically

nonexistent in this region, making it a paradise of figs, almonds, oranges and many other fruits. The Algarve is much more tuned to tourism than any other province, except perhaps Madeira.

The archipelagos of Madeira and Azores are also part of Portugal, although they enjoy a degree of autonomy. They have been compared, quite rightly, to jewels in the sea. Their lively traditions, food, crafts and religious festivities are very deeply rooted and actively maintained with zeal and love. In Madeira (a land popular with the English and a favourite haunt of Churchill's on his painting trips) agriculture is taken seriously in man-made, hard to reach terraces, irrigated by an ingenious system of canals called 'levadas', covering the island. Tropical flowers, bananas, sweet-potatoes, passion-fruit and many other kinds of fruit, sugar-cane and maize, are grown here, as well as the vines for Madeira wine, that most precious of the island's products.

The more remote and also incredibly beautiful Azores islands are true bird and flower havens. Every field and road is bordered with blue or white wild hydrangeas and deep pink azaleas, while blue-green lakes fill old craters. Here, too, agriculture is important, including the cultivation of fragrant pineapples, a large and very well cared for organic tea plantation (the Gorreana) and a limited but seriously taken wine production. An abundance of pasture land is translated into splendid cheeses, each island having its own specialities. The most famous of these is 'queijo da Ilha' (meaning island's cheese) referring to the magnificent cheddar-type produced in vast amounts at S. Jorge's.

Food and Tradition

What is a national dish? How best to classify an authentic regional delicacy?

Fialho de Almeida in *Os Gatos* (*The Cats*, 1893) had no difficulty in expressing what he thought: 'It is a culinary creation which resents being written down in manuals; it is characteristic, incapable of being expressed in amounts of ingredients, fractions of time and the quick or slow action of cold, heat, water, ice, the use of a strainer, a food-mill, a knife or spoon. . . . Like a national legend, a national dish is the product of collective genius: no one in particular invented it – it has been invented by all. When one is born, one is already crying for it, and when one is travelling very far from the country, it is what one remembers first – before even remembering father and mother.'

Having stated so eloquently what he considered to be authentic food, he then complains bitterly about loss of standards: 'Among us the art of cooking and eating is degenerating, like everything else at present. It is a lack of cohesion in people's tastes and it is also the fault of brainless innovators, for whom our national traditions never attain the level of the most uninteresting Anglo-French concoctions . . . I hope you will agree that this matter is well deserving of a patriotic crusade to reinstate the country to its former high standards. Defending their national cuisine, the people will be defending the territory. Armed invasion starts in the kitchen.'

Fialho de Almeida most emphatically declared that, '. . . without a shadow of doubt the Portuguese is the most refined, the most voluptuous and succulent cuisine in the world . . .' because, 'It is true to say that we had excellent masters, having for instance inherited from the Arabs the casserole and the art of frying, which was a lot; and that our voyages of discovery meant more than an outlet for the fighting moods and bad habits of those rowdy noblemen who were going bankrupt in the metropolis. We did acquire – thanks to the spices from the Orient, the tangy bits from Brazil and the art of using sugar from sweet-toothed countries, Turkey, India and the Moors of northern Africa – culinary skills, foods, delicacies, recipes, which turned us into a foremost gastronomic people. There is no other country that can boast such an array of national dishes.'

On a different note Almeida Carrett, another classic writer (1799-1854) in *Introduction to the Pilgrim* also demands fidelity to tradition: 'Let's be ourselves; let's see by ourselves; copy from ourselves – and forget about imitating Greeks, Romans or anybody else', and again, 'I have more faith in popular traditions than in all the books by chroniclers, archaeologists or commentators put together.' (*St Ana's Arch*)

These were the feelings of many patriots at the time, faced with the intrusion of foreign (mainly French) culture and customs in Portugal. They needn't have worried, though. Almost two centuries later tradition is very much in people's minds, especially as far as food is concerned.

The richness of the gastronomic heritage of a country may not be an appropriate yardstick for

that country's whole culture, but it is an important aspect of it. Eating is a basic need, yes, but eating well is an art. It is said that someone who does not care much about food – or, rather, who does not have much appreciation for really good food – is insensitive in other areas too. I wouldn't be surprised if that is true.

In Portugal, a separate country for about 870 years (since 1143) and with the oldest established frontiers in Europe (since 1267), we would be right to expect a rich legacy of culinary treasures and talents, and indeed, despite its small size, Portugal does have a refreshingly versatile cuisine.

A good deal of printed matter and manuscripts regarding Portugal's traditional cookery was lost when Lisbon suffered a major earthquake in 1755. The city was practically destroyed, over 15,000 lives were lost (some say 30,000 or more) and amid the destruction many books disappeared forever. So it was particularly lucky that Portuguese documents dating from the sixteenth century containing medieval recipes were found (only a few years ago) at Naples National Library, in Italy – when, in 1565, the Portuguese Princess Maria (1538-77) married the Duke of Parma, she took with her to Italy her personal library, including notebooks containing recipes and useful advice for the home. This material has now been transcribed into modern Portuguese (though keeping the savour of the archaic descriptions) and it suggests clearly that at least some of the recipes had already been handed down, pushing back their original date and thus making them all the more intriguing from the scholar's point of view. As far as we are concerned, they have the virtue of confirming the really old roots of many traditional Portuguese recipes.

However, recipes in documents such as these probably mirror the customs of nobility and royalty more than those of ordinary people. That would explain, for example, the use of Oriental spices (notably cinnamon and cloves) in a great number of these recipes. Many spices were available in medieval Portugal through *especieiros* –spice-men or spice-traders – but they fetched prices beyond the pocket of the man in the street, even after Portuguese explorers had reached India and the Far East by sea.

The cookery booklets belonging to Princess Maria are methodically and neatly divided into recipes for meat, eggs, milk and preserves. There are also some remarkable hints for the home, which I am sure would still apply – for example, a hearty version of chicken broth (p.36) was recommended for many lung sufferers of the time, and the following formula to treat *esquinecia* (*angina tonsilar* in modern Portuguese, *quinsy* in English). Take cinnamon, ginger and nutmeg, ½ oz (15 g) of each; 4 or 5 cloves; 1 oz (30 g) sugar, all pounded to a very fine powder. The patient must take as much of the powder as can be held between three fingers and push it through his 'gullet', as far as possible. Drink some cold water and repeat three times on three to four consecutive days.

A colourful recipe for milk tartlets, which might well be the precursor of the much loved cream tarts (p.174), says: 'Take a pan and put it over the fire with an amount of water equal to about 300 ml/½ pint and no salt. After reaching boiling point, add the milk and sugar – which should be 8 oz (225 g), if you want half a dozen tartlets. If this amount is not enough, add some more. Then take the flour, put it in a container with one dozen eggs, yolks and whites, and after it is all well beaten add to the milk; it should not be too thin. Pour this into the pan. Boil until cooked and remove from the heat, then prepare the dough, which must include a little sugar and 2 egg yolks and butter, all well beaten. Shape the tartlets and put them into the oven. They must not be overcooked. Then pour the boiled milk cream into them and when full pour butter on top. Return them to the oven. When cooked on top, remove.' The introduction of egg custard in Italy is credited to the Portuguese, and perhaps recipes like this one had something to do with it.

The few cookery books from the sixteenth century onwards which did survive the earthquake also give extremely interesting recipes. As in Maria's notebooks, they call for the use of cinnamon and, curiously enough, mix sugar with chicken, something still found in some regions. Here is a recipe for 'egg-coated chicken': 'Prepare the chicken and roast it, and after it is well roasted cut it into pieces. Coat each piece with beaten eggs, yolks and whites together. When the chicken is well coated in these beaten eggs, fry it in butter, in a frying pan which you must have over the fire. Using the same butter, afterwards fry slices of bread also coated in the beaten eggs. Dip the chicken and bread into a sugar syrup. Then put everything on a platter with the bread under the chicken and pounded cinnamon and the syrup on top.' Another sweet made with chicken breasts, cooked and pounded, mixed with ground rice and sugar, was very popular in the Middle Ages not only in Portugal but also in Spain and Italy (at least). An old recipe still followed in Coimbra is practically the same, step by step, and still given the same name, *manjar branco* –blancmange (p.161).

Things which are common in Portugal today, such as quince jam (*marmelada*), sponge cake (*pão-de-ló*) and cheese tarts (*queijadas*), as well as the use of marinades for rabbit and other meats, are all included in these medieval recipe books, which were, remember, themselves collections of old, traditional material.

Food – if not recipes proper – was the subject of various other surviving chronicles, reflecting Portuguese eating habits from the nation's earliest days and giving a vivid description of the seriousness of this matter, even then.

Kings, nobles and high-ranking military men would choose with great care the various servants whose task it was to wait at the table, serve the wine and keep an eye on the quality (and amount) of the food that went into their master's larder. These servants were accorded special privileges for their devotion and efficiency, and of course their work kept them busy all day, for they had also to care for the many cups, trays, basins and other implements (many of them made of silver) needed for the great number of guests normally present – with the ladies usually eating at separate tables.

Bread was an important item in the Middle Ages, and the best was made with wheat flour. Maize bread (p.51) commonly called *broa* nowadays, was then known as *borona* and is mentioned in documents dating as far back as 1258. It was made with millet and similar cereals, as corn arrived from South America only towards the end of the fifteenth century, subsequently completely replacing the cultivation of millet in Portugal.

Before the advent of metal or ceramic plates, rounds of bread would hold the solid food (meat, fish), and the rich would sometimes discard the bread which had become soaked in tasty gravy, giving it either to their dogs or to the many beggars crowding outside their doors. Cutlery was not much used in those days anywhere in Europe. Spoons had been around for a long time, but their main function was as a kitchen implement. The first 'tool' to make a regular appearance at table was the pointed knife, used for cutting meat and to spear food as a fork does now. Although two-pronged forks had long since been invented and used, albeit rarely, in some countries, most Europeans did not use them, in conjunction with the knife and spoon, until the seventeenth century. The more advanced three-and four-pronged forks were not in general use in Europe until the nineteenth century.

The advantage – if one can call it that – of not using cutlery was that people felt more obliged to wash their hands both before and after eating, which they did not always think necessary when its use was finally established.

What did they eat with their fingers? Mainly meat. There was apparently plenty of it around – at least for the higher classes. They ate it fresh, salted and cured: pork, beef, sheep, lots of poultry and an infinite variety of game. People felt deprived if they did not eat meat at every meal (a view still prevailing among many, even today). Fish was eaten mainly by the less affluent, as well as shellfish and plenty of eggs. People of means limited their fish intake to the days prescribed by the Church for that purpose. Vegetables were also regarded as food for the poor, but everybody seems to have consumed fruit, fresh and dried, especially as a snack, complemented by a large cup of wine. Wine was produced all over Portugal in the Middle Ages (see p.212) and was exported in large quantities, England being the main customer. Even nuns in the convents were quite free to drink wine (this was not discouraged until later), and an old document shows that in some convents they consumed something like 2½ pints (1.5 l) of 'daily wine'.

During the Middle Ages, the Portuguese had two main meals: dinner (the heavier of the two) started between 10 and 11 a.m. and would be finished by noon, followed by a 'siesta'; supper was around 7 p.m. Also, according to various chronicles, a drink of wine and some light food were taken on rising, and the same between meals and in the evening.

For the higher classes dinner would include soup, two or three (most likely three) meat courses, accompaniments and desserts. Supper was generally a version of the same but perhaps on a more reduced scale. Less affluent people would fashion their meals in the same way but with less variety and with just one or two meat courses per meal, and also some fish. The populace often had to content themselves with vegetables, pulses, chestnuts and large quantities of bread, all of it washed down with copious wine.

It is thought that the amount of food consumed in medieval Portugal was quite gargantuan, by our present standards, as it led to laws being passed, occasionally, to regulate the number of meat courses in proportion to the eater's station in life. King Duarte (r. 1433-7), who was called 'The Eloquent' for his culture and intelligence, wrote several books, in two of which (*How To Be a Good Horseman* and *Loyal Counsellor*) he advised, among other things, that people be frugal at table, have an interval of eight hours between the two main meals, and water down their wine. Duarte was one of the five outstanding sons of King João I and his English Queen, Philippa of Lancaster (daughter of John of Gaunt), and it seems that they all had moderate eating habits. That Fasting was practised by at least some of the princes may have been due to the influence of their pious mother.

Prince Henry 'the Navigator', who initiated the Portuguese voyages of discovery from which stemmed Europe's maritime expansion and colonization of new lands, was thus responsible for enterprises which were not only radically to change the course of Portugal's history but also the study of the products of these strange lands. New plants and seeds were brought back from these voyages and some successfully

adapted to the European climate. Others such as tea, coffee, cocoa, peanuts and tropical fruit were transplanted from one new territory to another.

The exodus of large numbers of settlers started with the colonization of the Atlantic Islands (Madeira and the Azores) in 1425 and 1439. Curiously enough, it was from these islands that some of the biggest contingents of Portuguese emigrants would, in time, go to the United States and Canada, and to South America (Venezuela, Argentina and, mainly, Brazil). From Portugal itself over the centuries scores of people followed in the footsteps of the early pioneers. They established themselves not only in Brazil but also in Africa, India and many other places besides. In fact, it is calculated that at present over 4 million Portuguese live abroad (though recent emigration has been within Europe, seeking work). That does not include second and third generations who have been assimilated into their host countries, especially in Brazil, Canada and the United States.

The Portuguese are extremely adaptable. If they were not, there would not be so many of them in all corners of the earth. But when it comes to food, they are forever complaining, when abroad. So, if they live as a family, they continue cooking Portuguese dishes, at least on special occasions, and get together with fellow-countrymen whenever possible, to share hearty meals and drink Portuguese wine, listening to and singing folk songs and the melancholy *fado* and talking with *saudades* about their country. Even the second and third generations keep at least some of the food traditions handed down from their parents and, when they visit Portugal, one of the main attractions is sampling traditional dishes at their source.

Of all the religious and secular celebrations in Portugal, Christmas is the most important as a family gathering occasion, an excellent excuse

and opportunity for the enjoyment of good food, prepared with love, time and the co-operation of all.

Christmas Eve supper is the real highlight of the season, a long drawn-out affair, after Midnight Mass. The classic writer Ramalho Ortigão (1836-1915) states in *As Farpas* (*The Arrows*): 'There is a kind of Portuguese banquet which completely surpasses any dinners you may have in Paris, and that is Christmas Eve supper . . .' Everybody is hungry, the smells from the kitchen are tempting, platters laden with food compete with each other for space on the table and spill over to sideboards and dressers, with fresh and dried fruit, nuts, the ever-present rice pudding and the many fried and baked cakes especially concocted for the season, all in lavish proportions, to last through to the end of the year.

A typical menu for Christmas Eve supper in Minho (the most celebrated of all and followed in many parts of the country, with variations) would include the following:

'Salt Cod with Everything' (*Bacalhau com todos* or *Bacalhau de Consoada*, p.67)

Octopus with Rice (p.95)

Salt Cod Cakes (p.72)

Golden Soup (a dessert, p.154)

Rice Pudding (p.144)

Fried Cakes (p.187)

Punch – Mulled Port (p.221)

Christmas lunch will probably start with a homely and fragrant chicken broth (*canja*, p.36) or, in northern provinces, with the salt cod mixture left over from supper and reheated with an olive-oil sauce. Then comes the turkey or one or two capons, with their trimmings, and similar desserts to the previous night.

Seasonal or celebratory dishes typical of Portugal's regions are indicated in the respective sections, but many of them are also prepared for other occasions, such as the Christmas fried cakes which are also made for Carnival or Easter, at least in the northern provinces. Carnival is still celebrated with great pomp in most Portuguese regions, and food specially prepared for this occasion reflects the care given to this kind of festivity. It follows the pig-killing season, so pork dishes naturally figure on the menu. The Trás-os-Montes province includes *Cozido à Portuguesa* (Boiled Meats, Portuguese Style, p.100), even though this is an otherwise everyday dish.

In the Madeira and Azores archipelagos Carnival is celebrated with street festivities, with young people in fancy dress, music, 'battles of flowers' and general amusements. The Azores reserves its 'fluffy cakes' (*fofas*, p.182) for this occasion. The Carnival is also celebrated with lively parades all over the Algarve province.

For Easter the custom is not so much to prepare special menus as to make sure there are plenty of sugared almonds in the house to eat and to give as presents to all the children in the family, as well as the Easter fancy breads (*folares*) decorated with eggs. In Braga (Minho province) Easter is celebrated with the most solemnity. One of the oldest cities in the country, it was 'Bracara Augusta' to the Romans and capital city for the Swabians. Its beautiful shrines, the cathedral and various important churches give Braga the name 'Portuguese Rome'.

Soon after the Holy Week, in the first days of May, Guimarães (birthplace of the first Portuguese king) and Barcelos – both in Minho – celebrate the Cross Festival, dedicated to the Passion of Christ. Pilgrimages are followed, as usual, by fireworks and a noisy country fair. Barcelos is a delightful Roman town, with many medieval buildings, an important centre for local crafts whose markets attract people from miles around, to sell and buy pottery and the region's traditional handicrafts, such as wood carvings, silver and copper-ware, embroidery and lace. Barcelos has become famous also for its cockerel, which many consider the symbol of Portugal (legend has it that a man wrongly accused of some terrible crime declared that to prove his innocence a roast fowl on the judge's table would crow. To the judge's great surprise the cooked cockerel got up and crowed – hence the man was pardoned.)

In popular festivities religion and pagan customs are apt to get mixed. All over Portugal, in old rites associated with Christian celebrations, saints are given certain protective roles as if they were pagan gods. All the year round, but especially in summer, and mainly in the north-west of the country, there is hardly a Sunday without a *romaria* (a saint's day) here or there, with song and dance, food and wine, after the particular saint of each town or village has been honoured and asked to perform specific miracles.

St Anthony (born in Lisbon, 1195; died in Padua, Italy 1231) is the patron saint of sweethearts. He must be one of the most burdened saints, pestered with requests for finding lost things and, especially, for finding husbands for single girls. St Anthony is celebrated all over Portugal but in Lisbon nobody fails to honour him and the other two so-called 'popular' saints: St John and St Peter. The festivities commence on 13 June and go on until the 29, coinciding with bygone pagan solstice celebrations. Altars are erected in suitable places in the old districts of Lisbon, and the whole night people sing, dance and eat grilled sardines. Everywhere little pots of fragrant basil are sold, to give as presents and to take home, as a sweet-scented souvenir.

At night young people make bonfires and leap over them, singeing thistles afterwards, to see whether they will flower the following day: a 'love divination' of old. Similar solstice festivities coinciding with St John's feast are held in other localities, the most famous of them being Vila do Conde, Braga and Oporto. St John's are, in fact, Oporto's greatest festivities of this kind. Everybody comes out onto the streets, saluting each other, holding a leek or lemon balm in their hands. Altars with various images are arranged throughout the city, and people dance and sing all night. Vinho verde goes well, then, with the roast kid traditionally eaten.

In the country, religious festivities and fairs demand those lovely pasties (*fogaças*) which are also made as offerings as well as sweet buns, fancy breads and bread pies, All Saints Day buns and cakes and other sweets.

Cake-shops and tea-houses thrive all over Portugal, for it is a Portuguese habit to eat cakes with coffee, tea or any other beverage. In Lisbon there are streets where almost every other entrance leads to a cake-shop, which also serves light lunches of savoury pastries, pies and prawn rissoles, generally eaten standing. For a more leisurely meal many of these shops do have tables, where people meet to chat, for business or to do their courting and where sometimes one is permitted to spend hours, having bought only a cake or two and a coffee or tea.

But eating out in Portugal does not consist only of going to pastry-shops. Not only big cities but even small towns and villages have a good number of eating-houses of various standards. The best policy is to choose those which seem to be preferred by the locals and to watch which dishes they ask for. Generally each restaurant will indicate on its menu the *pratos do dia* (dishes of the day) which always include typical Portuguese fare. People do not mind travelling long distances to a restaurant specializing in some particular regional dish. Some are available only in their authentic version in the areas where they originated. There are, of course, modern 'fusion' dishes, available at contemporary restaurants, but by and large tradition still prevails.

Food Festivals and Wine Routes

Portuguese gastronomy has been elevated by the government to the rank of 'National Heritage', following the success of many regional events and, especially, the impact of the National Festival of Gastronomy held at Santarém (Ribatejo) for 30 years now. This colourful festival lasts for over two weeks, in the Autumn, opening comprehensively from 12 to 16h and from 19 to 23.30h – a real magnet for family meals. It consists of a national representation of food, produce, crafts and folklore, all under one vast roof. Mini-restaurants, one from each region, serve full meals and samples of typical dishes, at very reasonable prices, while an upper-floor large dining-room concentrates on serving lunch with a carefully chosen menu dedicated each day to the specialities of a different region. The Festival is great fun and Portuguese families from miles around come every year at least for one week-end, while the locals try not to miss dinner there, every night, for the duration of the great feast. It is a place to partake of food, do some shopping, meet friends and spend time and is completely different from the food fairs we are accustomed to. Should you be interested in savouring the atmosphere and the many tastes of Portugal in Santarém, the Tourist Office will I am sure be obliged to give you details. Consult also www.festivalnacionaldegastronomia.com or write to them at: pturismo.santarem@mail.telepac.

Wine Routes for each province are also a feature, now, throughout the country. It is possible to request a wine tasting at some designated wineries and find out about the many and excellent regional wines. (See Portuguese Wines Chapter.)

Starters and Appetizers

Most good restaurants in Portugal used to have on their menus a good choice of *hors d'oeuvres* and a few still do. These 'acepipes' (the equivalent of tapas), as starters for special lunches or dinners, are very popular as the only fare at receptions or modern wine bars. When prepared at home they are ideal for a spread as a buffet for a party. These are traditional dishes normally chosen for this purpose:

SALT COD CAKES (p.72) – these are entirely indispensable in Portugal. They must be made small, shaping them with a dessertspoon before frying.

PRAWN RISSOLES (p.90) – also made small.

SALT COD FRITTERS (p.75) – again, these should be small.

FRIED ALMONDS – Fry whole peeled almonds in a little vegetable oil until golden. Cover the frying pan, to avoid splashing, but remember that the almonds will be ready in a couple of minutes (turn them now and then). When ready give the almonds a sprinkling of salt.

CHUNKS OF CANNED TUNA, SARDINES OR OTHER CANNED FISH (well drained).

PRAWN, LOBSTER, TUNA OR ANCHOVY SALAD – mix the chosen seafood, already cooked or drained from the can, with home-made mayonnaise (p.133), cold-cooked potatoes in cubes, sliced hard-boiled eggs, olives, a few fine slices of mild onion and some lettuce or watercress (or both).

BLACK-EYED BEAN SALAD – this is delicious cold and a must for this table (p.137). Boiled (cold) chick-peas are prepared the same way.

STUFFED EGGS – Boil the eggs for 10 minutes, plunge them in cold water before shelling and allow to cool. Then slice them in half lengthwise and scoop out the yolks. Mix these into a paste with a little home-made mayonnaise and some canned tuna or sardines (a teaspoon of each ingredient for each yolk used). Cut a small slice off the bottom of each egg 'boat', so they stand, and refill them with the prepared paste. Top each mound with a stoned black olive and parsley. Decorate the plate with sliced tomatoes and lettuce. Instead of canned fish you can stuff the eggs with some tomato flesh mixed with mayonnaise and the yolks into a paste and decorate as before.

SARDINE OR CANNED TUNA SPREAD – this is a kind of pâté which can be prepared in advance and kept in the freezer. To prepare mix very well equal amounts of good butter at room temperature and the chosen canned fish. Mash it really well, to form a smooth paste, season with a little lemon juice, salt and pepper to taste and use for canapés. This kind of spread can be frozen as a stand-by for snacks. Keep it well covered for a couple of weeks or up to a month.

COLD MEATS – *Presunto* (smoked ham), sliced raw good quality *chouriço*; fried *chouriço* in fine slices (fry until crisp in its own fat); slices of *morcela*, also fried in its own fat.

Tea and Coffee Drinking

The Portuguese word *cha* means 'tea' – *cha* being the word used where tea originated, in China, Japan, Indochina, India and Ceylon. The navigators brought the plant back and established it in some of Portugal's African colonies, in Brazil and in the Azores archipelago.

By the end of the seventeenth century tea was already being drunk – and much appreciated – by the Portuguese nobility, and it was popularized at the English Court by Catherine of Braganza when she married Charles II. One can only imagine the circle the Queen must have created around her, probably exchanging Court secrets while sipping tea, during the many idle moments palace life afforded. Catherine was an unhappy, barren Queen and, although the King did not repudiate her for this reason and had great respect for her, their married life was far from easy. But this had been a marriage of some considerable convenience, consolidating a then much needed alliance and affording England a vast dowry, consisting of a large sum of money, plus Tangiers, in northern Africa, and the Indian port of Bombay, a starting-point for subsequent English expansion in India.

Nowadays tea is still widely drunk in Portugal, served rather weak and without milk or lemon.

Afternoon tea and cakes are offered to visitors calling at the house and in pastry-shops. Tea and toast are a favourite snack for the ladies, especially the older generations.

Coffee, however, is the choice hot drink in Portugal. For breakfast, after meals and as a snack, coffee is drunk throughout the day, with or without milk. Cream is not used.

Coffee originated, it seems, in the Abyssinian mountains. It is said that a shepherd happened to notice that his goats became unusually lively when feeding on a certain plant. Word spread around and later the beans were also tried by the people. Eventually, as we all know, the whole world had the chance of sharing the goats' experience!

Although already taken in many eastern countries since the fifteenth century, it was only in the sixteenth that the first coffee-houses were opened, in Mecca. Europe acquired a taste for coffee in the seventeenth century, and it soon became well established. Portugal had the plant cultivated in her former colonies in Africa and Brazil and has enjoyed excellent coffee ever since.

The Portuguese are very particular about their coffee and always demand the best. Coffee is served in various ways, which are given peculiar names: *galão* (gallon) is a large glass full of milky coffee; *garoto* ('little boy') is a small cup or glass, again with milky coffee –one can ask for a *garoto escuro* ('dark little boy') if less milk is preferred; *bica* ('spout'), the most popular, is a small cup of strong black coffee, while *carioca* (the name given to a native of Rio de Janeiro) is a *bica* slightly watered down, for those who dislike too much caffeine.

People go to cafés, cafeterias and pastry-shops at all times of day, to drink their coffee, on its own or with cakes (or rolls, filled with ham, cheese, beef or omelette).

A popular drink for those who want to avoid caffeine is the *carioca de limão* (a lemon carioca) which consists simply of boiling water poured over lemon rind and allowed to stand in it all the while one is drinking the fragrant liquid. Very pleasant and refreshing as a change.

As a cool drink for quenching thirst, however nothing is better than a *limonada* made with cool water mixed with lemon juice (½ small lemon for each tumbler), some lemon rind and sugar to taste.

Much as the Portuguese love their wine (and their coffee and tea), they are also much inclined towards mineral water, of which the country offers a wide range, from the many celebrated and ancient spas dotting the north and centre of the country. In the south there is only one famous mineral water, that from the excellent and beautiful Monchique Spa, in the Algarve. The Azores archipelago also has two important spas, Varadouro and Furnas.

Throughout the country there are some forty-four healing waters competing, some of them bottled – such as the Vimeiro, Luso, Pedras Salgadas and Vidago. These waters are taken for health or just for pleasure. Some have to be taken on the spot itself, where treatment can be had for a variety of complaints, from liver conditions to skin and metabolic ailments. In Portugal it is very common to spend a regular spell at 'the waters' – a therapeutic holiday, combining treatment and rest, amid a beautiful landscape. And both at home and in restaurants the drink to have at the table is mineral water, when wine is not liked or advisable, for some reason. 'What are you having to drink?' the waiter will ask. If wine is refused, he will automatically suggest various mineral waters.

'The valet brought in, on a silver tray, two bottles of Vidago water, just opened,' wrote Eça de Queiroz in *A Ilustre Casa de Ramires* (*The Remarkable House of Ramires*). 'Not wanting to miss the marvellous fizz, Gonçalo immediately filled a big crystal glass: "What delicious water, man!" he exclaimed.'

Preparing to cook

Ingredients
Basic condiments and seasonings

From the fifteenth century Portuguese seamen were instrumental in bringing to Europe, from the Orient, rich loads of spices which, up to that time, were available only via the traditional overland routes and across the Red Sea, being then distributed by Italy throughout the Western World. As the Portuguese had the advantage of carrying and selling the goods direct, they were able to offer them at a cheaper price, and this caused the market for spices to shift from Genoa and Venice to Lisbon.

Despite that, simplicity remains the hallmark of Portuguese cuisine, using only discreet amounts of some spices, herbs and seasonings but nevertheless making the most of them in combinations that enhance the food and make it distinctly Portuguese. The variety of herbs on sale at markets (and sometimes given free of charge to anyone buying vegetables from the stall) is often confined to the most commonly used: flat parsley (hugely popular and included in most dishes), mint, bay leaf and fresh coriander (a great passion). It is curious to note that Portugal seems to be the only European country where traditional cuisine includes a great many dishes flavoured with fresh coriander, raw or cooked, from salads to stews and soups. The most likely explanation is that coriander (cilantro) was one of the many plants brought back from India, during the 15th and 16th Centuries, even though it existed in the Middle East and other places as well.

Here is a list of most herbs, spices, seasonings and flavourings used in traditional Portuguese cooking:

ALLSPICE (known as 'pimenta da Jamaica', widely used in the Azores)

ANISEED (seed and powder, a great favourite for chestnuts and cakes, can be substituted for fennel seed and star anise, but it is worth seeking it out)

BAY LEAF (Mild – known in some countries as Turkish bay leaf)

CHILLIES (known in Portuguese as 'piri-piri' and ready-made chilli paste in various guises)

CINNAMON (Portuguese best-loved spice) (stick and powder)

CLOVES

CORIANDER (fresh) – essential in many dishes (Cilantro in the US)

CUMIN (popular mainly in the Azores, Minho and Alto Douro)

GARLIC (another national addiction)

LEMON

MANDARIN

MINT

NUTMEG

ONIONS (i.e. the type known in the US as Yellow Onion)

ORANGE

OREGANO

PAPRIKA (called 'colorau', this is a popular seasoning made with powdered sweet-peppers. A paste is made with 'colorau', called 'massa de pimentão', used for marinades, roasts and as a seasoning for cured meats, such as the various kinds of *chouriço*)

PARSLEY (the flat variety, small leaved and very aromatic)
PEPPER
ROSEMARY
SAFFRON
SAGE
TARRAGON
VANILLA (stick and extract)
WINE (white, red, Port and Madeira)
WINE VINEGAR
WINTER SAVORY

I have already mentioned onion and garlic in the list but they do deserve a separate note with regard to Portuguese cooking. In fact, we might not have any Portuguese cookery at all without these two vital ingredients. An old Portuguese adage states that 'Salt cod wants garlic'. The truth is most traditional recipes, cod or not, want garlic. As to onions, they are fried together with olive oil or some other fat – the basic procedure for countless dishes. This mixture, sometimes with the addition of garlic and tomato, as well as parsley and bay leaf, takes the name of '*refogado*', and '*refogar*' is the frying process, which can be more or less lengthy, according to what it is being used for.

Tomatoes and peppers

As with so many other products, both tomatoes and peppers (all their varieties) originated in Central and South America and from there found their way to Europe and the rest of the world.

Both Spaniards (through Columbus' voyages to the West Indies) and the Portuguese (via Brazil), brought these strange fruits to Europe the first time. But because Portugal was already involved in going around Africa and thence to India and beyond, such products started showing up all along these lands, following the decision to study and exchange all manner of plants – and even animals. I've called this a *gigantic worldwide pollination operation...* In reality, given the difficult circumstances surrounding these voyages, such endeavours were something quite extraordinary.

Tomatoes grow profusely in Portugal, and are even exported to Italy, to bulk up the Italian canning industry. And since they are so good, they are included in countless dishes and even made into jam (see the Jams Chapter).

Peppers are now, of course, part of the Portuguese kitchen, as well, raw or roasted in salads, mixed in fish stews, processed into paprika, and so on.

The hot kind that grows more easily is a long pepper, called *malagueta*. But the small chillies (*piri-piri*) grow much better still where they were first introduced, i.e. Angola and Mozambique. So now they come from there to the Lisbon market... already dried.

While all these exchanges are taking place, these small chillies came to be cultivated also in South Africa, where they take the name of 'peri-peri'. And that's why the famous (now worldwide) Nando's chain, which popularized the mouthwatering 'chicken peri-peri' (barbecued piri-piri chicken), adopted the name of peri-peri for the dish. In reality, the very first Nando's restaurant was started in South Africa by a Portuguese cook named Fernando, who had left Mozambique – where he resided for some time. He then passed his restaurant on to the present company, and returned to Portugal – where, I am told, he is still cooking, but under another name…

In any case, perhaps you'd like to try Nando's chicken. It is really excellent, and they do have other dishes (including diets) and even sell Portuguese wines to go with their meals. Visit: www.nandos.com to find your nearest outlet.

And here is a thought: can you imagine India without chillies…

Olive Oil

Much has been written in the last few years about the virtues of olive oil. Nowadays most people have been converted to what is known as the 'healthy Mediterranean diet'. That is, one which includes red wine, tomatoes, peppers, garlic, onions, excellent bread and . . . lashings of olive oil, which imparts a very special and wonderful flavour to food. This style of eating has, of course, always been adopted by the Portuguese because, even though not strictly a Mediterranean country, the climate and therefore the crops, as well as past cultural influences, are all similar. You will find that the recipes given in this book, as examples of traditional Portuguese cooking, encompass all these ingredients, including exquisite spicy cakes made with olive oil. Vegetable soups, stews and roasts are also seasoned with it and both at home and at restaurants the cruet-stand will automatically be brought to the table when serving poached fish, boiled vegetables and salads. Olive trees have been cultivated and cherished in Portugal as far back as one can remember and so it is not surprising that olive oil is such an essential part in many dishes.

When eating in Portugal you will notice that most meals start with a soup and that most of these soups are splendid. Well, one of the secrets (apart from the fact that the vegetables actually do taste lovely) is the inclusion of olive oil. A further dash of raw oil added to the plate, just before eating, also enhances vegetable soups. Farm workers in Portugal like to eat large slices of toasted bread well soaked in freshly pressed olive oil. Dishes indicated in the menu as *à lagareiro* mean that they originate in the *lagar* – where olives are crushed.

It is nice to have at hand more than one kind of oil: some of the highest quality, for using in raw salads, mayonnaise, poached fish and so on, when its fruity taste can be fully appreciated, and a more ordinary oil for cooking. However, do not buy bad quality oils. It really is not worth the effort.

Olive oils are subjected to close scrutiny on the part of EU regulations and therefore all countries belonging to this Group are aware that if their installations are not up to standard, they will have to become so or face closure.

Within the EU Portugal is a main producer, though exports have been, up to recently, confined mostly to Portuguese communities spread all over the world. But production is increasing, with many more olive groves planted in the main regions (Douro, Trás-os-Montes, Beira Baixa, Ribatejo and Alentejo).

At present, with the latest methods and state-of-the-art installations, as well as an enthusiastic and capable group of technicians, Portuguese olive oil has acquired a high profile of excellence internationally, comparing extremely well with the best oils produced elsewhere, including the organic kind. Indeed, organic oils are those that are expanding faster, attracting foreign markets – i.e. Germany, France, Belgium, Holland and so on. Some producers actually sell most of their oils to Germany, and hardly keep up with demand.

Some of the best are, for example, Sardeiro, Romeu, CARM (Casa Agrícola Roboredo Madeira) with their Quinta da Urze, Quinta das Marvalhas and Quinta da Calábria, Alfandagh (Casa Aragão),

Rosmaninho, Ollivus, Coop. Valpaços, Quinta da Fonte, Quinta Vale de Lobos, Ourogal, Risca Grande (Serpa), Cortes de Cima, Herdade dos Coteis, Paço do Conde, Herdade do Esporão (especially their Private Selection), Trifas, Olidal, H.Monte Novo e Figueirinha, Coop, Ouro Vegetal, Quinta S.Vicente and many others. If interested in more information, please consult the useful information given at the end of the book, before the index.

Other cooking fats

Vegetable oils, other than olive oil, are also used in Portuguese cookery but never raw as a seasoning. Groundnut, corn and sunflower oils are the most popular. Butter is also used quite a lot. Another very popular cooking fat is lard, given the prevalence of pork meat. Sometimes recipes call for half lard and half butter or oil. Some cakes also include lard and are all the better for it. In fact, lard is the second most popular cooking fat in Portugal, after olive oil, as far as traditional dishes are concerned. When trying to buy lard please ensure it is of the highest quality, otherwise substitute it for butter.

Salt cod

Cod was one of the fish prized by the Scandinavian peoples, even one thousand years ago. In order to keep supplies all year round they used to dry the fish, which would become as hard as a piece of wood. Later, they started importing salt from the Portuguese coast. These contacts gave rise to an exchange of information and the subsequent interest of the Portuguese in cod (which does not occur in its territorial waters) and its preservation in salt, followed by sun-drying. What started as a curiosity led to a life-long passion, with a well-established fishing industry. Trawlers used to go every year as far afield as Newfoundland, from the 15th Century onwards. At present, the Portuguese do not do any cod fishing at all, getting their supplies mainly from Norway and Iceland. However, the use of this fish has never abated and although it is now much more expensive than it used to be, and therefore not considered as the food of the poor anymore, it is, nevertheless, very good value for money, given that it doubles in volume once it is soaked, and is packed with protein.

Salt cod sold at Portuguese shops abroad comes normally from the sustainable waters of Norway and Iceland, via Portugal.

Pork and pork products

Pork being such popular meat in Portugal, the art of curing ham and making sausages has developed to quite a remarkable degree. *Presunto* is smoked ham, laboriously prepared, extremely tasty and used as a raw snack, for sandwiches, with melon as a starter and to add to certain dishes. *Presunto* is made from whole legs of pork preserved with salt, paprika, wine and garlic. This mixture may vary from region to region. The meat is then left between layers of salt for a few weeks, after which the salt is scrubbed off and the meat is hung in the traditional *fumeiro* (smoking place). The smoking can last for up to two months, again according to each region. Once this operation is finished the ham is brushed with olive oil, sprinkled with paprika and then with a little borax, which acts as a preservative. The *presunto* is then ready for consumption, but, to be at its best, it must be left for several months, to mature. It is said that any *presunto* worth having must have been cured for a whole year. The best Portuguese *presuntos* come from the Lamego and Chaves regions, in Trás-os-Montes. Outside Portugal look for *presunto* at Portuguese shops. If this is not possible, substitute Italian *prosciutto* or Spanish *Serrano*.

There are a number of sausages found only in Portugal and even there varying from region to region. They form sometimes the chief part of a meal. Some are eaten fresh, others are smoked for a short time, but the majority is cured for a long period before eating. They can be grilled, baked, fried or boiled and a few are extremely good raw as a snack or sandwich filler.

Chouriço is the most popular of Portuguese sausages, highly seasoned and flavoursome. A few slices of it will improve enormously some soups and stews. When of good quality it is very good raw. Each region has its own versions of *chouriço*, varying the seasonings, but basically *chouriços* are sausages about 2.5 cm (1 inch) in diameter and either short (13-18 cm/5-7 inches) in length, or double that size, in which case they will be tied up in a loop. They are filled with lean and fat pork meat, garlic, red-pepper paste and salt, being thoroughly smoked at the *fumeiro*. *Linguiça* is a variety of *chouriço*, much thinner and longer.

Although similar sausages are made in many other countries, they do not seem to be exactly like *chouriço*, which has a very characteristic flavour and is, to my mind, very special indeed. For this reason I find it difficult to replace with seemingly identical sausages from other sources and prefer to substitute them for *presunto* or bacon. *Paio* and *salpicão* are not unlike *chouriço*, as far as taste is concerned, but these much thicker sausages are made with loin of pork and therefore much better still. The difference between *paio* and *salpicão* is that the former contains very little fat. The spices used also vary.

There are various kinds of very meaty black sausages, which include blood (just as the black pudding does). They are filled with pork meat, bread, blood and wine, apart from other seasonings. Look for *morcelas*, *chouriço mouro* and *chouriço de sangue*. They are all excellent fried or barbecued and are included in dishes like bean stews. They are not suitable for eating raw.

Alheiras are rich sausages made with a variety of lighter meats, such as chicken or game, bread, as a binder, and lots of seasonings in which garlic is prominent. They are delicious grilled or fried, and their colour is yellowish.

Farinheiras are still another type of sausage, also lighter in colour, and, as the name suggests (*farinha* is flour, in Portuguese) made with flour, mainly, pork fat (no meat) and seasonings, including wine. They are very nice cooked together with other sausages in some dishes, although they are an acquired taste, really.

Another pork product included in many dishes is pure pork fat, that is to say, a kind of bacon fat, called *toucinho*. It can easily be substituted for bacon.

If you have no access to a Portuguese shop it is better to postpone certain recipes until you can get hold of these specialities.

Wines and wine vinegar

Many Portuguese dishes rely heavily on marinades (generally made with white wine but sometimes also with red). Wine is also used in some recipes even without a marinade and almost all meat recipes will, in any case, improve with a dash of wine. Other dishes call for the use of a little wine vinegar diluted in water. Do not, please, ever use malt vinegar or such like, which would completely alter the character of the dishes. However, I find that cider vinegar gives good results. Port and Madeira wines are also used to enrich some dishes.

WINE AND GARLIC MARINADE

'Garlic and pure wine lead to safe harbour'
Portuguese proverb.

The objective of a marinade is to tenderize and flavour some meat dishes. The basic mixture is simply wine and garlic but bay leaves, parsley, olive oil, paprika and other seasonings can also be included, depending on the recipe. In the absence of wine (generally white) one can use a couple of tablespoons of wine vinegar diluted with the same amount of water. Some marinades can also be enriched with orange or lemon juice. As a rule, use marinades for poultry and game, lamb, kid and pork. Here is a basic recipe:

150 ml/¼ pint dry white wine	1 bay leaf
2 tablespoons of olive oil	2-3 cloves of garlic, crushed or well chopped
1 teaspoon of wine vinegar, for sharpness	a little salt and pepper

Optional ingredients might be some chilli paste (what is known as piri-piri), a coffeespoon of paprika and 1 tablespoon of lemon juice.

Mix well the ingredients and steep the meat in the marinade for a few hours. Some of the liquid may be used to cook the dish. Each recipe will indicate the procedure.

Coarse cornmeal (maize flour)

Maize grows profusely in Portugal, including Madeira and Azores, so it is used for much more than just feeding farm animals. Cornmeal bread (*broa*) is a great speciality (see recipe in the Bread Dishes Chapter), as well as a kind of soup, called *papas*, which can either be savoury or sweet (in which case it serves as a dessert, sprinkled with more sugar on top). In Madeira and Azores it is used as an accompaniment to fish and other dishes, and, for this purpose, it must be much thicker, more or less like mashed potato. In Madeira this mash is spread out in a tray or large dish, then allowed to cool, cut into small squares and fried (*milho frito* – fried maize). This is of course *polenta*, which has become popular through Italian restaurants. In Portugal maize flour is also used as a thickener for some soups.

Citrus fruits

These precious fruits were introduced into the Iberian peninsula by the Moors who had themselves brought them from eastern countries. They grow all over Portugal but are cultivated mainly in the Setúbal and Algarve regions. Oranges from the Algarve are the best for the table: big, seedless navels, fragrant, juicy and very sweet. These, however, were brought from China by the Portuguese navigators and then introduced also in Brazil. Oranges from Setúbal are smaller and used both for the table and for jams and preserves.

Citrus fruits are widely adopted as a flavouring for cakes and pudding and for delicious homemade liqueurs (see wines, p.222). Both lemons and oranges are cut into wedges or slices to garnish fish or meat dishes at the table. Their peel can be candied and is very popular for cakes (especially *Bolo-Rei*, King's Cake, p.203) or to eat as a sweet, together with candied *abóbora* (white pumpkin) and candied cherries, small whole mandarins, figs, pears, apricots and plums. Candying fruit is perhaps too laborious to be attempted at home, but candying orange peel is not very difficult, and many Portuguese housewives still do it (p.172). I actually still do it, myself...

Almonds

Almond trees grow quite freely in Portugal, especially in the Algarve province, where they cover extensive areas, although lately other trees have been substituted, as agriculture in the Algarve becomes more diversified.

Almonds are eaten as a snack, either roasted or fried and sprinkled with salt or covered with a hard sugar coating for the Easter table, but mainly they are used in confectionery, after being ground. Many beautiful sweets include ground almonds, together with egg yolks and sugar. In the Algarve marzipan sweets are a speciality.

A delightfully romantic legend tells of a Nordic princess who came to the Algarve, having married its Moorish ruler. Winter arrived and, missing the snow-covered fields of her distant native country, she became sad, pensive and tearful. Then her loving husband had an idea: he would have the land covered with almond trees, and at blossom time (around February) they would look like snow. And so it was done. When the trees blossomed, the princess gazed through the window and lo and behold, the fields seemed to be covered in snow! She clapped her hands and laughed, something she had not done for a long time, and she lived happy ever after.

Chestnuts

'Caetana, once she thought of eating many chestnuts and black pudding, foods she was particularly partial to, immediately started putting on weight.'

Camilo Castelo Branco (1825-90), *Noites de Lamego* (*Lamego Nights*)

The northern inland provinces have many chestnut trees and provide chestnuts for the whole country, when in season (some of them also exported, in recent years). Chestnuts are very popular as a dessert or snack, boiled in water flavoured with salt and a handful of aniseed (which imparts a wonderful fragrance to them), baked in the oven or roasted over charcoal in special earthenware pots full of holes. Many chestnuts are dried and then eaten as a snack, or soaked and used in savoury dishes.

In olden times, when there were no potatoes around, chestnuts were used as an accompaniment to many dishes. In Trás-os-Montes this custom is still in evidence. I am told by my friend Maria de Lourdes Paixão, whose family comes from that province, that in certain remote villages they still follow the old habit of burying fresh chestnuts – it seems that they last much longer that way.

It is possible to buy excellent dried chestnuts at health-food shops, and it is worth getting used to their mildly sweet texture.

For cooking, dried chestnuts are best soaked for twenty-four hours and then boiled for about one hour, using the soaking water (having drained it of any loose skins).

Turnip-tops and *grelos*

It is sad to see how some vegetables do not seem to be acceptable for the table in some countries. Turnip-tops fall into this category in Britain. In Portugal they are much appreciated as a delicate vegetable for soups and for accompaniments. They must, of course, be very tender, otherwise they will be suitable only for soups which are to be blended and sieved.

The best turnip-tops are gathered before the turnips are actually formed, looking like the larger radish leaves. If you cannot get any grower to supply you with this vegetable, try to grow it yourself, if you have a garden. They grow very easily and are ready to eat within three to four weeks. Sow the turnip seeds thinly on well-prepared soil and watch the results. Small turnip-tops cook in a couple of minutes.

The leaves of fully grown turnips are also good to eat, at least the smaller ones, and can be used like those above, although they will have to be boiled for longer, like cabbage leaves. They enhance vegetable soups and should not be thrown away.

Just before the turnip-tops go to seed, they present handsome tops, *grelos*, like little bunches of flowers ready to bloom. They are similar but less compact than broccoli heads.

At this stage, the bigger leaves have become a bit tough, but the pinnacles of sprouts and smaller leaves, surrounding them, are tender and delicate; they have long been a favourite green with the Portuguese. They are prepared just by boiling in salted water, to accompany any fish or meat dish, just as one would prepare boiled cabbage or spring greens. If you have a chance to cultivate or buy this vegetable, I am sure you will agree how good it is.

Sweet potato

Sweet potatoes, which the Portuguese have introduced to India, as well as potatoes proper, have been cultivated in the mild climates of Algarve, Madeira and Azores, for centuries. In Madeira, especially, they have become a staple food, being used for countless recipes, as an accompaniment. Despite their sweetness, they are excellent with savoury dishes, but are also used as a main ingredient for cakes. In Algarve sweet potatoes are very much appreciated as a snack, or even dessert, either baked whole and unpeeled, until they burst, with the skin almost caramelized (eat them whilst still warm), fried in thick slices and then sprinkled with sugar and cinnamon, or boiled, then mashed and made into a kind of jam with sugar syrup, to form a thick filling for special turnovers, eaten mainly during the Christmas season.

Quinces

Quinces have been used for jams and jellies for centuries, and in Portugal they have never lost favour, unlike in some other countries, especially in northern Europe.

There are two distinct kinds of quince trees in Portugal (the Japanese quince bush is not known there). One is the *marmeleiro*, which gives *marmelos* – hence the name *marmelada* given to the jam ('marmalade', the word used in English for bitter orange jam, may be derived from *marmelada*, quince jam in Portuguese) and the other is *gamboeira*, whose fruit is a variety of *marmelo*, called *gamboa*, which is bigger, smoother and sweeter than its counterpart but which has the same kind of flavour and perfume. Both are used for jellies and jams, and once in this form they are indistinguishable one from the other.

'Quince cheese' is the name given in English to Portugal's *marmelada*, because quince jam, once dried, can be cut like cheese. Quinces are also nice just boiled with sugar and some water, as a dessert (cooked as you would apples) or baked in the oven (whole and unpeeled), sprinkled with sugar at the table (after peeling, once baked) and eaten still slightly warm.

Quince trees grow almost wild in mild climates. In Portugal one can see them along hedges, and in people's backyards. They are common in Cyprus and Turkey, from where they are imported into Britain. Even large supermarkets now stock them, when in season (around autumn) but ethnic shops sell them, as well. Having an affinity with apples, one can treat them as such, for cooking, although they are too acid to eat raw. See recipes in the Jams and Jellies section.

Salt in cooking

When mentioning SALT in the recipes, I am always referring to sea salt. That is the kind used in Portugal. Normally it will be a bit coarse, as it does seem to give a much better taste, although at the table you may have a container with fine salt.

The most luxurious is the salt called *Flor de Sal* (Flower of Salt), delicate flakes that one can also add at the table, over some dishes. It is very expensive to extract from the salt flats, as it demands intensive, old-fashioned hand harvesting.

There are various regions with splendid salt pans in the country. Aveiro (North), Setúbal (South of Lisbon), the Alentejo coast and especially the Algarve: the Sapal do Castro Marim salt pans and the Ria Formosa Natural Park (well worth a visit).

Flor de Sal is exported also to top chefs in France and elsewhere.

Cheeses

In Portugal cheese is not normally used for savoury dishes, except in more modern recipes, as a topping. But cheese is certainly a very important ingredient for many cakes and puddings and also, of course, to be eaten as a snack, sandwich filler and to serve as a dessert or even a starter (especially if we are talking of small fresh or dried cheeses). The country has always offered a variety of wonderful cheeses (ewe's, goat's, cow's and mixtures of these) but lately many more have appeared on the market and I am glad to report that the problem is one of choice – there are so many, so good.

Small cheeses generally follow their own 'season' and so one may find them either fresh, half-cured or cured. Many are soft and creamy, others hard (if becoming too hard they sometimes are kept in large jars, covered with olive oil, although this may be found mainly at farmhouses). Each region has various specialities, always worth trying, which differ from each other even when made with the same kind of milk. The old saying *pão e queijo e a mesa está posta*, meaning 'bread and cheese and the table is laid', shows that one does not really need anything else for a good meal and indeed many country folk do just that, when working in the open, until they can have a proper dinner later on.

Many of these cheeses are made all over Portugal as a cottage industry and sold at markets or small shops, but larger producers turn out a large range and many regions have now become demarcated for cheese, just as they are for wine or olive oil. Some of the most famous small cheeses are those from the Ribatejo and Alentejo provinces and they can be made with goat's milk or, more often, ewe's. Some are also a mixture of these, plus cow's milk. The label will clarify this point. Near Lisbon, and destined principally for its consumption, there are lovely small fresh cheeses made in the Sintra and Mafra areas. Fresh cheese is also found as a large cheese, sold by the kilo at supermarkets, all the year round. It is generally made with cow's milk, and absolutely delicious.

Among small and medium-sized dried cheeses the best known are perhaps *Évora*, *Nisa*, *Azeitão*, *Serpa*, *Saloio* and *Rabaçal*. Trás-os-Montes province has larger cheeses made with ewe's milk and some also with goat's. They are both excellent, the best makes being *Queijo Terrincho* and *Queijo de Cabra Transmontano*, both DOP. *Monte* is another Northern cheese, and, from *Castelo Branco*, a cheese of the same name, which is as strong as they come – to the delight of many. However, the king of Portuguese cheeses and certainly a great cheese anywhere, is the unique *Serra* (Mountain), about 7 inches (18 cm) in diameter, which comes from Serra da Estrela (Star Mountain, the highest in Portugal) in the Lower Beira region, just above Alentejo. It is made with pure ewe's milk and exceedingly creamy, which makes it possible to be spread like butter during the winter (hence its category as 'amanteigado', buttery). At this stage it needs to be kept with a bandage of muslin, to avoid it collapsing. It is served from the top, by the spoonful. Later it hardens and becomes cured, when it can be sliced easily though keeping a creamy texture. There are many other so-called *buttery cheeses* up and down the country, known as 'tipo Serra' – mountain-type – which can be good but never as good as their role-model.

Widely available in the country and very prized as well is the *Queijo da Ilha* (island's cheese), produced mainly in São Jorge's island, sometimes slightly crumbly, with excellent flavour and hint of pepper. Other cheeses from the Azores are not unfortunately produced in sufficient quantity to be exported to mainland Portugal. This is a great pity, because there are many beautiful cheeses in each island, all of them different – though all made with cow's milk.

For most cheese cakes or puddings, however, the Portuguese generally use *requeijão*, which is made with the whey of the milk and sold fresh everywhere. Its taste and texture are similar to that of *ricotta* cheese, which can be substituted in the recipes.

Hard cheeses – and even *requeijão* – combine very well with quince jam (*marmelada*) and in some provinces pumpkin jam is served instead of quince. See Jams and Jellies section of this book.

I have mentioned here the basic traditional cheeses made in Portugal but there are other kinds, which follow foreign methods, resulting in very acceptable local versions of, for example, Edam and Camembert.

Bread dough

In Portugal it is possible sometimes to purchase prepared bread dough, ready to bake by itself or, more likely, to include in some of the various recipes for fancy breads (with the addition of meat) or even to prepare homely fried cakes during the Christmas season. If fresh unbaked white dough cannot be bought, make up the amount needed for whatever recipe, or make more and bake the rest just as bread.

Portuguese country bread is more substantial than ordinary white bread, and I would suggest that you use strong, unbleached flour, to achieve a good texture, so different from the 'woolly' type of bread.

When preparing dough, all utensils should be kept warm, if possible, and try to ensure that the kitchen is free from draughts. All this has an influence on the finished product. Please see examples of bread dough and bread-based dishes after page 50.

Syrup

Many Portuguese sweets include a syrup made with sugar and water and boiled to various consistencies according to the recipes. Generally speaking this is a very simple procedure, in which a little practice will enable one to become quite proficient and bold, dispensing with tables, thermometers and so on. But if you are not familiar with the methods, follow these hints:

Mix thoroughly the given sugar (granulated) with the water and bring to the boil over low heat, using a strong and roomy pan (to avoid overflowing when bubbling).

Try not to boil the mixture for longer than is necessary, or the syrup will get thicker and eventually turn into caramel; after that, it will burn. If the syrup becomes too thick, add a little water and simmer again to the point needed.

When talking about a light syrup, one has in mind the first stage (smooth), which is achieved very quickly, almost immediately after reaching boiling point (101°C/215°F), while a heavy or thick syrup would be at the stage known as 'the blow'. The table below shows those sugar-boiling stages likely to be met in the recipes, their approximate temperatures if you have a thermometer, and the behaviour of the syrup if you do not have one and want to test the stage you have reached.

The smooth stage (101°C/215-220°F)

The sugar starts boiling at this temperature. The syrup formed at this stage is thin, very liquid and leaving a spoon dipped into it shining and dripping.

The thread stage (103-106°C/225-230°F)

This stage is achieved when a small amount of syrup put between thumb and finger forms a fine thread, when they are separated.

The pearl stage (106-108°C/230°F)

This is reached immediately after the previous stage. The syrup will present pearl-like bubbles on its surface.

Caramel (154°C/310°F)

The consistency of the syrup is very dry, resembling sand, and then turns into a golden liquid. The caramel is then boiled a little further, with great care, until the desired colour is reached.

CARAMEL FOR PUDDINGS

FOR A LARGE MOULD:

140 g/5 oz granulated sugar   1½ tablespoons water

Place the sugar and water in a small saucepan and bring to the boil until a brown spot appears. This means the sugar is turning to caramel. Reduce the heat and continue boiling, stirring with a wooden spoon, until it acquires an overall dark toffee colour. Pour immediately into the mould and turn it round, covering the bottom and sides with the help of the wooden spoon if necessary. It is only too easy to burn the caramel – and thus ruin it. As soon as it reaches the desired colour, remove from the heat and use.

SOUPS

In Portugal it would be unthinkable not to have soup every day, at least for dinner, if not for lunch as well. Generally speaking, soup is a must.

There is always, as the Portuguese say, room for the soup. ('What is the soup today?' is the first question to housewives from their hungry family on arriving home from work). Some people eat their soup as a last course, instead of as a starter.

Some countryfolk like to eat a good bowl of soup for breakfast, if there is any left over from the previous day. This will provide enough sustenance for a hard morning's work, especially if it included some meat or bacon fat, pulses and vegetables.

It is good to see that in many other countries soups of the 'a meal in themselves' variety are also taken seriously. Soups can be very nutritious and satisfying. In fact, why not elect soups as the next best idea for 'fast food' – with a difference?

There are countless soup recipes in Portugal, and they tend to be thick and chewy, blending only the basic thickener (potatoes, beans, chickpeas or whatever) and leaving the rest as it is (cut into small pieces, of course). Consommé-type soups are also popular, the best loved being *canja*, a broth made with pieces of chicken or just the giblets, with or without the addition of *chouriço*, for more flavour, and rice or small pasta. Fish and shellfish are also ingredients of splendid Portuguese soups. On the other hand, bread is sometimes the main ingredient of a soup (apart from being used as a garnish, as croutons).

GREEN BROTH
Caldo Verde

MINHO PROVINCE, BUT USED WIDELY ALL OVER THE COUNTRY • Serves 4 to 6

This soup, extremely simple but very tasty, is perhaps considered the most typical of Portuguese soups nowadays. It is rather appropriate that it originated in the northern province of Minho, as it reproduces the emerald colour of the countryside.

The real version of *caldo verde* includes a little garlic sausage (*chouriço*, see p.25) and, in some places, a tiny amount of onion. A simpler version, with only the shredded cabbage, mashed potatoes, olive oil and perhaps a very small clove of garlic, is really all that is needed. The cabbage must be very finely shredded, which makes it look like little mounds of grass. Because of this, a misinformed British journalist wrote, a few years back, in one of Britain's leading papers, that the Portuguese people are so poor that they even make soup with grass!

Whenever a Portuguese émigré manages to get a little plot of land, he will invariably grow some of these special cabbages (called *galegas*, meaning that they came originally from Galicia, the neighbouring Spanish province), which are tall, similar to the kale and Brussels sprout plants and from which one can go on gathering leaves all the way up the stem. As this variety of cabbage is not normally available outside Portugal (unless in the private gardens of émigrés), I have experimented with other kinds and find that curly kale is remarkably similar to *galega* cabbage. Tender spring greens, when in season, can also be substituted, when nothing else is at hand, although the 'real' thing must be made with *galega* cabbage, of course. My friend David Leite (based in New York), an excellent food writer, says that he uses collard greens, with success.

450 g/1 lb tender kale or spring greens, very finely shredded	2 tablespoons olive oil
	enough water and salt
4 medium floury potatoes	½ small onion, chopped
1 small clove of garlic, chopped	4-8 thin slices of *chouriço*

Cook the potatoes and garlic, as well as the chopped onion in salt water, while you prepare the greens. For this you must gather up the clean leaves, free from the hard core, and roll them up, to be able to cut them evenly with a sharp knife. Secure the rolled leaves against a wooden board. You will probably need to make up several bunches of rolled-up leaves to facilitate the shredding. This is a very easy procedure which you will be able to follow immediately. If not, just cut the leaves as finely as you can, by any other method you prefer. Mash the potatoes with a fork, return the mash to the broth, add the olive oil and the cabbage. Bring back to the boil and cook for just a few minutes.

The cabbage will take more or less time to cook according to how tender it is, but given the fact that it is so finely shredded, it normally cooks in a very short space of time. Besides, *caldo verde* must not be served with mushy cabbage. Allow 4-5 minutes, check, correct seasoning and serve at once. Add a drop of olive oil to each plate, if you like.

In Portugal they will give you a piece of that wonderful cornmeal bread which is so typical of the countryside (see p.51). Otherwise you can serve the soup with fresh wholemeal bread. Place 1 or 2 slices of *chouriço* in each soup bowl. Add a side dish of small black olives, if you can.

VARIATIONS   The basic potato thickener can be used for straightforward similar soups, all very popular with the Portuguese. Instead of kale, use watercress (purslane), turnip-tops (see Ingredients, p.28) or very tender green beans, adjusting the cooking time for these vegetables. Chinese leaves are also good for this kind of soup.

CHICKEN SOUP
Canja
Serves 4 to 6

> Still suspicious, he [Jacinto] tried the fragrant chicken broth and looked up at me . . . His eyes shone in surprise. Another spoonful, and still another, fuller, more consistent. And he smiled, astonished: 'It's good!' And it was: divine. It had liver and gizzard. Its aroma was endearing. And thrice, with great fervour, I attacked that broth. 'I'll have some more as well,' Jacinto exclaimed, thoroughly convinced. 'I am so hungry!' he said. 'God! I haven't felt this hungry for years!' . . . The rich aroma from the soup in the tureen was simply mouthwatering. On a large platter, a succulent chicken covered with moist rice and garnished with sausages had the magnificence of a meal fit for the lord of the manor.
>
> Eça de Queiroz, *A Cidade e as Serras* (*The City and the Mountains*)

Apart from *caldo verde* (see p.34), *canja* is perhaps the best-known Portuguese soup. It is mentioned in the classics, ingrained in popular tradition and considered a particularly good food for the infirm. As far back as the fifteenth and sixteenth centuries, *canja* was being recommended as a food suited to those suffering from consumption. The Princess Maria medieval cookery booklets (see p.11) advised for this complaint a concentrated broth made from one chicken cooked in a minimum of water and then pounded into a purée, which was then pressed through a sieve, to extract all its goodness. This 'dose' had to be repeated daily until the person felt better. The current version is simple enough but always a winner.

1 medium chicken and giblets
140 g/5 oz rice
1.2 L/2 pints water
salt

4 small sprigs fresh mint (optional)
A few dashes of lemon juice in each plate
   (optional)

Clean and prepare the chicken. Cut it into convenient-sized pieces. Bring to the boil together with the giblets and cook gently until tender. Skim the broth once or twice. When tender, drain the meats and set aside. Cook the rice in the broth, taste for salt and add more water, if needed. Serve the soup garnished with a few pieces of cooked chicken and the edible giblets, diced. Some people like to add a small sprig of fresh mint to each plate.

   Use the remaining chicken for other dishes.

VARIATIONS

1 Small pasta or noodles can be used, instead of rice. Also, for a rich tasting broth (and provided it is

not intended for sick people), add a few pieces of *chouriço* (p.25) towards the end of cooking.

2   The broth can be served on its own, as a consommé, perhaps with a few cubes of toast floating in each soup bowl.

NOTE: A simpler *Canja* can also be prepared just with the giblets, provided these are meaty enough. In this case, add a good chicken cube or granules, to enhance the stock. Nowadays there are trustworthy brands you can try.

STONE SOUP

Sopa de Pedra
RIBATEJO PROVINCE • Serves 4 to 6

There is a delightful story attached to this soup, which, in spite of its name, is very rich and wholesome.

A monk used to travel up and down the country, taking nothing with him in the way of provisions or money, so he was forced to beg for food now and then. He would knock at some door, asking for a little bowl of soup. If the people answered that they had no soup to offer him, he would suggest that they let him in to show them how to prepare a very nice soup out of a stone. The astonished hosts would then follow the monk's instructions: 'Please get a clean, biggish pan and add some water to it. Bring it to the boil and, in the meantime, wash a medium-sized stone and place it inside the pan.' 'Perhaps,' he would go on to say, 'we could find a piece of bacon and some bones with meat, and maybe a few carrots. If you could also manage some cabbage and onions . . .' and so forth.

'Stone soup' became well known in the Portuguese countryside. Here is the recipe – although this is the kind of soup to which one can add almost any vegetable and meat that may be available.

1 L/1¾ pints water	175 g/6 oz onions
200-225 g/ 7-8 oz boiling ham or bacon	1 medium turnip
1 medium-sized knuckle of bacon (ham hock)	175 g/6 oz carrots
a few beef marrow bones (optional)	350 g/12 oz potatoes
1 medium-sized black pudding	110-140 g/4-5 oz cabbage
90 g/3 oz *chouriço* (p.25)	1 small clove garlic
175 g/6 oz red or butter beans	1 bay leaf

If wanted, instead of beans use double the amount of vegetables (except the onion) or 175 g/6 oz of soaked chickpeas.

Bring the meat to the boil in the water and simmer together with the previously soaked beans (if used) and bones. When everything is almost tender, add the other ingredients, chopped. Skim off the soup and simmer until everything is collapsing. Correct the seasoning and the amount of liquid (the soup should be thick, like a chowder). Serve from a large tureen, whilst very hot, with crusty bread.

BEEF STOCK SOUP

Sopa de Caldo de Carne

Serves 4

This is a soup intended to use up any left-over beef stock or the broth which hopefully still remains after one of those big *cozido* meals (p.100).

enough stock or left-over *cozido* broth (for 4 people)

4 slices of good-quality white bread, dried in the oven and crumbled roughly

4 small sprigs of mint

Bring the liquid to the boil (you can add some stock made from a good cube, if you need to resort to this) and pour over the bread. Serve with one piece of mint in each plate.

VARIATION   Another way of using the above liquor for a good, everyday soup, is to cook some small pasta in it (1½ tablespoons of pasta per person), until tender.

BEEF SOUP

Sopa de Carne

Serves 4

750 ml/1½ pints beef stock
2 tablespoons small pasta
1 small potato, diced very small
1 medium carrot, thinly sliced
1 small turnip, thinly sliced
¼ medium-sized cabbage (or equivalent amount spring greens), shredded
salt

Simmer all ingredients until tender (20-25 minutes). Add more stock if needed, taste for salt and serve very hot.

VARIATION   A few slices of *chouriço* (p.25) or a little smoked bacon can be added half-way through cooking, as well as small pieces of boiled beef, for a richer flavour and texture.

FESTIVAL SOUP

Sopa da Romaria

MADEIRA • Serves 4

The Madeira and Azores archipelagos have long-standing religious traditions, which they keep faithfully, due no doubt to their insularity. This soup will be comforting after the merrymaking of the *Romaria*.

450 g/1 lb beef (brisket or shin, cut into small chunks)
1 medium tomato, peeled, seeded and chopped
1 large onion, chopped
2 large carrots, thickly sliced
4 medium potatoes, quartered
salt

Simmer the beef in enough water with some salt, until almost tender. At this point add all other ingredients and boil everything for about 40-50 minutes, over a low flame. The idea is to have both the vegetables and the meat really soft and mushy, like a very thick chowder. Serve piping hot, with crusty bread.

DRY SOUP, MINHO FASHION
Sopa Seca do Minho
Serves 4

The Portuguese housewife is thrifty and imaginative. Very little is thrown away in her kitchen, and it is considered almost a sin to discard good food only because it was left at the table. On the other hand another of her traits is being a little too generous with the amount she cooks. So these are two good reasons to create different recipes out of left-overs. *Cozido* (p.100) is a dish you can count on for this, the meat being suitable for various fillings, and the vegetables and broth for soups. But if you happen to have *cozido* left over as well as some cooked chickpeas, try this substantial 'dry soup', which is a meal in itself.

enough mixed cooked meat (for 4 people)
some cooked cabbage (the amount depends on
   whether you use green beans or not) and about:
280 g/10 oz cooked chickpeas
200 g/7 oz cooked green beans (if in season)
2 tablespoons chopped parsley

2 medium onions, chopped
2 medium tomatoes (peeled, seeded and
   chopped)
6-8 slices of bread
2 tablespoons olive oil

Fry the onion in the oil until transparent, add the tomatoes and parsley and fry again for 3-4 minutes. Add this to the pan with the cooked meats and some stock. Boil for 4-5 minutes. Set aside.

   Line a deep, buttered fireproof dish with half the bread. Assemble layers of cubed meat, chopped vegetables and chickpeas. Cover with more bread. Pour some of the liquor over all, to moisten, and leave in the oven (190°C/375°F/Gas 5) until golden brown and crusty on top. Serve at once.

WILD RABBIT (OR HARE) SOUP
Sopa de Coelho Bravo (ou Lebre)
INLAND PROVINCES • Serves 4 to 6

Soups made with game are always extra-special and worth a little extra trouble. Instead of using a whole rabbit or hare, one can of course use only part of it and the carcass, plus any trimmings especially reserved for the soup (the more the better, obviously) and the offal, if this is in good condition.

1 small wild rabbit (or part of it, see above)
90-110 g/3-4 oz smoked ham or good bacon,
   cubed
1 tablespoon lard
1 tablespoon butter

150 ml/¼ pint white wine
3 tablespoons port (or dry madeira)
1 large onion, chopped
2 bay leaves
2 medium carrots, diced small

2 cloves garlic, chopped
3 stalks parsley, chopped
4-6 peppercorns
1.2 L/2 pints chicken stock or any good meat stock

without a very marked flavour, so as not to influence the overall taste
1 tablespoon cornflour, diluted in a little water
garnish – a handful of croûtons for each person

Prepare the rabbit (or equivalent amount of hare), the cubed ham or bacon and all the other ingredients (except the port and flour) and cook until everything is tender. Strain it all, keep the stock aside and discard all bones and unwanted bits. Bone and cut the meats and vegetables, add to the stock, bring to the boil and add the cornflour. Simmer for a few minutes, to thicken. Add more stock or water, if necessary, and the port or madeira. Correct seasonings and serve with the croûtons.

VARIATION   From the same regions, another, slightly different wild rabbit soup:

1 medium-sized wild rabbit, cleaned and cut into
    pieces
110-140 g/4-5 oz fatty bacon, in chunks
300 ml/½ pint white wine
2 large carrots, halved
1 large onion, chopped
1 medium potato, halved

3 sprigs parsley, chopped
2 cloves garlic, chopped
freshly ground pepper
salt
900 ml/1½ pints water
3 slices stale bread

Prepare a marinade with the wine, garlic, a little water, salt, some pepper and the parsley. Steep the rabbit in this and leave for 4-6 hours. Bring the remaining water to the boil with all the other ingredients, add the rabbit mixture (with the wine) and cook until the meat is tender. Drain everything in order to get hold of the rabbit pieces. Bone them. Mash the carrot and potato roughly. Return to the broth the boned meat and mashed vegetables. Add more water and salt if needed and boil again for 3-4 minutes, to blend it well. Thicken the soup with a few pieces of stale bread soaked into it.

PARTRIDGE SOUP

Sopa de Perdiz
MOST INLAND PROVINCES • Serves 4

Any stock left when preparing partridges should be used as a basis for this lovely soup. However, any other game would be appropriate for a soup of this kind, and it can be enriched with all sorts of things, such as cream, egg yolks and port wine. Try your own experiments on a small portion first, before committing yourself to the whole stock.

900 ml/1½ pints partridge stock
90-110 g/3-4 oz smoked ham or lean bacon
1 tablespoon butter
1 tablespoon lard

1 large onion, chopped
enough slices of bread for croûtons (toasted or
    fried)
seasonings to taste

Taste the stock and see whether you are satisfied with the seasoning. If not, add perhaps a few peppercorns, or just pepper. Do not add any salt until after cooking the smoked meats. Fry the onion in the fats until transparent. Add to the stock, boil with the cubed meats until tender. Pour into a tureen, add lots of croûtons and serve.

VARIATION   Rice and shredded cabbage could be considered in addition to the suggestions above, for variations using this stock. If you don't have partridge stock, try the recipe using chicken stock.

PRAWN (OR SHRIMP) AND MUSSEL CHOWDER
Sopa de Camarão e Mexilhões
DOURO LITORAL PROVINCE • Serves 6

This is a very substantial soup, of the 'complete meal' kind.

675 g/1½ lb prawns (or shrimps) in the shell
675 g/1½ lb mussels (live, in the shell)
1 large onion, chopped
2 tablespoons butter
4 hard-boiled eggs
150 ml/¼ pint white wine

2 tablespoons flour
100 ml/3½ fl oz double cream
1 coffeespoon paprika
3 peppercorns
salt and pepper

Prepare a pan with enough water to cover the shellfish (which must have been thoroughly cleaned) and add the wine, the paprika, peppercorns, some pepper and salt. Bring to the boil. Cover. After 3-4 minutes remove from the heat and strain. Discard the mussels that have not opened, and remove the flesh from the others. Peel and clean the prawns (or shrimps). Keep the prepared shellfish aside. Crush the shells of the prawns to extract their juice and use the stock to wash them, strain through a fine sieve. Now bring the stock to the boil with the onion, and boil for 8-10 minutes. Add the flour (made into a paste with water), stir well and boil, to thicken. Add more water if needed, taste for salt, add the shellfish, reheat and serve immediately, garnished with the boiled eggs, cut into small dice, and with little 'islands' of cream floating in the middle. Serve with chunks of fresh bread.

VARIATION   For a more exotic version of this soup add some coconut milk, 1 teaspoon of curry powder and a dusting of cayenne pepper.

SHRIMP SOUP

Sopa de Camarão

LISBON AREA • Serves 4

Shrimps impart a very distinctive and exquisite flavour to this soup, and those with a taste for hot food will no doubt find it excellent with some chillies added.

450 g/1 lb shrimps	4 tablespoons olive oil
1 large tomato, peeled, seeded and chopped	1 dessertspoon cornflour
1 large onion, chopped	1.2 L/2 pints water
1 large clove garlic, chopped	4 medium slices of fried bread, cubed
3 sprigs parsley, chopped	salt and pepper
1 bay leaf	a few chillies (optional)

Bring some of the water to the boil, with salt. Meanwhile, wash the shrimps really well. Cook them in the boiling water for 3-4 minutes. Set aside to cool until the temperature allows you to handle the shrimps. Drain and shell them, keeping the liquor and the shells, which you then mash, using a pestle and mortar. (This will help extract all their juices and flavour.) Boil the mashed shells and the chillies, if using them, in the remaining water for 8-10 minutes. Drain, discard the shells (and chillies), keep the liquor. Meantime, fry the onion and all other ingredients (except the peeled shrimps) in the oil, over a low heat. Add the strained liquor (both lots) to the fried mixture. Bring to the boil and add the flour, mixed into a paste in a little cold water. Cook for 4-5 minutes, stirring, until it thickens. Add the shrimps. Boil again, correct the seasonings and serve over the cubes of bread.

FISH SOUP, MADEIRA STYLE

Sopa de Peixe da Madeira

Serves 4 to 6

This is a chowder-type soup, like most fish soups in Portugal. The difference in this Madeira version is the use of different herbs, which gives the soup a distinctive flavour. Scabbard fish is used in Madeira, but you can use any fish of the smooth flesh variety.

450 g/1 lb fish, plus its head and tail	4 tablespoons white wine
450 g/1 lb tomatoes, peeled, seeded and chopped	280-310 g/10-12 oz stale white bread, cut roughly
6 tablespoons olive oil	2 sprigs savory
1 large onion, chopped	1 coffeespoon oregano
2 large potatoes, peeled and thickly sliced	salt and pepper

Cook the fish in enough salted water to cover, then bone it and discard all skin and bones. Pound the fish slightly and set aside. Fry the onions and tomatoes in the oil until soft (8-10 minutes), add to the fish stock with more water, the potatoes and herbs. Boil until the potatoes are tender, then add the fish pieces and the wine. Boil again for 3-4 minutes, taste for salt and correct the amount of liquid. Serve over the bread.

FISH SOUP, ALENTEJO FASHION

Sopa de Peixe
Serves 4

This is a rich soup with plenty of fish, which makes it a complete meal.

560 g/1¼ lb skate or similar (white) fish
100 ml/3½ fl oz wine vinegar
4 tablespoons olive oil
2 cloves garlic, chopped
8 sprigs coriander, chopped

2 bay leaves
1 dessertspoon cornflour
1 coffeespoon paprika
stale bread
salt

Make a marinade with the vinegar, bay leaves, paprika and salt. Steep the fish (thickly sliced) into this and leave for 2½ hours or so. Then sweat the coriander and garlic in the oil. Add the fish and marinade and enough boiling water to cover. Cook until the fish is tender (10-15 minutes). Remove the fish, and bone it if the slices are not perfectly presentable, otherwise leave them whole. Keep warm. Mix the cornflour with some water and add to the stock. Mix well and bring to the boil for 3-4 minutes, to thicken. Taste for seasoning and add more water if needed. Place the stale bread (cut small) in a tureen, put the fish on top and pour the boiling soup over all, or serve directly in individual bowls.

FISH SOUP, CHOWDER TYPE, ALGARVE FASHION

Sopa de Peixe
Serves 4

The objective of this soup is to make use of a fish head and stock. Generally a sea-bass or hake is chosen and, needless to say, the fish must be impeccably fresh.

1 large white fish head (or 2 smaller ones), cleaned
450 g/1 lb potatoes, thickly sliced
4 tablespoons olive oil
3 sprigs parsley, chopped
1 large red pepper, seeded and finely sliced
1 large onion, chopped

5 medium tomatoes, peeled, seeded and coarsely
    chopped
4 slices of stale bread
4 poached eggs
salt
1.2 L/2 pints fish stock, made with fish trimmings
    boiled for 20-25 minutes, then strained

Make a *refogado* (p.22) with the oil, onion, tomatoes and parsley. When soft, add the fish stock and bring to the boil. Add the potatoes, the red pepper and some salt. When half cooked (10-15 minutes), place the fish head in the pan. Cover again and cook for a further 15 minutes. Taste for salt. Prepare poached eggs. Put the slices of bread in a tureen, pour the soup over it, then the poached eggs, and crown with the fish head, as a garnish. Serve piping hot.

SHELLFISH SOUP

Sopa de Marisco
ALGARVE PROVINCE • Serves 4 to 6

Clams and all kinds of shellfish are very abundant and delicious in Algarve and their use is therefore very widespread. People go to the beaches to gather them, so they could not be fresher.

675 g-1 kg/1½-2 lb live shellfish	2 bay leaves
1.2 L/2 pints fish stock	2 medium onions, chopped
90 g/3 oz rice	2 medium tomatoes, peeled and seeded, chopped
6-8 tablespoons white wine	2 tablespoons olive oil
1 clove garlic, crushed	pinch paprika
4 stalks parsley, chopped	salt and pepper

Clean the shellfish and leave it with its shells on in salted water for a while. In the meantime bring the stock to the boil, together with all other ingredients, except the parsley. Cook for 10 minutes, then add the rinsed shellfish and boil for a further 5-6 minutes. Skim off the scum. Drain the shellfish and set aside. Cook the rice in the liquid. Meanwhile, remove the shells from the shellfish and discard. When the rice is tender, add shellfish to the soup. Taste for seasonings and add the chopped parsley. Boil for 1-2 minutes. Serve with crusty bread.

CLAM SOUP, MINHO FASHION

Sopa de Ameijoas
Serves 4 to 6

Clams are found not only in the southern coast. Minho and other coastal areas have their share as well, and Minho offers a lovely soup made with them.

1 kg/2 lb live clams	3 sprigs coriander, chopped
(or mussels)	4 slices stale maize or wholemeal bread
4 tablespoons olive oil	salt and pepper
1 large clove garlic, chopped	water or fish stock
1 sprig parsley, chopped	

Prepare the shellfish, wash thoroughly and bring to the boil with a little water or fish stock, the oil and seasoning. While the shellfish open and cook for 4-5 minutes, break the slices of bread into rough small pieces and share them between the soup bowls. Remove the pan from the heat, taste for salt, add more stock if needed. Share out the shellfish between the individual bowls, using a slotted spoon. Then serve the stock, with the ladle, pouring it over the shellfish and bread. The amount of liquor you use depends on how thin you want the soup to be.

CHICKPEA SOUP

Sopa de Grão

Serves 4 to 6

This is a wonderfully tasty soup, a filling starter for a good lunch. It can use left-over chickpeas. Try to prepare double the quantity, to keep half for reheating in a couple of days.

350 g/12 oz chickpeas
310 g/11 oz tender turnip-tops (see Ingredients, p.28) or spinach, or a bunch of watercress
2 medium onions, chopped

2 cloves garlic, chopped
3 tablespoons olive oil
salt

Soak the chickpeas overnight and cook them with the onion and garlic in 900 ml/1½ pints boiling water until tender (it rather depends how old the chickpeas are, but it may take over an hour, unless you use the pressure-cooker, which would finish the job in less than half the time). Liquidize, sieve (to ensure a very smooth purée) and put aside. Meanwhile cook the chosen greens in a minimum of water. Mix (with their liquor) with the purée, season and add a little more water, if necessary.

VARIATION   Omit the greens and add 110 g/4 oz boiled rice. Mix well.

BEAN AND CABBAGE SOUP

Sopa de Feijão

Serves 4

A great stand-by, one of the most common, nourishing and tasty of everyday soups in Portugal. It can be varied by adding bacon, *chouriço* (smoked sausage, p.25), smoked ham, a piece of fatty pork, or beef.

200 g/7 oz red kidney beans, well soaked overnight
1 small cabbage, shredded
2 tablespoons olive oil
1 medium onion

1 clove garlic
1 bay leaf
1.2 L/2 pints water
salt and pepper

In a large pan put the water and beans and bring to the heat, together with the onion and seasoning (except the salt). Boil for 10 minutes and then cook over gentle heat until the beans are tender. Discard the bay leaf and sieve or liquidize, reserving a few whole beans for garnishing. Add the cabbage and salt and cook. Taste for salt, add more liquid if needed and serve, putting a few whole beans in each plate. Add a little raw olive oil to each serving.

VARIATIONS   Instead of cabbage use sweet potato cut into small cubes and cooked until very soft; or opt for some pasta (like macaroni) or rice.

BROAD BEAN (FAVA BEAN) SOUP

Sopa de Favas

ALL NORTHERN INLAND PROVINCES • Serves 4

This very substantial and tasty soup can be served as a complete meal in itself and goes extremely well with cornmeal bread or any close-textured wholemeal loaf. Alternatively, croûtons can be added.

450 g/1 lb broad beans (after shelling)	60 g/2 oz rice
90 g/3 oz smoked ham, cut into small cubes	2 tablespoons olive oil
1 large onion, chopped	salt and pepper
1 medium carrot, diced small	4 sprigs of fresh coriander

Peel the shelled broad beans for a really velvety soup. Cook them in water together with all other ingredients, until tender. Blend, if you prefer a completely smooth, cream-like soup. Serve with one of the breads indicated or croûtons.

VARIATIONS

1   Instead of fresh broad beans (fava beans), use dried ones, after soaking them overnight. Liquidize and sieve, after cooking. Possible additions are small sprigs of cooked cauliflower and an egg yolk beaten in, just before serving, whilst the soup is still at boiling point.

2   Vegetarians can simply omit the smoked ham and add a little soya sauce, instead.

PEA SOUP

Sopa de Puré de Ervilhas

This soup is made like the broad bean soup (previous recipe) using either fresh or dried (and previously soaked) peas. Croûtons are the classic garnish for this most delicious soup.

The same variations also apply, or create your own.

VEGETABLE PURÉE

Sopa de Legumes

Serves 4

A homely soup, full of goodness, easily prepared with a blender or sieve, for a creamy texture.

175 g/6 oz potatoes	1 small bay leaf
175 g/6 oz turnips	2 tablespoons olive oil
175 g/6 oz carrots	salt
110-175 g/4-6 oz pumpkin (optional)	600 ml/1 pint boiling water
1 medium onion	garnish – croûtons and a little chopped parsley
1 small clove garlic	

Cook all ingredients together for 25 minutes or until tender. Remove the bay leaf and liquidize. Add more liquid if necessary. Taste for salt and serve with the parsley and croûtons.

VARIATION I like to make this soup omitting the turnip and adding a good tablespoon of finely cut fresh coriander leaves, during the last two minutes of boiling. In this instance I omit also the parsley garnish.

TOMATO, EGG AND BREAD SOUP

Sopa de Tomate, com Ovo e Pão

LISBON REGION • Serves 4

This is a very homely dish, belonging to the thick soup kind, and is easily transformed into a light meal by itself. It is pleasant and nutritious, and really simple to prepare. I use it very often for my family when wanting to produce something wholesome, cheap, quick, colourful and tasty.

600 ml/1 pint water, to start with
225 g/8 oz ripe tomatoes
175 g/6 oz onions
300 g/10 oz potatoes
4 eggs
4 thick slices of day-old farmhouse-type bread
2 tablespoons good olive oil
2 sprigs of parsley, chopped
1 small clove of garlic, peeled and crushed with
    some salt
bay leaf
¼ teaspoon paprika (optional)

Put the oil in a saucepan and gently fry the sliced onion until golden. Add the peeled and seeded tomatoes, cut into small pieces, and add the bay leaf, garlic, parsley and paprika, if using. Sweat all this together for about 5 minutes, then add boiling water. Add the potatoes, peeled and thickly sliced, and some salt. Cover the pan and simmer, until the potatoes are tender (about 25 minutes). Try for salt and see whether it needs any more water (it should have the consistency of a hotpot after adding the bread, which, of course, will absorb some liquid, so allow for this). Serve in soup bowls containing a slice of bread, and top with a poached egg for each person. Traditionally the eggs are poached in the soup itself, before removing from the heat and after checking the amount of liquid and seasoning.

GREEN BEAN SOUP WITH TOMATO
Sopa de Feijão Verde com Tomate
RIBATEJO PROVINCE • Serves 4

When green beans are in season, the Portuguese use them very often, either as a vegetable for meat and fish dishes or in soups. Apart from a kind of *caldo verde* soup, as indicated in variations for *caldo verde* (p.34), green beans make a delicious tomato-and-onion-based soup, as used in Ribatejo.

225 g/8 oz very tender green beans	110 g/4 oz ripe tomatoes, peeled, seeded and
1 medium onion, cut into rings	chopped
2 sprigs parsley, chopped	4 medium floury potatoes
1 small clove garlic, finely chopped	pinch of oregano (optional)
1 small bay leaf	salt
2 tablespoons olive oil	enough water for 4 people

Fry the onion in the oil over gentle heat for 4-5 minutes. Add the tomato, parsley, garlic and bay leaf and fry for another 2-3 minutes. Add about 900 ml/1½ pints boiling water and some salt, as well as the potatoes, peeled and cut in half. Allow to boil for 5 minutes, then add the finely cut green beans and cook everything until tender, over a low flame. Remove and discard the bay leaf, remove the potatoes and mash, adding the purée to the soup again (do not worry if the potatoes have broken a little in the soup), taste for seasoning and serve piping hot. Add a little oregano to each plate, after serving.

VARIATION A richer version of this soup is obtained by adding a few pieces of homemade bread to each plate, before pouring the soup, and a poached egg, topping the bread. In this case do not sprinkle with oregano.

DRIED CHESTNUT SOUP
Sopa de Castanhas Piladas
NORTHERN PROVINCES • Serves 4

The chestnut season is not very long, and dried chestnuts are sometimes used. They have a chewy texture and a mild sweetness all their own.

90-110 g/3-4 oz dried chestnuts, soaked overnight	3 tablespoons olive oil
(keep the water afterwards)	1 medium onion, sliced
60 g/2 oz rice	salt
90 g/3 oz butterbeans (soaked overnight)	

Fry the onion in the oil, until soft but not coloured. Set aside. Bring the beans and chestnuts to the boil (use the water from soaking the chestnuts). When almost tender, add the rice and more liquid if necessary, plus salt and the oil and onion mixture. Cover and cook. When everything is tender, taste for salt and correct amount of liquid. Serve very hot, on cold days.

CORNMEAL PORRIDGE
Papas de Milho
MOST INLAND PROVINCES • Serves 4 to 6

See Ingredients, p.27. This savoury dish can be classed as a soup, and its thickness rather depends on personal taste. Generally, it is served like a pap, with the consistency of a thick custard. On cold days, it is a comforting and filling first course. See also sweet cornmeal porridge, p.164.

200 g/7 oz coarse cornmeal
900 ml/1½ pints water

2 tablespoons olive oil
salt

Bring half the water to the boil. Meanwhile mix the meal with the remaining water. Add to the pan. Combine well, over low heat and add the oil and a little salt. Cover and cook for 15-20 minutes, stirring from time to time to prevent its becoming lumpy. Add more water if you find it too thick. Taste for salt and serve piping hot. Once tried, one is sure to want *papas* occasionally.

VARIATION Use half the amount of cornmeal flour and add to the pan a bunch of prepared watercress or similar amount of spinach, or turnip-tops.

NOTE Cornmeal porridge is what is known as *polenta* and has become popular lately. In Portugal, however, it is seasoned with olive oil – except in Madeira, where they use butter – but never with cheese. The recipes given here are a thinner version of the *polenta* that can be served as an accompaniment and has a thickness similar to that of mashed potato. Nowadays most shops sell a kind of easy-cook *polenta* quite acceptable for these dishes.

BREAD AND BREAD DISHES

Bread has always been an important staple in Portugal and is ever present at the table, at every meal. The Romans brought wheat to the territory, but maize and rye are also used. There are many traditional bread recipes all over the country, comprising soups, main dishes and desserts – so many, in fact, that they deserve a chapter all their own.

There are the *Açordas*, which generally consist of bread boiled with a few other ingredients, forming a lumpy sort of mixture (do not be put off by the description, because even though bread dishes may not always look terribly glamorous, they are extremely attractive to the palate); the *Ensopados*, which are a kind of stew; the *Migas*, another variation on *Açorda* but with some significant differences; the 'dry soups' and *Gaspachos*; and the sweet dishes – to crown it all.

These recipes have the obvious advantage of using up stale bread lying about the house. In Portugal there is a very high bread consumption which explains why it gets to be left over in sufficient quantities to justify cooking it. There is an old Portuguese saying: 'Broth without bread only in hell.' In the countryside there is a very common snack called *Sopas de Cavalo Cansado* (Tired Horse Soup). It consists of pieces of bread soaked in red wine in a large bowl and then generously sprinkled with sugar. It is a wonderful reviver: hence the name. If it can revive a horse it can revive anyone.

Bread used in *açordas* and all other bread dishes must, nevertheless, be of good quality. In country homes there will perhaps be homemade bread, though now less frequently. But all over Portugal it is possible to buy the so-called peasant loaf, which is not quite white but not wholemeal either – a mixture of the two. Greek and Italian breads are similar. They are much more solid and close-textured than an ordinary white loaf. An unbleached stoneground white flour will be the nearest to the flour used for this bread. Although most good breads can be used for the recipes, the dish may turn out slightly different from its Portuguese original. Avoid, please, those excessively white, 'lifeless' breads of the 'cotton-wool' variety, which would produce a bland, less appealing pap.

Bread dishes may have started as a cheap solution for a square meal, but they went on to occupy their rightful place among the most original and tasty Portugal has to offer.

CORNMEAL BREAD
Broa de Milho
Makes one cornmeal loaf

This heavy round loaf came originally from the northern provinces but is now common all over Portugal and is typical peasant bread at its best. *Pão de Milho* or *broa* is now available in every town supermarket, but I am sure my tastebuds do not deceive me when I compare the long-lost *broa* my grandmother used to bake when I was a child most favourably against the current commercial version.

When it is properly made, cornmeal bread crumbles very easily and is ideal to thicken soups (*caldo verde*, for example, which is traditionally served with a slice of cornmeal bread by the side, see p.34). It is also good to eat with those delicious small black olives so typical of Portuguese tables or with cheese or, when freshly baked, just on its own, to appreciate fully its thick crust and mealy texture.

In some Portuguese provinces where white corn prevails, the *broa* is obviously made with whitish cornmeal, but ordinary yellow corn is most commonly used. The results, with either, are similar. The proportion of wheat (which is always added, as cornmeal by itself would be too heavy) varies from region to region. Recipes for maize bread are handed down from mother to daughter and followed automatically – nothing written down, just the eye and the experienced hand for measuring and calculating. I would advise beginners to start with half the amounts stated. Do not be put off by the 'boiling water method', which is an essential part of cornmeal breadmaking.

300 ml/½ pint boiling water	for sprinkling
110 g/4 oz cornmeal (coarse maize flour)	1 sachet (7 g) easy blend yeast
225 g/8 oz strong white bread flour – plus a little	1 teaspoon sugar and a teaspoon of salt

(This is a light cornmeal bread recipe, to get you used to it. A traditional loaf uses equal amounts of both flours or even twice as much cornmeal. Whatever proportion you decide to adopt, the preparation method is still the same, and the end result always delicious.)

Place the cornmeal in a large bowl and pour the boiling water over it. Using a spatula (to avoid burning your fingers) mix both very well, for a couple of minutes. Set aside to cool a bit (for about 8 minutes), then add the other ingredients, previously well mixed together. Work and knead the dough until smooth. You may need to add a little tepid water or some flour, depending on whether the dough is too dry or too wet. Cover with a tea towel or oiled polythene and place in a warm spot, to rise (40-45 minutes). It may not double in volume, but do not worry – this is a heavy loaf. Knock the dough back and knead for a couple of minutes. Shape into a ball and roll it well in wheat flour. Place on baking tray, cover again and let it rest for 40 minutes or so. Meantime turn the oven to 220°C/425°F/Gas 7. Bake the loaf for around 30-35 minutes, until it sounds hollow when tapped underneath. The loaf will have lovely yellow cracks all over, amongst the whitish thick crust. Place on a wire rack to cool. Cornmeal bread keeps well (place it in a plastic bag, inside a bread tin, after cooling). It also freezes well. Serve it to accompany soups, to make dishes as indicated further on, and to eat with olives or cheese.

WHITE BREAD/ROLLS

750 g/1½ lb strong bread flour
1 sachet (7 g) easy blend yeast
60 g/2 oz fat (half butter, half light olive oil)

2 teaspoons salt and a coffeespoon of sugar
450 ml/¾ pint warm water (more than tepid)

Using a large bowl, mix the fats, salt, sugar, yeast and flour. Add the warm water and work the ingredients into a soft dough. Place now on a floured surface and knead for 10-12 minutes. Divide the dough, shaping it into two small loaves or, if making rolls, shape about 10-12, placing them into a greased baking tin. Set aside, in a warm place, to rise, covering with cling film or greased polythene. When doubled in size bake in a pre-heated oven (230°C/450°F/Gas 8) for about 35 minutes, if you shaped the dough into loaves, or 190°C/375°F/Gas 5 if making rolls.

AÇORDAS

BREAD-PAP, PORTUGUESE STYLE
Açorda
Serves 4

This is the simplest version of *açorda*, but none the worse for it. It is surprisingly tasty. Nowadays perhaps it has lost favour as a stand-by dish for feeding infants, but not long ago it was still very commonly used for this purpose – although grown-ups never turned away from it either. Like many other forms of *açorda*, it is suitable as an accompaniment to fried or grilled fish.

300 g/10 oz stale bread, in small chunks
1 large clove of garlic, finely chopped
2 tablespoons olive oil

300 ml/½ pint salted boiling water
1 large or 2 small eggs (optional)

Mix the olive oil and garlic with the boiling water, add the bread, bring to the heat. Cook gently, while stirring, until it becomes a soft pap, with the consistency of thick porridge (about 10 minutes).

You can enrich it with the beaten eggs, added just at the end of cooking. Mix thoroughly and serve at once. Discard the garlic.

CORIANDER (CILANTRO) BREAD SOUP-ALENTEJO
Açorda Alentejana

Serves 4

This is the most aromatic of bread dishes, and the Portuguese are extremely fond of it. Fortunately it is very easily made, but the use of plenty of fresh coriander is an absolute must. Should you be unable to get it, postpone preparing this *açorda* until such time as you have this delectable herb at hand.

  450 g/1 lb day-old bread (follow hints on the
    bread to use for açordas on p.50)
  4 tablespoons olive oil
  4 eggs, poached
  3 cloves garlic
  900 ml/1½ pints boiling water
  8-10 good sprigs fresh coriander (cilantro)
  salt

Process the garlic and coriander (or crush with some salt with a pestle and mortar) and place this pulp in a large serving bowl or tureen. Add the boiling water, salt to taste, and the oil. Break the bread into small chunks and add to the water. Soak it well. Divide among 4 soup bowls and place a poached egg on each. Serve at once.

This is meant as a soup, and it should not be excessively dry. It all depends on the kind of bread used, but you may need to add a little more boiling salted water, in order to have some liquid around the bread.

This *açorda* can be served with a side dish of fried or grilled fish and olives.

VARIATION A very light version of this soup can be made omitting the bread and serving the fragrant broth in a cup, with a quail egg on top.

SEAFOOD AÇORDA

Açorda de marisco

ESTREMADURA, MAINLY THE LISBON AREA • Serves 4 to 6

This kind of *açorda* is typical of the Lisbon area and has become extremely popular in recent years, with many restaurants specializing in it. It has an absolutely glorious taste and is very filling, so do not think of adding anything else to the meal when choosing this as a main dish.

560 g/1¼ lb mixed seafood (prawns, clams, cockles) weighed after cooking and cleaning, discarding the shells
300 g/10 oz fish (with firm white flesh, such as monkfish)
560 g/1¼ lb stale white bread, in chunks

3 tablespoons olive oil
4 eggs
2 cloves garlic, very finely chopped
600 ml/1 pint liquid
6 sprigs fresh coriander, chopped
salt and pepper

If the shellfish has been prepared at home, keep the resulting liquor and strain it. Cook the fish and flake it. Keep this liquor, too, and measure the amount needed for the recipe. If there is any liquid left, keep it in case you need to add some of it towards the end, should the *açorda* become too dry. The consistency should be like that of thick porridge.

Put the liquid, garlic, salt and pepper to taste, and the oil, in a roomy pot. Add the bread and bring to the heat. Cook gently, while stirring all the time, until a pap is achieved. Add the coriander, fish and seafood, reserving a few prawns for decoration. Boil again, mixing. Taste for seasoning, and just before taking the *açorda* off the heat add the beaten eggs, stirring it all up. Put the reserved prawns on top and serve at once in the same pot. This is traditionally cooked in an earthenware pot, but any other will do. In restaurants it is served in individual earthenware pans.

VARIATION Prawn *açorda* is a richer version of seafood *açorda*, using only prawns (or lobster, or a mixture of the two), although in some restaurants they will also bulk it up with some firm-fleshed fish, as above. The liquid should be fish stock or, much better still, the strained liquor left after cooking the prawns or lobster, if you do cook them at home. The idea is to have a marked seafood taste in these *açordas*.

SALT COD AÇORDA

Açorda de bacalhau

NORTHERN PROVINCES • Serves 4 to 6

In the very religious northern provinces of Portugal, people try to refrain from eating meat during Lent. Salt cod *açorda* is a dish especially eaten at that time of the year.

400 g/14 oz good-quality stale white bread, thinly sliced

350 g/12 oz salt cod, soaked for up to 24 hours, changing the water a couple of times

2 medium tomatoes, peeled, seeded and chopped

4 eggs

1 clove garlic, chopped

2 medium onions, thinly sliced

5 tablespoons olive oil

1 bay leaf

salt and pepper

600 ml/1 pint water

a few olives for garnishing

Fry the onion in the oil for a couple of minutes, then add the tomatoes, bay leaf and garlic. While this basic *refogado* is cooking, rinse the cod, then skin, bone and flake it and cook in half the given water, until tender (about 15 minutes). Add the remaining water, boil, taste for salt and add pepper (if liked) and the bread. Simmer for a short while, stirring. After 8-10 minutes it should be cooked. Take off the heat and add the beaten eggs. Do not boil again. Serve immediately. The consistency will be like that of mashed potato.

VARIATION Instead of beating the eggs, they can be poached on top of the *açorda*.

AÇORDA MADEIRA STYLE

Açorda Madeirense

Serves 4 to 6

The tradition of *açorda* travelled to Madeira, where a local version has been created. It is a winter supper dish (though winters are almost non-existent in Madeira). It is made more substantial by serving it with a side dish of boiled or baked sweet potatoes cooked in their skins (sweet potatoes are very abundant in Madeira).

400 g/14 oz stale bread cut into 2.5 cm/1 inch cubes

3 cloves garlic, well crushed

1 tablespoon thyme

3 tablespoons olive oil

4-6 poached eggs

salt and pepper

100 g/3½ oz cooked corn (optional)

1.2 L/2 pints salted boiling water

Place the bread in a large serving bowl or tureen with the corn, if used. Sprinkle with the crushed garlic and thyme. Add the oil and the boiling salt water (usually the water used for poaching the eggs). The liquid will be almost completely absorbed by the bread. Serve at once with the side dish (sweet potatoes, or simply olives, if you do not like or do not have the potatoes).

MIGAS

Like *açorda*, *migas* are dishes full of flavour and goodness, in spite of lacking elegance.

In some places to make *migas* (*fazer migas*) really means just soaking crumbled maize or peasant bread into some liquid. Coffee *migas*, for instance, is simply bread crumbled on black coffee, sprinkled with sugar, served very hot in a small bowl, and eaten slowly with a spoon. I still remember having coffee *migas* for breakfast (followed by the most gorgeous fresh figs), when as a child, I used to spend holidays with my grandmother at her farm in the Ribatejo province. She was an early riser and, as soon as I heard her about the kitchen, on her own, I would get up and rush to have my *migas* with her. This was our little secret, because I wasn't really allowed to have coffee without milk.

The dividing line between *açorda* and *migas* is slightly blurred sometimes and may depend only on local terminology, although *migas* tend to have a different texture and to be drier, looking sometimes like omelettes (either rolled up or flat).

MIGAS RIBATEJO STYLE
Migas do Ribatejo
Serves 4 to 6

This dish has a rich texture, being made with that glorious cornmeal bread which is so common in the Ribatejo, Minho, Trás-os-Montes and Alto Douro provinces.

350 g/12 oz cornmeal bread (p.51) – or use the heaviest kind of wholemeal bread, medium sliced

2 cloves garlic, chopped
150 ml/¼ pint olive oil
enough salted boiling water to cover the bread

Place the slices of bread in a deep, roomy frying pan and cover with enough salted boiling water to absorb it. Boil gently for 5 minutes, stirring. Mix in the olive oil and the garlic, and shape the mixture like a roll, with the help of two wooden spoons or spatulas. Cook for a further 5 minutes, shaking the pan. The bread should become quite solid, like a rolled-up omelette with a golden crust. Serve as an accompaniment for fried fish or sausages.

MIGAS BEIRA LITORAL STYLE
Migas à moda da Beira Litoral
Serves 4 to 6

This *migas* is made with more substantial ingredients than most of the other *migas* recipes, the resulting dish being appropriate for wintery days. The actual origin of the recipe is the Lousã mountain, in the Beira region, where winters can be bitterly cold.

400 g/14 oz cornmeal bread (p.51) in little chunks
1 bunch sprouted turnip-tops (see Ingredients, p.28) – about 450 g/1 lb after discarding the tough parts of the vegetable

200 g/7 oz cooked butterbeans, with their cooking liquid
2 cloves garlic, finely chopped

Cook the greens until tender. Have the beans boiling in their cooking liquid (enough to cover them). Fry the garlic in the oil. Keep everything very hot. In a warm tureen assemble alternate layers of beans, bread and greens. The first layer must be beans, and the top one greens. Pour the oil with the garlic over the surface and serve immediately, accompanying baked Portuguese sausages (*chouriço*) or pork chops, fried in lard and seasoned with chopped garlic and a dusting of paprika. The bean liquor should be just enough to soak the bread through.

If you cannot get or do not want the trouble of preparing cornmeal bread, the heavier kind (organic), wholemeal bread can be substituted.

NOTE   You can use other kinds of beans and greens, as available.

MIGAS BEIRA BAIXA STYLE
Migas à Beira Baixa
Serves 4 to 6

400 g/14 oz stale bread, thinly sliced	4 tablespoons olive oil
60 g/2 oz smoked ham, thinly sliced	4-6 eggs fried in oil
90 g/3 oz *chouriço* (p.25) sliced	1 teaspoon paprika
2 cloves garlic, chopped	450 ml/¾ pint salted boiling water
2 sprigs parsley, chopped	

Boil the water with the seasoning (paprika, garlic and parsley). In a separate deep container assemble layers of bread, ham and sausage. Pour the seasoned water over this and leave it for an hour or so, to get completely moist. Put half the oil in a large frying-pan, warm it up and transfer the bread mixture to this, flattening it with a wooden spatula to look like a pizza. When golden underneath, turn it over (with the help of a plate which you use as a lid and then turn upside down, sliding the *migas* again into the pan, where you have added the remaining oil). Fry till golden and serve topped with the fried eggs.

MIGAS ALENTEJO STYLE
Migas Alentejanas
Serves 4

400 g/14 oz loin of pork	1 coffeespoon paprika
100 g/3½ oz fatty bacon	400 g/14 oz stale bread, thinly sliced (see hints on
150 g/5 oz *chouriço* (p.25)	bread to use on p.50)
2 large cloves garlic, chopped	300 ml/½ pint salted boiling water

Cut the bacon and fry slowly until all the fat has been extracted from it. Put the cracklings aside. In this fat fry the garlic, the sausage and the meat, cut into 2.5 cm/1 inch cubes. Season with salt and the paprika, and keep turning the meat until ready (10 to 15 minutes at the most). Put the meat aside, keep warm and reserve the fat and juices. In a separate container scald the bread with the water, and mash it, to resemble mashed potato. Put the mixture in the frying pan containing the fat and juices of the fried meat, and bring to the heat. Fry while shaping the *migas* like rolled-up omelette. Serve after it has acquired a golden crust, surrounded by the meat.

ENSOPADOS

Bread is also one of the ingredients in *ensopados* – which means 'soaked in'. *Ensopados* consist of wet stews where the excess liquid is absorbed by the bread, which, in this case, serves the purpose of a thickener.

Ensopados are popular dishes in Portuguese homes, not so much at restaurants. They can be prepared with either meat or fish. I give here one example of each.

KID ENSOPADO
Ensopado de Cabrito
ALENTEJO PROVINCES, BUT USED COUNTRYWIDE • Serves 4 to 6

1 kg/2 lb kid meat (or very tender lean lamb)
4 tablespoons olive oil
1 tablespoon processed lard
1 large onion, chopped
1 medium tomato, cleaned and chopped
150 ml/¼ pint white wine
1 tablespoon wine vinegar

½ teaspoon paprika
2 cloves garlic, chopped
1 bay leaf
450 ml/¾ pint meat stock – it can be prepared with cubes
4 thick slices of very good day-old bread
salt and pepper

Prepare a marinade with the wine, vinegar, garlic, bay leaf, paprika, salt and pepper. Cut the meat into medium-sized pieces and allow them to marinate for two hours. In a roomy pot fry the onion in the fat and oil. Strain the meat and fry it until browned. Add the marinade, tomato and stock. Cover the pot and cook gently until the meat is tender. Correct seasonings and serve over the slices of bread, in individual plates, adding more bread if too wet.

VARIATION This recipe can be made using rabbit, hare or any other game, or veal.

FISH ENSOPADO
Ensopado de Peixe
THE ALGARVE • Serves 4 to 6

1 kg/2 lb filleted fish (for example, monkfish/sea bass/fresh cod)
150 ml/¼ pint white wine
1 tablespoon lemon juice

1 tablespoon olive oil
3 tablespoons butter
1 medium onion, chopped
2 sprigs parsley, chopped

3 yolks of eggs

4-6 large slices of toasted bread

salt and pepper

Fry the onion in the butter and oil, until transparent. Add the cleaned fillets of fish, sprinkled with salt, and the wine. Cover and simmer until tender (about 10 minutes). Drain the fish and keep warm. Beat the egg yolks with the lemon juice and add to the juices in the pan, stirring very well. Boil gently, to thicken a little. Divide the toast between the plates and place the fish fillets on top of them. Cover with the sauce, sprinkle with the parsley and serve at once, with boiled, sauté or mashed potatoes.

DRY SOUPS

These dishes should not really be classified as soups, and neither are they dry. The name has probably been given centuries ago and nobody I asked seems to know why. A dry soup is very much like a hotpot, but with the addition of bread. Dry soups are simple, wholesome meals and can be adapted to use up left-overs.

DRY SOUP MINHO STYLE

Sopa Seca do Minho
Serves to 4 to 6

400 g/14 oz chicken

200 g/7 oz lean beef

100 g/3½ oz smoked ham

100 g/3½ oz *chouriço* (p.25)

100 g/3½ oz bacon

1 medium-sized white cabbage, cut into large chunks

300 g/10 oz stale white bread, sliced

1.8 L/2½ pints salted water

1 sprig fresh mint

Simmer all the meat in the water until almost tender (start with the beef), then add the cabbage. Simmer again. When cooked, remove the meat from the liquid in order to cut it up. Transfer the soup to an ovenproof container. Add the meat, the chopped mint leaves and finally the bread. Press a little, to get the bread soaked into the liquid. Bake in a preheated oven at 190°C/375°F/Gas 5, top shelf, until the bread is golden brown (about 15 minutes).

VARIATION For a more substantial *sopa seca*, Minho people add 4 or 5 potatoes, 2 carrots, a medium onion and a turnip, all thickly sliced and cooked together with the meat and cabbage. These vegetables are then layered with the meat before covering with the bread. In this case, instead of mint use chopped parsley.

GARLIC DRY SOUP

Sopa Seca de Alho

ALTO ALENTEJO • Serves 4

This is really more like *açorda*, with the difference that it is cooked partly in the oven. This recipe is the simplest of all *sopas secas* but, even so, rich tasting and filling.

400 g/14 oz stale bread (see hints on the bread to
    use, p.50)
3 cloves garlic, finely chopped
4 tablespoons olive oil

1 egg
1 coffeespoon sweet paprika
600 ml/1 pint boiling water
salt and pepper

Fry the garlic in the oil till golden. Add the paprika and the boiling water, salt and pepper to taste. Place in an ovenproof dish. Add the bread, press it in to soak well, and cover the top with the beaten egg. Bake on the middle shelf of a preheated oven (190°C/375°F/Gas 5) till golden brown (20-25 minutes). To complement the dish, serve fried, poached or scrambled eggs or fried fish.

SALT COD DRY SOUP

Sopa Seca de Bacalhau

Serves 4 to 6

It would be strange if salt cod did not come into the dry soups as well. This recipe is very tasty (as is everything prepared with salt cod) and a good alternative to the dry soups made with meat. This would be a way of using left-over cod and chickpeas to advantage.

350 g/12 oz cooked salt cod
350 g/12 oz cooked chickpeas
225 g/8 oz sliced stale bread
1 large onion, chopped
4 tablespoons olive oil
2 cloves garlic, finely chopped

2 sprigs parsley, chopped
600 ml/1 pint liquid (if you kept the water in
    which you cooked the cod, use this; if not, use
    seasoned boiling water)
salt and pepper

Fry the onion, garlic and parsley in the oil, till golden. Use this mixture between layers of flaked cod, chickpeas and bread, assembled in a deep ovenproof dish. The top and bottom layers should be bread. Pour the boiling liquid over the mixture and bring to the middle shelf of an oven preheated to 190°C/375°F/Gas 5 until golden brown, about 20 minutes.

GASPACHOS

Gaspacho soup has become well known to visitors to Spain, where it is served quite often during the summer months (*gazpacho*, in Spanish). The Portuguese provinces of the Alentejo and Algarve have their own versions of this soup. The main difference is that in Portugal *gaspacho* is not reduced completely to a pulp, thus keeping the crunchy texture of some of the ingredients.

Gaspachos are refreshing soups, very welcome on the hot summer days you get in both the Alentejo and the Algarve.

GASPACHO, ALENTEJO STYLE
Gaspacho Alentejano
Serves 4 to 6

200 g/7 oz day-old bread, diced very small
900 ml/1½ pints salted iced water
2 cloves garlic, thoroughly crushed with some salt
  (use a pestle and mortar for this)
2 tablespoons olive oil
2 tablespoons wine vinegar

2 medium-sized ripe but firm tomatoes (peeled
  and seeded)
½ medium-sized cucumber
1 small green pepper, cleaned
½ coffeespoon dry oregano
salt

Mash one of the tomatoes into a pulp and mix with the oregano, the crushed garlic, oil and vinegar, forming a purée. Put this into a tureen or serving bowl. Dice the remaining tomato very small, and the cucumber. Cut the pepper into matchsticks. Place all these vegetables in the tureen. Add the iced water. Taste for salt. (You may also like to add a little more vinegar.) Mix in the bread and serve while it is cold.

GASPACHO ALGARVE STYLE
Gaspacho do Algarve
Serves 4 to 6

This soup also takes the name of Arjamolho, in this province. It is practically the same as the previous recipe, except that it does not include cucumber. Here half the ingredients are liquidised together with the garlic. The other half is cut in small pieces. Otherwise it is the same.

VARIATION Drain some of the liquid of either version of *gaspacho* and serve in a small cup, as a delicate pink consommé.

BREAD PIES

FOLARES OR BOLAS

MOST INLAND PROVINCES, BUT ESPECIALLY THE NORTHERN ONES • Serves 6

Folares or *bolas* can be sweet or savoury, so I will give here the savoury versions, which can be translated as 'bread pies'.

Folares and *bolas* are made with a kind of bread dough enriched with many lavish additions. They are made for special occasions, mainly Easter, but this does not preclude serving them at any time, and lately they have become standard 'ready meal' fare in some good bakers. The difference between *folares* and *bolas* is minimal and depends only on regional terminology. I would recommend them as picnic-basket fillers, as they make a perfect out-of-doors meal, with a salad.

At summer fairs, all over Portugal, one can find stalls selling nothing but deliciously fragrant hot rolls filled with *chouriço* (baked inside them), which are small versions of bread pies.

DOUGH

450 g/1 lb flour	2 tablespoons butter
1 sachet (7 g) easy blend yeast	3 large eggs

FILLING

140 g/5 oz *chouriço* (p.25)	225 g/8 oz smoked ham

Add the yeast to a small amount of tepid water and a pinch of salt and mix. Add the flour and combine thoroughly, adding drops of tepid water, until smooth. Cover and allow to rest for 6-8 minutes. Beat the eggs with the melted butter and mix with the dough until well blended. Mix in a little more flour if you find the dough too runny. Beat it very well until fluffy and airy. This dough should be considerably softer than plain bread dough. Butter a square 23 cm/9 inch baking tin (or an oblong one of the same capacity). Divide the dough into three equal parts. Place one at the bottom and sides of the tin, cover with half the filling (sliced and with the *chouriço* free from the outer skin), then assemble another third of dough, cover with the remaining filling and finally cover the pie with the last piece of dough. Leave the tin in a warm place to rise, for 45-60 minutes, covering it with a cloth. Bake at 200°C/400°F/Gas 6 for 25-30 minutes or longer, until golden. Take out of the tin, brush with butter and leave the bread in a wire rack until it cools down.

VARIATIONS

1   A good recipe of bread pie with game, comes from the Entre Douro and Minho provinces. Serves 6.

about 1 kg/2 lb bread dough, made with wheat and rye flours, if possible	200 g/7 oz stewing veal
450 g/1 lb rabbit meat (wild or tame)	175-225 g/6-8 oz *chouriço* (p.25)
1 large chicken leg	90 g/3 oz smoked ham
1 quail (or another chicken leg, if quail is unavailable)	1 large onion
	4 tablespoons olive oil
	salt and pepper

To prepare the filling, fry the chopped onion in the oil until golden. Add the meat, seasoning and just a small amount of water or stock, as necessary, and cook until tender over gentle heat. Check seasonings,

bone the meat and cut it into bite-sized pieces. Set aside.

Generously grease a deep baking tin 30.5 x 30.5 cm/12 x 12 inches. Spread two-thirds of the bread dough over the bottom and up the sides of the tin, leaving a little over the rim, all round. Fill the dough case with the meat and its juices (which should be reduced, if too abundant). Place the rest of the dough on top, bringing the borders over this lid, to make sure all the meat juices remain inside. Bake an hour later, in a preheated oven (210°C/425°F/Gas 7) and reduce to 190°C/375°F/Gas 5 once the pie is inside the oven. It will be ready when nicely browned (25-30 minutes). Brush the top with butter to make it shiny, when ready, and leave to cool on wire rack. It is equally good hot or cold.

2   Bread pies can be varied just by ringing the changes with the fillings, providing the stew used is rich and well seasoned. The bread dough can also be varied, according to taste.

CHOURIÇO ROLLS

These little gems deserve a mention here. They are scrumptious... They appear in stalls at country fairs, still warm, and are a delicious snack not just at fairs, but at any time.

To make *Chouriço* Rolls, you simply prepare some bread dough (see recipe at the start of this Chapter, or use your own recipe). Mould the dough into rolls, open them through the middle and fill with thick slices of the best *chouriço* you can find. Close the rolls again and bake until golden.

If you do not relish the idea of preparing dough, you can just use any rolls freshly baked and of the best quality, open them, fill with some *chouriço* slices as above and wrap in foil. Take them to the oven for a few minutes, to allow the *chouriço* juices to melt inside the rolls, and serve.

SEAFOOD

Thousands of years ago fish was one of the main foods of the peoples settled along the coast of the land that would become Portugal. This is still true today and one of the blessings of Portuguese gastronomy. Some of the cheapest fish is also, fortunately, some of the tastiest (such as sardines and *carapaus* – horse mackerel). Hake is a national love and always prominent and so is a long, narrow fish called *peixe espada*, scabbard fish, which is silvery, has no scales and is excellent fried and grilled. There are many splendid varieties of sea bass and sea bream, turbot, tuna, skate, dogfish, sole, conger eels and other eels, trout, mullet, swordfish, grouper and many others, as well as shellfish and molluscs.

As salt cod plays such a large role in Portuguese cookery I shall start this chapter giving it the place it deserves, right at the beginning.

SALT COD

There are many dozens of different recipes for salt cod in use, all over Portugal, with new ones cropping up at regular intervals. It is said that one could have a different salt cod dish every day of the year, but whether this is an over statement or not, its versatility makes this assumption quite credible. Salt cod is very obliging, lending itself to one's creativity. The *fiel amigo* (faithful friend), as the Portuguese call it, is indeed terribly accommodating and if you are afraid of being put off by its strong taste, try the milder recipes first and you will start to understand what all the fuss is about. See, for example, the salt cod cakes, the fritters and the very sophisticated salt cod with a rich béchamel sauce with cream.

BASIC PREPARATION Most recipes demand that salt cod be well soaked before cooking it. Rinse well, under the tap, to wash away some of the salt, and place in a roomy bowl, covering it well with cold water. Change the water 4 to 5 times, for a period of 12 hours for thin cuts, and 24 hours for thicker ones. Before cooking taste a few strands to make sure it is not over salty anymore, although it should retain some saltiness, or it will be too bland. Most dishes ask for the fish to be skinned and boned after soaking – which is a much easier operation than for fresh fish. For poaching and charcoal grilling it is nice to keep the skin, and in this case one should scale it, as for any ordinary fish. In fact, after being reconstituted by soaking, salt cod is treated as fresh fish and takes very little time to cook.

Remember that you should not add salt to any dish containing salt cod until you taste it, to take into account the salt remaining in it, which will probably be enough, or almost, for seasoning the whole dish.

TIPS The weight indicated in the recipes refers to the salt cod before soaking.

If you intend cooking salt cod occasionally soak a bit more than you need and keep the excess in the freezer, well wrapped up in a plastic bag, or box, and use within 1 month.

If you do not use the salt cod immediately when you buy it, keep the parcel inside a plastic bag and place in the lower part of the fridge. This will prevent it drying too much and any fishy smell pervading the fridge. Use within 2 weeks.

See reference to Salt Cod – page 24.

CHRISTMAS EVE COD (COD WITH EVERYTHING)
Bacalhau de Consoada (Bacalhau com Todos)
ENTRE DOURO AND MINHO PROVINCES BUT USED IN MANY OTHER REGIONS

For Christmas Eve supper, make abundant quantities of 'Cod with Everything'.

Boiled salt cod (soaked previously, as usual – see above), having, of course, chosen the best middle slices

Potatoes, boiled in their skins and peeled whilst still hot

Cabbage. If possible, use the so-called typical Portuguese cabbage, a variety which is not found easily outside Portugal but which can be substituted by any good cabbage of one's choice

Hard-boiled eggs

All these items must be cooked at the last minute, before serving, so as to be brought to the table at their best. They are served on big platters, separately.

Oil and vinegar from the cruet-stand are the usual table seasonings for this kind of dish, together with chopped garlic, salt and pepper.

For this occasion some people prepare a sauce with olive oil:

3 tablespoons olive oil per person
1 clove garlic per person

1 teaspoon wine vinegar per person (or less to taste)

Bring the oil and garlic to the boil, remove from the heat, add the vinegar, beat well and serve in a sauce boat.

Any cod, potatoes and so on left over from this meal are reheated the following day and served as a starter, before the turkey.

To reheat, use 1½ tablespoons olive oil and ½ clove garlic per person. Fry gently until the garlic is golden. Add the left-over cod (flaked and free from bones and skin), the potatoes and cabbage, all cut in small pieces, and mix with the oil. Turn carefully to reheat through. Serve at once. This starter is called 'roupa velha' (old clothes).

NOTE Although for Christmas Eve the chosen vegetable will be cabbage, 'cod with everything' is also served with sprouted turnip-tops when these are in season (see p.28).

SALT COD GOMES DE SÁ FASHION
Bacalhau à Gomes de Sá
OPORTO • Serves 4 to 6

When there are many variations to a popular dish, the most elaborate one is generally the original. This is no exception as far as Gomes de Sá cod is concerned. It is said that a salt-cod merchant by that name, who lived in Oporto, created it first. The recipe given below is, according to the experts, the real one, having been carefully passed on by Gomes de Sá's descendants (there is still a generation of the family today). The secret of the real recipe resides in the use of milk, to soften the cod.

450 g/1 lb salt cod, from the thick middle slices
675 g/1½ lb potatoes (boiled in their skins, then peeled and sliced)
3-4 hard-boiled eggs
300 ml/½ pint hot milk
2 medium onions, sliced

2 cloves garlic, finely chopped
120 ml/4 fl oz olive oil
2 sprigs parsley, chopped
salt and pepper
20 black olives, for garnishing

Soak the cod really well for 24 hours, changing the water various times. Place it in a pan with enough boiling water to cover it. Do not bring to the boil. Leave it soaking in the boiling water for 30 minutes. Then drain, skin and bone it. Flake it carefully with your fingers, and put the pieces into a deep dish, pouring the hot milk over. Leave to soak for 2 hours. Put the oil, onions and garlic in a large pan and

fry until golden. Add the sliced potatoes and the flaked cod (having drained off the milk). Taste for salt, and sprinkle with pepper. Heat the whole mixture in the oil, over a low flame, turning it now and then, without actually allowing it to fry. Transfer it to a fireproof dish (or an earthenware one, if possible) and bake for 20 minutes, in a preheated oven (210°C/425°F/Gas 7). Serve at once, garnished with the sliced boiled eggs, olives and chopped parsley.

SALT COD BRÁS FASHION
Bacalhau à Brás
ESTREMADURA PROVINCE • Serves 4 to 6

It is not quite known who Brás was but the dish he invented is certainly very tasty and popular in most Portuguese restaurants.

560 g/1¼ lb potatoes
350-400 g/12-14 oz salt cod, thoroughly soaked
5 eggs
2 cloves garlic

1 tablespoon chopped parsley
salt (if needed) and pepper
oil for frying

Prepare the cod as usual (p.67). Skin, bone and wash again (without cooking it). Pull it into small strips, using your fingers. Pat the raw cod dry with a cloth or kitchen paper. Peel the potatoes and cut them as for very thin chips (like short lengths of spaghetti). In a roomy frying pan warm up the oil, fry the cloves of garlic (to transfer their taste to the oil, then discard them) and fry the potatoes slowly, turning them to cook through but without browning. Drain and set aside. Slowly sauté the pieces of cod in the same oil, for about 5 minutes. Add the potatoes to the pan and mix both. Taste for salt (you may not need any). Sprinkle with a little pepper and mix in the beaten eggs with a large fork, so the mixture does not set like an omelette but stays rather like scrambled eggs. When the egg is set (try not to overcook), remove the pan from the heat at once. Sprinkle with the parsley and serve with a side salad and olives.

VARIATION Use the same recipe but add a large onion thinly sliced and fried in the oil until transparent, mixing it with the other ingredients before adding the eggs.

BOILED COD AND CHICKPEAS
Meia-Desfeita com Grão
ESTREMADURA PROVINCE • Serves 4 to 6

A rich, heavy and delicious luncheon dish, rightly famous all over the Estremadura province. In Lisbon there used to be various small restaurants specializing in this dish. They do not, alas, seem to have survived but the dish is still available at many places and is easy enough to prepare at home as well.

350 g/12 oz best salt cod, from the middle thick slices

350 g/12 oz chickpeas

2-3 hard-boiled eggs, sliced

1 medium onion, finely chopped

1 clove garlic, finely chopped

3 stalks parsley, chopped

150 ml/¼ pint olive oil

1 tablespoon wine vinegar

salt and pepper

Soak the cod for 24 hours or longer (assuming the slices are thick) in cold water, changing it several times. Soak the chickpeas separately, overnight. Start cooking the chickpeas first (as they take 1½-2 hours if not done in the pressure cooker, which could reduce the cooking time to 25-30 minutes) in enough boiling water and salt. Scale and boil the cod in enough water to cover it, until tender (15 minutes). Do not add salt but check at the end whether it needs any, taking into account that you have soaked it long enough. Prepare the garnish, mixing the onion, garlic and parsley, all very finely chopped. In a separate bowl, mix the oil and vinegar. For serving, place the cod at the bottom of a deep serving dish and cover it with the cooked and drained chickpeas. Pour the oil mixture all over this, sprinkle the onion-garlic-parsley garnish on top and decorate with the sliced boiled eggs.

NOTE To save time you can use a good brand of canned chickpeas.

SALT COD WITH TOMATO SAUCE
Serves two for a main dish

This dish can be prepared in advance, then re-heated.

350 g/12 oz salt cod

400 g/14 oz potatoes

4 tablespoons olive oil

tomato sauce (see recipe, p.129)

flour and dried breadcrumbs for sprinkling

Prepare the salt cod as indicated at the start of this chapter. When soaked, skin it and cut into smallish fillets about 2.5 cm/1 inch square or a little more (do not worry about this, as they will later be covered with the sauce). Then cut them across, to give a thickness of about 0.5 cm/¼ inch or slightly more – again do not worry about accuracy. In practice there is no problem about this. Pat the pieces dry in a piece of kitchen paper, dust with flour and fry briskly for a couple of minutes on each side, in the warm olive oil. Set aside. Cook the potatoes until tender and slice them in thickish rounds. Have the tomato sauce ready (you may prepare it the previous day). Use a fireproof deep dish, well greased with olive oil. Place a few spoonfuls of tomato sauce at the bottom, then make a layer with the potatoes, cover them with a little sauce, then place the pieces of cod on top. Spread the remaining sauce on to the cod, covering it well. Sprinkle with some dried breadcrumbs, to form a little crust and bake in a preheated oven (210°C/425°F/Gas 7), top shelf, for 10 to 12 minutes. If you would like to prepare the dish in advance you can have it all ready up to the point of when you cover the cod with the sauce. Then, before serving, finish it – adding now the breadcrumbs and taking the dish to the oven. Do not overcook, to avoid drying the sauce too much.

SALT COD CAKES
Pasteis de Bacalhau
Makes 24 to 30 fishcakes

'She went home to eat fishcakes. Every day, both at dinner and supper, she would eat fishcakes, made with salted cod.'

Camilo Castelo Branco, *Noites de Lamego* (*Lamego Nights*)

Here is a great Portuguese favourite. Although their real origin is the north, cod cakes became so popular that they were adopted as a truly 'national speciality'. Cod cakes are ideal fare for snacks (hot or cold) and feature at every Portuguese function, from the most sophisticated to the humblest. If there is anything really engrained in the Portuguese palate, loved by everyone, this is it. Snobs may be somewhat derogatory about cod cakes, afraid of admitting that they too love this 'poor-man's dish', but do not believe them. They will probably eat them all the same, when nobody is looking.

Salt cod cakes are sold at delicatessens, patisseries, road-side cafés, tavernas – everywhere in Portugal. If you cannot find or do not like salt cod, they are also very nice made with fresh cod, although not as nice as the real thing.

280 g/10 oz thick salt cod (soaked as usual, see p.67)
400 g/14 oz floury potatoes
1 small onion, very finely chopped
2 tablespoons finely chopped parsley leaves
3 eggs
oil for frying

Prepare the cod, soaking it and changing the water several times (see p.67). Boil the potatoes (in their skins, for preference, so they do not absorb water); peel them and mash well or sieve. Meantime, simmer the cod in enough boiling water to cover it, until tender (about 12 minutes). Drain, discard the skin and bones and flake it as much as you can with your fingers, then with a fork, to reduce it to threads. (The proper way of doing this is to place the flaked cod inside a clean cloth, fold it and squeeze and pound the contents of the cloth with your fists. In this way you will have mashed cod.) Mix this mass with the mashed potatoes and add the eggs, one by one, and the onion and parsley. Taste for salt but you may not need to add any, as the cod itself retains enough saltiness, in spite of being soaked and boiled. (Avoid having cod cakes which are too salty.) The mixture should be quite stiff, enabling a spoon to stand up in it. If you find it excessively dry, add one or two tablespoons of milk. Allow this to cool completely before deep frying, as you would deep fry fish or chips. With two tablespoons, shape the fishcakes like large eggs and place in the hot oil, turning them three or four times to get nicely browned all over. As they fry, lift them with a big fork or slotted spoon and place in kitchen paper, to absorb excess fat. Go on moulding and frying until you use up the mixture. Serve hot (with cod rice, or tomato rice, and/or salad), or cold with salad, or simply on their own or with olives. Delicious.

NOTE You can, of course, use a food processor for mashing the salt cod effectively.

SALT COD WITH CREAM

Bacalhau com Natas

Serves 4

This is a more modern, yet already quite traditional dish, which is very showy and tasty, but very mild. It can be used for a special occasion, to tempt friends who do not know much about salt cod. This will prove to them that here is something sophisticated and elegant, that they can become addicted to! The title of the recipe –with cream – may imply that it is too rich, but cream does not in fact need to be used to make the béchamel sauce and what I generally do is use half cream (single) and half milk.

450 g/1 lb salt cod	3 tablespoons butter
450 g/1 lb potatoes	3 tablespoons grated cheese (can be mild
350 g/12 oz onions, sliced finely	cheddar)
600 ml/1 pint milk and single cream (half and half)	vegetable oil for frying
3 tablespoons flour	salt and pepper

Prepare the salt cod as usual (see start of this chapter) and boil for 10 minutes. Flake it after skinning and boning it thoroughly, once it has cooled enough to handle. Set aside. Peel the potatoes and cut into small wedges. Fry them together with the cut onions in sufficient oil, to cover. Do not allow the mixture to take colour. The idea is simply to get these ingredients to soften. Set aside. Make a béchamel sauce using the butter, flour and cream/milk mixture. The sauce should be thickish. Season it with a little salt and pepper. Grease very well a fireproof dish with butter and assemble the dish, placing a little sauce at the bottom, then layers of cod and potato/onion. Finish with the remaining sauce and sprinkle with the cheese. Bake on top shelf of preheated oven (210°C/425°F/Gas 7) until golden – about 15 minutes.

IMPORTANT NOTE You will notice that I did not indicate salt for seasoning the potatoes and onions. This is because the cod will still be slightly salty even after all the preparations. Go careful on this, to avoid ruining such a delightful dish, then taste everything first to gauge what to do in way of salt. Remember also that the cheese itself contains salt. On the other hand, you do not want a salt cod dish to taste bland. This dish can be prepared earlier and warmed up. It also freezes well.

SALT COD STEAKS WITH OLIVE OIL

Bifes de Bacalhau com Azeite

If you love olive oil and garlic this dish is for you. The cod must be from the middle pieces (thicker and more meaty). Serve it straight after cooking with boiled potatoes.

1 piece of cod per person	1 garlic clove per piece
3 tablespoons of olive oil per piece	dried breadcrumbs

Soak the cod as usual (see start of this chapter), skin and bone it and cut into large squares. If the cod is very thick you can also cut these squares across. Pat dry the cod in kitchen paper and fry gently in half the oil for about 5 minutes, turning once. Then coat the pieces of cod in breadcrumbs and take to a warm grill for 5 minutes on each side, to finish cooking and acquire a nice crust. Sprinkle with a little of the oil while it is cooking. Do not keep under the flame for too long, to avoid drying. Serve the cod with the remaining oil, really hot – having fried the sliced garlic cloves in it. Pour it all over the fish.

NOTE A good addition to the dish is a tablespoon of finely cut fresh coriander sprinkled over the cod just before serving, and a fresh lettuce and watercress salad.

SALT COD FRITTERS
Pataniscas
Serves 4

Pataniscas are very popular all over Portugal, though they originated in Algarve. There are a few versions in use and this is the sort of salt cod dish which you can modify as you wish, creating new versions of it yourself. *Pataniscas* are generally served as a snack, or starter, in which case they are accompanied just with a few olives. But they can be transformed into a good lunch dish if served with a salad and/or tomato rice.

225 g/8 oz salt cod
½ small onion very finely cut or grated
1 egg
1 clove of garlic, very finely cut or crushed
3 tablespoons of flour
1 tablespoon olive oil
oil for frying
1 tablespoon finely cut parsley
milk, lemon juice and pepper

Desalt the cod as indicated at the start of this chapter. Remove the skin and bones, and flake it roughly or, if preferred, cut into small pieces. Place it in a soup bowl or other bowl and cover with a little milk and a sprinkle of lemon juice. Leave in this sort of marinade for a while (at least 1 hour). Drain the cod and set aside. Prepare a thickish batter with the flour, diluted in some water, the egg, the olive oil and a dusting of salt and pepper. Add the parsley, onion and garlic and beat really well, to mix all the flavours. Add the cod pieces and fry in vegetable oil by the spoonful until golden on both sides. According to whether this is going to be for a lunch dish or a snack you can decide upon the size of the fritters. They are nicer whilst hot but also good cold. If you would like to reheat them just place them for a few minutes in the oven, to crisp up again.

SALT COD STEW

Bacalhau Guisado

Serves 3 to 4

Very simple to prepare and tasty. A nice lunch dish, to serve with a side lettuce salad.

225 g/8 oz salt cod
450 g/1 lb potatoes
1 medium onion, sliced fine
1 large clove of garlic (or 2 small)

1 medium ripe tomato, skinned, seeded and cut
3 tablespoons olive oil
parsley, fresh coriander, piri-piri (a little of each, to taste)

Desalt the cod as usual (see start of this chapter), skin and bone it and cut into smallish pieces. Fry the onion and garlic in the oil until soft, add the tomato, boil for about 5 minutes and add some water to cover. When boiling, add the potatoes cut into thickish slices or cubes (these will cook faster, so you may choose). After about 5 minutes add the pieces of cod and parsley and cook over gentle heat until the potatoes are done (the cod will also be done by then). Taste for seasonings, add some piri-piri if you like and the coriander (a few sprigs) well cut. Simmer for another couple of minutes, taste again and serve. Should you have too much liquid in the stew just serve it over a slice or two of bread, to soak it up.

GRANDMOTHER'S SALT COD

Bacalhau da Avó

Serves 4

This was my grandmother's creation and we all loved it. It is a great lunch dish, maybe for the weekend, with all the family around. It is served with boiled potatoes, as so many cod dishes – they have great affinity for each other. The recipe marries all those very Portuguese tastes – garlic, cod, olive oil, fresh coriander. Sublime.

450 g/1 lb salt cod
2 large cloves of garlic
4 tablespoons olive oil

6 sprigs of fresh coriander
wine vinegar – 1 coffeespoon (optional)

Desalt the cod as usual (see beginning of this chapter). Keep the skin (no need to scale it) and the bones, at this stage. Pat the pieces of cod dry and brush them generously with part of the olive oil. Take the cod to a moderately hot grill and cook for about 8 minutes on each side, turning, once or twice. Do not keep for longer under the heat, or it will go too dry. When done and as soon as you can handle it, bone and skin the cod, flaking it with your fingers. Place in a serving dish and cover with the remaining olive oil, which you have heated up meantime. Sprinkle the finely cut coriander leaves and the garlic over the fish and serve immediately with the boiled potatoes.

NOTE: If you do not like raw garlic you can fry it (finely sliced) in the oil, until golden, before adding to the dish. I do not, personally, like to add vinegar, but some people do. It is up to you to add a few drops of it over the dish before serving.

SALT COD RICE
Arroz de Bacalhau
Serves 4 to 6

This is simple fare indeed, but really tasty and wholesome. It can be served on its own (maybe with a side salad and/or black olives) following a soup, for a splendid everyday lunch, or as an accompaniment to salt cod cakes (p.72). Traditional books indicate this dish as originating from the northern coastal provinces but it is really a national dish, much loved by everyone. The quantities may vary, according to whether it will be served on its own or as an accompaniment. Amounts given here will be suitable for the latter. Otherwise, they can just be doubled.

200 g/7 oz rice
110 g/4 oz salt cod (soaked for 6-7 hours
   beforehand)
2 tablespoons olive oil
2 sprigs parsley, chopped

bay leaf
2 medium tomatoes, peeled, seeded and chopped
1 medium onion, chopped
a little salt
water – 2½ times the volume of rice

Put the oil in a saucepan and make a *refogado* (p.22) with the onion, tomatoes and parsley. When soft, add the cod (free from bones and skin, and flaked or made into small strips, by hand), toss around, add the water. When boiling, add the rice and the bay leaf and cover. Simmer until the rice and cod are tender. Taste for salt, add a very small amount of pepper (optional) and serve at once. This rice should ideally be on the wet side.

SARDINES

Fresh, grilled sardines are another of those Portuguese flavours that one cannot forget, once tasted. Fresh sardines can of course be cooked in various ways, apart from grilling – they can be stewed, fried and, when very small, they can be treated the same as whitebait fried in a batter, in threes and fours. Very small sardines are called *petingas*. They are much prized as a delicacy and equally good hot or cold, as a snack. But grilled sardines deserve an entry, all of their own.

CHARCOAL GRILLED SARDINES
Sardinhas Assadas

Apart from the ubiquitous salt cod, fresh sardines are, of course, one of Portugal's national dishes *par excellence* and (in their charcoal-grilled version) what foreign palates take most readily to, when visiting Portugal. The characteristic smell of grilled sardines can be detected everywhere, during the summer months, when tonnes of them are consumed in open-air restaurants, tavernas, sea-side cafés, funfairs and, of course, private homes. It would be impossible to disguise this mouthwatering smell, which immediately conjures up a superb meal out of doors. Fortunately sardines are at their best precisely during the summer months. The quantities are tricky to calculate, because it is really easy to go on eating sardines without realizing how many one has already had. It also depends on their size. But let us say that for 4 people we need:

16-24 medium-sized fresh sardines

675-1 kg/1½-2 lb boiled potatoes

8 medium tomatoes (rather firm, slightly under-ripe), sliced

2 medium onions, finely sliced

4 green peppers (optional)

seasoning for the salad (oil, vinegar, salt and pepper)

An essential requirement for this dish is that the sardines be impeccably fresh. They can, of course, be bought from a fishmonger who has them standing on ice, but on no account must they be soft or limp. Wash the sardines (do not scale, gut or behead them) leaving them whole, so as to keep their flesh moist whilst grilling (gutting and scaling them would have the effect of drying them too much). Sprinkle the sardines with sea salt and leave for an hour or so on a wooden board or in a large container. Wash them again and pat dry with a clean cloth or kitchen paper. Grill on charcoal, using a grid, barbecue style, in the open air, preferably. Failing this, use any ordinary grill, though this does not give the same results as the charcoal. While the fish is grilling (you have to do it in batches and keep warm those already done), boil the potatoes and prepare the salad. If using peppers, you must also prepare them, either raw with the other salad ingredients, or Portuguese style – that is, grilled, the classic accompaniment for sardines, together with the salad and the potatoes.

To prepare the peppers, first wash them, pat dry with kitchen paper and place under the grill, keeping them whole. Turn them around until the skin becomes burnt and blistered, by which time they are ready. Carefully peel all burnt skin and cut the flesh into strips, discarding the centre of the peppers. Keep in a side dish.

Make a salad with the tomatoes and onions, seasoning to your taste, and serve also in a side dish. Drain the potatoes and put them in a separate container. The sardines must be served on a very large warm platter and put in the middle of the table, for the great feast.

To ensure that everything is ready at the same time and served at once, it is customary to have two people engaged in the cooking, or at least to count on a spare pair of hands at some stage. One person attends to the grilling and turning of the fish and keeps the batches flowing, giving undivided attention to this task, and the other does the peppers, salad and potatoes.

FISH STEWS/CALDEIRADAS

Some of the tastiest and best-known Portuguese dishes come under the description of *caldeiradas* that is, a kind of fish stew or chowder, quite wet (hence the etymology of the word, which derives from *caldo* – broth). They are traditionally served at seaside places, since the fish must ideally have just been caught. Obviously fishermen are the best cooks of *caldeiradas*, and some have established simple restaurants, which are always overflowing with people. At some of them, one must wait for the *caldeirada* to be cooked there and then, with the latest catch just brought in by a colourful small boat, handled by one or two men.

Fishing in Portugal can still be a one-man affair, but generally a few more join in the venture, to

provide a living for their families. When the boats are not at sea, fishermen's wives help with mending the nets while their men repair and clean the boats, gaily decorated in vivid colours and with a large eye painted on the prow, to ward off evil.

There are famous *caldeiradas* in the north, centre and south of the country, varying according to the kind of fish and seasonings used. But basically *caldeiradas* are made in similar fashion, and all of them are magnificent, filling and not difficult to prepare. The idea with *caldeirada* is to serve more fish than potato (if potato is used at all), so don't be surprised by the seemingly imbalanced quantities in the list of ingredients.

RICH FISH STEW
Caldeirada Rica or Caldeirada à Fragateira
LISBON AREA • Serves 6

The principle is still the same as for the previous versions of *caldeirada*, but in this case the fish must be of various kinds (hence the title 'rich'), bringing a variety of flavour and texture to this super dish. 6-8 different kinds of fish are normally used but, if this doesn't seem practical, try to use at least three or four, knowing, however, that the more variety, the better. Use, for example, conger eel, monk fish, sea bass, fresh sardines, ray, eels, skate, squid. Add a few prawns, if you like. The fish must be of the firm flesh kind and, this being a 'rich' stew, it contains a still higher proportion of fish than other recipes.

1.45 kg/3 lb mixed fish (in more or less equal amounts, to add up to the given total)	3 sprigs fresh coriander, chopped
675 g/1½ lb ripe tomatoes, cleaned and chopped	2 bay leaves
4 medium onions, thinly sliced	1 chilli, chopped
450 g/1 lb potatoes, peeled and very thinly sliced	1 green pepper, cleaned and chopped (optional)
2 cloves garlic, sliced	3 tablespoons dry white wine, or 1 tablespoon wine vinegar
120 ml/4 fl oz olive oil	salt and pepper
3 sprigs parsley, chopped	

Start by cleaning and preparing the fish, cutting it into pieces, according to variety. Do not cut the pieces too small (3-5 cm/1½-2 inches). Have all the other ingredients prepared and at hand.

Use a roomy casserole with a thick base, to prevent sticking. Put half the oil in first and assemble alternate layers, starting with the onions, then tomatoes, potatoes, fish, sprinklings of salt and seasonings, and so on, leaving the most fragile fish for the top layer. Sprinkle a bit more salt, add the wine and the rest of the oil, and enough water to barely cover. Bring to the boil, then reduce to simmering, to avoid burning. Do not stir but merely shake the pan now and then. Cook for 25 minutes. The potatoes must be very thinly sliced, to make sure they will be tender. Serve in the same pan, after trying for salt.

You will have a good deal of delicious liquid left over. Strain it and use as a soup, as indicated for the eel stew, or use it as a stock for your own version of fish soup.

VARIATIONS Apart from those already indicated, there are many more variations of *caldeiradas*, made just by adding or omitting parsley, fresh coriander, tomatoes, paprika, peppers and wine (or a little

vinegar instead of wine), and varying the fish. Another version does not include potatoes at all: the fish stew is served over thick slices of good stale bread, which must be placed on the plate, before pouring the stew on top of it. The bread may be fried, if wanted. Do not overcook the fish.

EEL STEW, AVEIRO STYLE
Caldeirada de Enguias de Aveiro
Serves 4 to 6

Eels are very good and plentiful in and around the picturesque northern town of Aveiro (the Portuguese Venice, so called because of its canal). Aveiro is surrounded by saltflats, lagoons and beaches. It has good hotels and restaurants, some of them well known for their own version of *caldeirada de enguias*, followed by the local dessert, *ovos moles* (soft eggs), a very delicate, sweet confection (see p.150), relished by the Portuguese.

1 kg/2 lb very fresh eels (they should be live ones, if you can bear cutting them up)	4 tablespoons olive oil
2 medium onions, sliced	30 g/1 oz lard
450 g/1 lb potatoes, peeled and cut into thin slices	2 sprigs parsley, chopped
1 clove garlic, finely sliced	1 bay leaf
120 ml/4 fl oz dry white wine	½ teaspoon saffron
	salt and pepper

In a large saucepan or, better still, an earthenware pot, place the wine, the fat and oil, a little salt, the other seasonings and then the potatoes and onions, in alternate layers. Barely cover with boiling water and simmer for 12-15 minutes, shaking the pot occasionally, to prevent sticking. In the meantime, prepare the fish, cleaning it carefully and cutting into 2 inch (5 cm) lengths. Place the fish on top of the parboiled potatoes, sprinkle with some more salt and add some water if, at this stage, you think it is needed, as the stew must be kept quite wet, like a thick soup. Simmer for a further 10-12 minutes, until everything is tender. Taste for salt. Take the pan to the table and serve immediately, with chunks of bread.

If there is any liquid left over, strain it and use it as a fish soup, adding some fried cubes of bread and a sprinkling of finely cut coriander leaves.

SARDINE STEW
Caldeirada de Sardinhas

The same as before, substituting fresh sardines for the eels. The sardines must be scaled, beheaded, gutted, and left whole, if small, or cut into halves if medium or large. With the sardine stew use one teaspoon of paprika, instead of the saffron.

VARIATION Omit the wine and use three medium-ripe tomatoes (seeded, peeled and coarsely chopped), placing them between the layers of onion and potatoes.

OTHER FISH DISHES

FISH FILLETS IN BATTER – (FISH AND CHIPS)
Filetes de Peixe Albardados

Fish fried in batter has always been a popular dish in Portugal, normally prepared with hake – or, in the case of small sardines, a way of cooking them in threes and fours. But you will probably be surprised to hear that this was actually the inspiration behind the creation of 'Fish and Chips' – that most iconic of British fare. According to research done by Claudia Roden (foremost expert on Jewish cookery), Portuguese Jews ate fish in batter, like everyone else in Portugal. When they were forced to leave (during the Inquisition, if they refused to convert to Christianity) they established themselves in various other parts of Europe and the Middle East, where they obviously continued to eat what they were used to before.

Many generations later – and still eating fish in batter – a certain Mr. Joseph Malin opened the first 'Fish and Chips' shop – London, 1860. The rest, as they say, is history. The only problem was, of course, the accompaniment. Tomato rice or salad (the usual backup for this dish) wouldn't be appropriate for a take-away. So Mr. Malin 'borrowed' chips from the French, who had just invented that most delicious method of cooking potatoes (hence French fries…). The British contribution is the liberal sprinkling of malt vinegar over the whole thing – which would be totally abhorrent to both the French and the Portuguese.

The idea of frying things in batter had been adopted also by the Japanese, under the name of 'Tempura', and had the very same origin, manifesting itself at the other side of the world. (See Chapter on 'Vegetables and Accompaniments', page 135

2 hake fillets per person
Salt/lemon juice/garlic

For the batter:
60 g/2 oz white plain flour
1 egg
Salt/oil for frying

Rub the fish fillets with a clove of garlic cut in half lengthwise, sprinkle with a little salt and drops of lemon juice and set aside for an hour or so. Meantime, prepare the batter with the other ingredients (use a little water to dissolve the flour). Pat dry the fish and dip really well into the batter, drain with a slotted spoon and fry in hot oil until golden on both sides. Serve with Tomato Rice (see Accompaniments).

'HAKE WITH EVERYTHING'
Pescada com todos
LISBON AREA, BUT EATEN COUNTRYWIDE • Serves 4

Hake is one of the most popular fish in Portugal – and one which has gone up in price considerably in the last few years, except in its frozen form. It is a fine sea fish with white, delicate flesh, suitable for poaching, frying and filleting. It can be obtained in most countries, but fresh cod can be substituted, or haddock, large whiting or any other fish which will poach well.

'Hake with Everything' is the simplest fish dish there is, and it makes an excellent and nourishing lunch (somehow it does not seem right in the evening). All restaurants in Portugal serve it, as well as every household.

The 'everything' is made up of hard-boiled eggs, boiled potatoes and greens in season (cabbage, broccoli, cauliflower, green beans or spring greens, and add a few carrots if you like). The meal is presented in a large serving dish, with a saucer full of black olives by the side and cruet-stand containing olive oil and wine vinegar. If you prefer, you can season the dish with a little melted butter. But it can also be enriched with a nice-looking and tasty dressing called *molho vilão*, p.130.

4 good pieces of fish	4 eggs
8 medium potatoes	greens in season

Clean and salt the fish an hour before cooking, to allow the salt to penetrate the flesh. Wash and cook it in just slightly salted boiling water (remember the fish has already been seasoned). Use enough water to cover the fish. Cook for about 10 minutes, taking care that it is cooked but not overdone. In a separate pan boil the potatoes and the greens, and in another boil the eggs, for 10 minutes. When everything is ready, place the drained ingredients in a large serving dish and serve immediately.

You can boil the potatoes in their jackets and peel them after cooking, in which case they should be cooked on their own.

NOTE In the same way as you prepare 'Hake with Everything', you can also produce 'Cod with Everything' – see p.67 for its special Christmas version.

BAKED FISH
Peixe Assado
Serves 4

For this dish, much appreciated in Portuguese households, the fish should be on the big side and cooked whole (after gutting and cleaning but leaving the head on). One can, of course, opt for thick slices of fish instead of a whole one, if not available in the right size. Sea bream and sea bass, turbot or even fresh cod would be the best choice. Plaice, sole and any oily fish would not be suitable.

1 kg/2 lb fish	¼ teaspoon paprika
6 tablespoons white wine	1 tablespoon lemon juice
4 tablespoons water	3 tablespoons olive oil
1 medium onion, chopped	1 tablespoon melted lard
2 sprigs parsley, chopped	salt and pepper
1 clove garlic, finely chopped	

Scale and gut the fish (leaving its head on, for better appearance), or use thick slices of fish. Sprinkle it with some salt. About an hour later wash and drain the fish and pat dry in kitchen paper. Give it a few cuts across the thickest part. Put it in an oiled ovenproof dish and sprinkle it all over with the solid

seasonings, finely chopped. Mix in a bowl all the liquid seasonings (and fat and oil) and pour this mixture onto the fish. Bake at 190°C/375°F/Gas 5 for 35-40 minutes, basting 2 or 3 times. If the fish is not very thick, or if you used sliced fish, about 20-25 minutes baking will probably be enough, or it might get too dry. Test with skewer or fork. Serve at once with boiled or mashed potatoes, with the fish juices. Or you can put some parboiled potatoes cut into small cubes around the fish at the beginning, dotting them with butter. Turn them over when basting the fish.

VARIATION   Some families prefer a few tomatoes, peeled and chopped over the fish, instead of using water.

GRILLED RED MULLET SETÚBAL FASHION
Salmonetes Grelhados

Red mullet is very common in the Setúbal fishing area (south of Lisbon), where they seem to be at their best. Perhaps the Romans who lived on the beautiful Troia peninsula, in Setúbal's estuary, knew this, for some of the many remains there (although excavations have not been extensive) reveal that they used the site as a residential area and turned it into an important fishing centre in the first to fourth centuries, producing *garum* paste – a mixture of fish, oysters, roe and crabs, which must be the precursor of our modern 'spreads'.

1-2 red mullet per person (according to size)   1 lemon in wedges for garnishing
1 tablespoon butter for each fish

SAUCE
90 g/3 oz butter   1 tablespoon lemon juice
the livers of the fish (if available)   3 sprigs parsley, chopped
salt and pepper

Clean the fish (leaving the heads on) and salt it for an hour. Wash and pat dry in kitchen paper. Grill under a gentle flame, brushing with the butter and turning once or twice until done (5-6 minutes each side). Prepare a sauce with the mashed livers (if available) simmered for 3-4 minutes in 6 tablespoons of water. Add the butter, the juices from the grilling pan, lemon juice, salt and pepper. Sieve, to obtain a smooth sauce, taste for seasoning, simmer again for a minute to reheat and add the parsley. Pour this sauce over the fish. If livers are not available, the sauce will consist only of the melted butter with lemon juice and parsley. Serve with boiled potatoes and garnish with lemon wedges.

VARIATION   The fish can be half grilled first and then finished in the oven (190°C/375°F/Gas 5) for just a few minutes, moistening it with 1-2 tablespoons of water and melted butter to prevent drying.

COLD TROUT, BEIRA ALTA STYLE
Trutas Abafadas

This dish is served cold and is therefore suitable for a summer menu. Trouts abound in the northern rivers and, when prepared with this kind of marinade, last for at least two days. In fact, they are better served 24 or 48 hours after cooking.

1 trout per person
2 tablespoons olive oil
1 tablespoon wine vinegar per trout
2 tablespoons water
2 cloves garlic, chopped

1 bay leaf
3 sprigs parsley, chopped
¼ coffeespoon nutmeg
salt and pepper

Mix the oil, water and vinegar in a fish kettle or large pan and bring to the boil. Add all the seasonings and the fish (gutted, scaled and washed). Cover and cook until tender (10-12 minutes). Take off the heat, lift the fish carefully and set aside, in a deep serving dish. When cold, cover the fish with the strained cooking liquor and keep until the following day, at least. Serve cold, with potatoes boiled in their skins and peeled.

TUNA STEAKS
Bifes de Atum
THE ALGARVE • Serves 4

Tuna is the one 'big' fish caught off the Algarve coast and one of the riches of that province. Apart from eating it fresh, the Algarveans have a flourishing tuna-canning industry, providing for the whole country and export. The thrills of catching tuna have led to organized tourist tuna fishing.

675 g/1½ lb filleted fresh tuna (or halibut, if tuna is not available)
1 large onion, chopped
2 cloves garlic, chopped

110 g/4 oz lard or a mixture of butter and lard
3 tablespoons chopped parsley
salt and pepper
lemon wedges for garnishing

Melt the fat and add the fish fillets, alternating them in layers with the onion and other seasonings. Cover and cook very gently for 15 minutes or until tender, turning the fish once, with great care. Add water only if absolutely necessary. Shake the pan now and then. Bring to the table in the same pot, garnished with lemon wedges and a side dish of boiled or fried potatoes.

VARIATION In Madeira, a similar dish includes more onion (sliced) and tomatoes, to enrich the sauce.

STUFFED FISH

Peixe Recheado

AZORES

In Azores the fish chosen for this dish is grouper but one can use any other large fish, of the bream family.

1 whole fish, weighing about 750 g/1½ lb (or up to 1 kg/2 lb)
1 large clove of garlic
1 medium onion

3 tablespoons of white wine
1 tablespoon of tomato concentrate
2 tablespoons of olive oil

FOR THE FILLING

110 g/4 oz white, fresh breadcrumbs
1 tablespoon of olive oil
1 small onion
1 small clove of garlic
60 g/2 oz stoned black olives

1 beaten egg
dash of wine vinegar
3 sprigs of finely cut parsley
salt and pepper

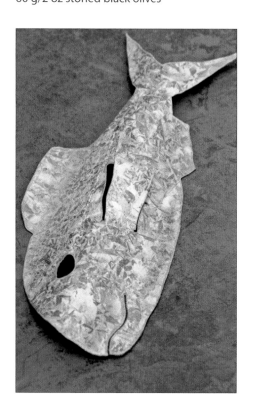

First scale and clean the fish, gutting it in such a way that it is not open too much. Wash it well, make a few diagonal cuts and sprinkle with some salt on both sides. Now prepare the filling. First soak the bread in a little warm water (fish stock would be better), squeeze and mash roughly, mixing with the olives, cut into small pieces, the parsley, a dash of vinegar and the beaten egg. While you are doing this have the finely cut onion and garlic sweating in the oil over a low flame. Add it all together, taste for seasonings and fill the fish (after washing off the salt). Secure the filling by sewing the fish, if necessary, or you can tie it up with a string. Place the stuffed fish in a greased fireproof dish, sprinkle it with the finely cut garlic, spread over it, the onion cut into fine rings and mix together the olive oil, the wine and the tomato concentrate, to season the fish overall, taking it to bake in a preheated oven (200°C/400°F/Gas 6) for about 25-30 minutes. Baste it a couple of times. Serve with mashed potato and a side salad.

SHELLFISH

Seafood should never be overcooked. This is especially important regarding shellfish, which becomes hard and rubbery if cooked for too long. Clams and mussels will be ready to eat as soon as they open.

Portuguese clams are quite small. You can use cockles or other small-type clams, such as littlenecks – see 'purging' method of recipe for 'Clams, Bulháo Pato Fashion'. Mussels could be substituted, as well.

STEWED LOBSTER
Lagosta Suada
PENICHE, ESTREMADURA PROVINCE • Serves 3 to 4

1 large lobster
3 medium onions, chopped
4 medium tomatoes, skinned, seeded and
    chopped
2 cloves garlic, chopped
2 tablespoons butter
2 tablespoons olive oil

4 tablespoons white wine or, better still, dry port
    or Madeira
1 bay leaf
2 sprigs parsley, chopped
½ teaspoon paprika
salt and pepper

Of course, the lobster must be impeccably fresh (there are places where they are available alive and where the fishmonger or fisherman will kill them for you). There is no such problem in Peniche and other coastal areas of Portugal where lobsters are plentiful – though always on the expensive side, nowadays. As you may know, a live lobster is rather dark in colour and turns orange only after cooking.

Have your lobster cleaned and cut into pieces. Save the liquid that escapes from the lobster whilst cutting. While you are doing this, have all other ingredients, except salt and wine, boiling gently for 4-5 minutes in a large earthenware pot, if you have one, otherwise in any roomy pan. Transfer all the lobster pieces to the pan. Do not add salt at this stage. Cover and cook gently until tender (about 15 minutes), shaking the pan now and then. Taste for seasoning and add the amount of salt you think necessary (a little at a time – do not overdo it). Add the chosen wine and boil for another couple of minutes. It is then ready to serve with white rice and a side salad, but if you can prepare it in advance and reheat it, so much the better.

PRAWN RISSOLES

Rissois de Camarão

ESTREMADURA • Makes about 12 large rissoles or 18 to 20 smaller ones.

Here we have the most delicious kind of rissole one can dream of. They are sold at every *patisserie* in Portugal, freshly made every day, and eagerly eaten by discerning customers. This is an obligatory savoury for parties, snacks and light lunches.

One can substitute prawns for shrimps in the rissoles, which are a little troublesome to prepare at home (hence their popularity ready-made). The pastry is of the cooked type and, when left to the following day, tends to harden, so the rissoles lose a lot of their appeal. Thus they should be made and eaten on the same day.

PASTRY

250 g/9 oz flour	100 ml/3½ fl oz milk
1 tablespoon butter	½ teaspoon salt
300 ml/½ pint water	

COATING

2 eggs	oil for frying
dried breadcrumbs	

FILLING

200 g/7 oz cooked and shelled prawns or shrimps	salt and pepper
300 ml/½ pint milk	dusting of nutmeg
3 tablespoons flour	1 coffeespoon chopped parsley
1 coffeespoon lemon juice	

To make the pastry, first bring the water and milk to the heat, with the butter. When boiling, remove from the heat and add the flour. Beat thoroughly and bring to the heat again to cook the flour, stirring continuously until a crust has formed at the bottom of the pan and the dough comes away from the sides (about 5 minutes). Remove from the heat, beat and work the dough lightly until smooth. Allow to cool.

Meantime, prepare the filling. Make a thick white sauce with the butter, flour and milk – that is, melt the butter, add the flour to make a roux (over a very low heat), cook for a few seconds, remove from the heat and add the warm milk little by little, stirring very well; cook again until thick. Add salt, the remaining seasoning and the prepared shellfish. Mix well and set aside to cool.

Roll out the pastry to 3 mm/⅛ inch thickness, taking care not to break it. Cut into rounds. These can be small or large, according to whether the rissoles are intended for a party or ordinary snack or meal. Small ones would be 5 cm/2 inches across, the larger 9 cm/3½ inches. Divide the filling among all the rounds of pastry, wet the edges with beaten egg, fold in half and press well. Dip each rissole in beaten egg, then in breadcrumbs. (They will gain by being left in the refrigerator for 1-2 hours before frying.) Deep fry until golden brown, turning once. Serve on their own or (hot or cold) with a salad.

VARIATION Cheaper rissoles can be made replacing the prawns with an equal amount of cooked fish (or half and half). You can also improvise your own version, using ready-made puff-pastry, but in this case the rissoles should be baked – not fried.

CLAMS, BULHÃO PATO FASHION

Ameijoas à Bulhão Pato

ESTREMADURA PROVINCE • Serves 4

Bulhão Pato (1829-1912) was a poet, writer and scholar who also translated into Portuguese various foreign works, including Shakespeare's *Hamlet* and *The Merchant of Venice*. This dish was apparently created by a cook who admired him. Clams Bulhão Pato Fashion make an exquisite dish and are available as a starter in many Portuguese restaurants and as an appetizer for drinks in beer-houses. It is a very simple recipe which can be adapted to other shellfish. Bear in mind that the dish should not be salty, so go very easy on salt and taste before adding any.

1 kg/2 lb clams	3-4 stalks fresh coriander, chopped, plus 2 for
2 cloves garlic, sliced	garnishing
1 medium lemon in wedges plus juice of ½ lemon	salt and pepper
3 tablespoons olive oil	

Prepare the shellfish in advance, as it needs to stand in salted water for about half a day, after the first wash. Use 5-6 tablespoons salt for each 1.2 L/2 pints of water for soaking. After soaking, wash again in plenty of cold water to remove the sand (see note). Fry the garlic gently in the oil until golden. Add the coriander, some salt and pepper and the shellfish. Bring the flame up a little, shake the pan until the clams open (3-5 minutes) and remove any which does not, discarding it. Squeeze the lemon juice on top, turn and serve at once, in the same pot, garnished with the lemon wedges.

NOTE It is possible that the fishmonger has already purged the clams, in which case you don't need to do it. Make sure of this.

CLAMS IN A CATAPLANA PAN

Ameijoas na Cataplana

THE ALGARVE • Serves 4

A *cataplana* is a special vessel usually made of copper which interlocks perfectly, permitting a complete turning. A good saucepan with a tight-fitting lid will have to do when a *cataplana* is not available.

1.25 kg/2½ lb clams	2 sprigs parsley
60 g/2 oz smoked ham (or lean bacon)	pinch paprika
60 g/2 oz *chouriço* (p.25)	2 small, red chillies, sliced
1 tablespoon olive oil	salt (a sprinkling, only)
1 tablespoon lard	1 lemon, cut into segments
3 tablespoons white wine	

Wash the clams and leave in salted water for half a day. Then wash again. (See note – previous recipe.) Fry the onion (in thin slices) very gently in the fat and oil in the pot, until transparent, together with the seasoning. Add the meats, in small cubes and parsley. Cover and cook gently for 10-15 minutes.

Add the clams and cook for 5-7 minutes. Serve adorned with the lemon. Discard any unopened clams.

NOTE See 'Pork Dishes' for a recipe from the Alentejo using clams with pork in similar fashion.

SQUID, CUTTLEFISH AND OCTOPUS

Squid, octopus and cuttlefish are very common all along the Portuguese coast, as well as in Madeira and Azores. Not surprisingly, they are served very frequently and constitute one of the great attractions at some restaurants. Squid is so plentiful that many fishermen still use the tougher ones, cut up, as bait.

Squid and cuttlefish can be cooked in the same fashion and have identical taste and texture. Logically, the smaller they are the quicker they will cook. If small they will be ready quite fast, getting tender before the potatoes, for example. If larger they may need boiling for much longer (one has to try now and then and see when they are ready, adding some more liquid to the pan, if necessary). However, if you leave them for longer than they need, they will actually become tougher, for a while. In this case you will have to prolong the cooking further, because they will eventually get tender again. In other words, there are two stages of tenderness: the first, quite fast, then again, much later. Such are their vagaries. Another warning is that they do tend to get tough if one adds salt at the start. So this seasoning must be added only towards the end. Even so, they never need much salt, anyway.

As to octopus, there is a consensus that it needs to be beaten hard, in order to soften its flesh, before cooking. Well, fresh octopus actually gets very obedient following this procedure: you prepare the octopus, washing it very well and cutting it if too large (the actual initial preparation will be done for you by the fishmonger, hopefully). Have a roomy pan containing a whole large onion, peeled, and nothing else – no water, no salt. Put the octopus in it and take to the boil, over a very low flame. The onion and the mollusc will create enough moisture for cooking. Keep an eye on the pot, because as soon as the onion is soft, the octopus will also be tender, having meantime acquired a nice colour. Take it out, discard the onion, cut it as needed for your recipe and use as fresh fish. Rice or potatoes and whatever other ingredients can now be added to it, as well as enough liquid for the dish. Do not add salt, however, because for some reason it contains quite a pronounced salty taste and it is possible you do not need much salt in the end – if any. Taste carefully. As you can see, this is a simple enough operation and one does not need fear cooking octopus anymore.

STEWED CUTTLEFISH (OR SQUID)
Chocos guisados (or lulas)
ALL COASTAL AREAS • Serves 6

1 kg/2 lb cuttlefish or squid (can be the larger ones)
150 ml/¼ pint fish stock (can be made with a fish cube)
4 tablespoons olive oil

1 large onion, chopped
3 sprigs parsley, chopped
175-200 g/6-7 oz ripe tomatoes, seeded, peeled and chopped
salt and pepper

Prepare the fish, removing the ink sac (perhaps the fishmonger will be kind enough to do it for you), wash it well and cut it in small pieces. Fry the onions, tomatoes and parsley for a couple of minutes, then add the fish and some of the stock, keeping the rest for gradual additions whilst cooking. Add salt and pepper towards the end of cooking, boil again for 5 minutes and serve with potatoes or rice.

You may enrich the stew with 2 tablespoons of white wine or a teaspoon of wine vinegar diluted in a little water.

VARIATION   Setúbal, south of Lisbon, offers a rich version for squid (or cuttlefish) stew. Serves 4:

675 g/1½ lb squid	¼ coffeespoon cayenne pepper
4 tablespoons olive oil	1 large clove garlic, chopped
4 tablespoons white wine	salt
½ teaspoon paprika	garnish – 2 hard-boiled eggs, sliced

Clean the squid (or cuttlefish), remove and discard the ink sac, and cut it into small pieces, including the tentacles. Fry the garlic in the oil until golden, add the wine and fish, cover and cook gently until tender, adding a little fish stock or water, as needed. The sauce should be rich, so add the liquid little by little, or reduce it at the end. Garnish with the sliced eggs and serve with chips. Do not overcook (please see instructions on page 93 regarding Squid, Cuttlefish and Octopus). Be careful also with the use of salt.

STUFFED BABY SQUID – ALGARVE FASHION
Lulinhas Estufadas à Moda do Algarve
Serves 4 to 6

1 kg/2 lb baby squid	**Cooking Sauce**
100 g/3½ oz Prosciutto	1 medium ripe tomato, cleaned and chopped
75 g/2½ oz rice	1 medium onion, chopped
1 medium tomato (ripe), peeled, cleaned and cut	1 clove of garlic, chopped
1 medium onion, well chopped	2 sprigs of parsley, chopped
1 clove of garlic, well chopped	2 tablespoons olive oil
2 tablespoons olive oil	3 tablespoons white wine
2 sprigs of parsley, well chopped	1 bayleaf
2 tablespoons white wine	dusting of cayenne pepper

Wash and clean the squid very well, discard the heads and keep the tentacles. Cut them into small pieces, for the stuffing. Cook and cool the rice. Set aside. Fry the onion and garlic in the oil, to soften. Add the tomato pieces and parsley. Cook gently for 5 minutes. Now add the ham cut into small bits, the tentacles and wine. Mix everything now and cook for 6-7 minutes in low heat, turning once or twice. Taste for salt and perhaps a little pepper. Set aside to cool, then stuff the squid with this mixture, without filling them too much (the stuffing expands a little). Close the squid with tooth-picks. Set aside. For the sauce, fry the onion and garlic in the oil until transparent. Add the other ingredients and cook gently for 5 minutes. Now place the stuffed squid on top of this sauce and simmer for 20 minutes. Shake the pan now and then, add a little boiling water if it becomes dry. Taste for salt.

Serve with mashed potato and sprinkle with coriander leaves.

OCTOPUS WITH RICE
Polvo com Arroz
MINHO PROVINCE • Serves 6

This is one of the dishes normally included in Minho Christmas fare. The Portuguese are very partial to octopus, anyway, fresh, half dried and fully dried. You will see it hanging in those specialized shops selling only salted and dried fish (salt cod mainly). The taste for octopus seems to have been acquired long ago, when the sailors who braved the seas, in the fifteenth and sixteenth centuries, during the 'discoveries era', packed dried food to eat during the voyages. This recipe is for fresh octopus.

1 fresh octopus, about 1 kg/2 lb	2 tablespoons wine vinegar
4 tablespoons lard	½ teaspoon chilli powder
4 tablespoons olive oil	400 g/14 oz rice
2 medium onions, chopped	salt and pepper
3 stalks parsley, chopped	

Ask the fishmonger to clean the octopus for you. Wash well and tie the sides of the head over it, like a hood, cutting the tentacles into pieces. Meanwhile fry the onion and parsley in the fat and oil for 3-4 minutes. Then add the fish, vinegar, chilli powder and enough boiling water almost to cover the octopus. Replace the lid and cook gently until tender (45-50 minutes or even longer), checking whether more liquid is necessary in the meantime. When tender, *and only then*, add the salt and boil again for 2-3 minutes. Lift the fish, set aside. Measure enough liquor to cook the rice (2½ times its volume). If you have too much liquor, boil it for a little while, to reduce to the proper amount. Add the rice and cook, until tender (about 25 minutes) – the rice should be on the 'wet' side. Taste again for seasoning and add the octopus, cut into pieces. Bring to the boil, to reheat through, and serve with a side dish of black olives and chunks of crusty bread.

VARIATION The addition of rice makes this dish more substantial, but it can also be served with chunks of crusty or slices of fried bread.

NOTE: Fresh octopus needs careful attention when cooking because it tends to harden if overcooked after the 'tender stage'. However, there is a 'secret' way of preparing octopus so it always remains tender. This was revealed to me by my friend Maria Aria Barata. See method on page 93.

MEAT

A popular Portuguese saying declares 'Fish does not pull a cart' ('*Peixe não puxa carroça*'), meaning that fish does not give enough strength. This is a conviction still held by many people, in spite of the fact that research has proved them wrong. On the other hand, there are many others fully prepared, nowadays, to admit that meat is not the be-all and the end-all of good food. Still, meat is much used by the Portuguese. Beef, veal, kid and lamb are used, but kid and pork are especially relished and used in many varied and imaginative recipes, as are domestic rabbit, chicken and also game (mainly wild rabbit and partridge). The Portuguese are also good at creating dishes out of offal and tripe.

NOTE: Kid, lamb, mutton and goat can all be cooked with the same recipes, varying only the length of cooking and taking care not to allow the meat to dry up. In the same way, poultry can substitute for game when necessary, perhaps adjusting the seasonings accordingly.

BEEFSTEAK

Fried steak is one of the most popular and sought-after quickly prepared lunches in Portugal, be it at restaurants or in the home (especially so in urban areas). The price factor may have curbed the demand somewhat, but steak used to be almost the staple diet of some people – or at least for Sunday lunches, much as the British have their joint.

Steak is called *bife* in Portugal, pronounced the same as 'beef', which clearly indicates its original inspiration. It derives from the British influence (after all the Anglo-Portuguese alliance is already into its seventh century) and, amusingly, *bife* is the name given colloquially to an Englishman. Portuguese acquaintances, in the course of conversation, have said to me: 'So you are married to a *bife*?' This is not intentionally pejorative – it is just a mild slang, if you like, and it is used much less nowadays than was the case years ago. Portuguese people love to give nicknames and fond diminutives to almost anything that lends itself to it – or even if it doesn't. Referring to steak, for instance, they may say: '*Vai um bifinho?*' ('Will you have a "little" steak?') – not meaning a *small* steak but a *lovely* one, inferring that it would be a good choice.

STEAK WITH EGG ON HORSEBACK
Bite com Ova a Cavalo
ESTREMADURA PROVINCE • Serves 4

4 rump or sirloin steaks
2 tablespoons butter plus enough butter to fry the eggs
4 sprigs parsley
4 small cloves garlic
1 bay leaf
4 eggs
salt and pepper

Clean and prepare the meat as for ordinary steaks. Rub each one with its own crushed clove of garlic, sprinkle with salt and pepper and leave for 10 minutes. After that melt the fat in a large frying-pan, add the parsley and bay leaf and fry the steaks, turning once or twice. They are generally slightly underdone. In the meantime, fry the eggs and serve one on top of each steak. At restaurants the steaks are cooked and served in individual earthenware pans. The classical accompaniment is thick chips (*batatas fritas*).

STEAK IN A ROLL
Bife no Pão (Prego)

For this you must have a roll baked on the same day, or bake your own. *Prego* is the most wonderful quick lunch or snack you can have... Prepare a steak as for recipe above (half that amount, so it fits into the roll). Omit the egg. Cut the roll in half and fill it with the steak, with all its lovely juices. Eat immediately.

STEAK MARRARE FASHION
Bife à Marrare
LISBON • Serves 4

This recipe for steak was allegedly created by a chef named Marrare who came to Lisbon from the north of Spain, or from Naples – there is a dispute over his birthplace among culinary experts; what they do agree on is the excellence of his invention. Anyway, the Marrare Café, which used to stand in the centre of Lisbon, became famous for its superb steak and was frequented by the most distinguished nobility and politicians of the nineteenth century.

4 good-sized fillet steaks
4 tablespoons single cream
4 tablespoons butter

2 cloves garlic, crushed
salt and freshly milled pepper

Rub the meat with the garlic. In a heavy pan melt half the butter. Fry each steak on both sides, over medium heat, to avoid losing the meat juices. Dust with salt and pepper as you take the steaks off the pan. Keep warm. When they are all fried, add the remaining butter to the pan and the cream. Stir well and allow to simmer, to thicken. Taste for seasoning. Add the fried steaks, to reheat. Serve immediately, with a side dish of chips (*batatas fritas*).

STEAKS WITH ONION
Bifes de Cebolada
ESTREMADURA PROVINCE • Serves 4

This recipe produces a steak completely different from the usual, on account of the seasoning, onion and tomato.

4 rump steaks
2 cloves garlic, chopped
2 tablespoons olive oil
1 tablespoon lard
2 large onions, thinly sliced

4 medium tomatoes, peeled and seeded, coarsely
  chopped
2 bay leaves
3 sprigs parsley, chopped
salt and pepper

Use a casserole or saucepan for this. Place the fat and oil at the bottom of it and assemble layers of steak, onion, tomatoes and the seasoning. Cover the pan and cook gently for 30-35 minutes. You may need to reduce the sauce a little towards the end. Serve with mashed potatoes or plain rice. This dish is prepared very quickly and successfully using a pressure cooker (8-10 minutes).

ROAST BEEF

ALCATRA
Roast Beef with Spices
AZORES • Serves 6 to 8

The islands have very good cattle, so beef is a popular meat. In this dish we have spices that are typical of the Azores (and even Madeira). This reminds us that these Atlantic archipelagos were –and are – on the route where all navigation stopped. Now it may be because of the popularity of cruising holidays, but centuries ago they were used for refreshing tired sailors and gathering much needed provisions for their long voyages. Ships would stop on their way to and from the Americas, and spices coming from Jamaica eventually gained favour locally. Allspice, called 'pimenta da Jamaica' (Jamaican pepper) in Portuguese, did of course come from the West Indies, being introduced in the Azores, where it is liberally used in many dishes, sweet and savoury. *Alcatra* is the name given to rump, but the dish includes various other cuts. However, one can choose any beef which is appropriate for roasting, but ideally should include some meat from the tail end, because of its gelatinous quality. As the dish is cooked for a long time it does not really matter if choosing relatively cheap cuts of beef, provided they are not stringy.

3 kg/6 lb beef (see above suggestions)	2 tablespoons of butter
90 g/3 oz smoked bacon	1 tablespoon of wine vinegar
2 large onions, sliced	6 peppercorns
2 glasses of red wine	1 small piece of cinnamon
6 grains of allspice	salt

Prepare the meat leaving it in large chunks. Grease very well a deep roasting tin and cover the bottom with a layer of sliced onions. Spread a little of the bacon, in small cubes. Now place a layer of meat and so on, until you use up the ingredients, not forgetting the wine and vinegar, which must be diluted with 2 tablespoons of water. Add also some salt between the layers. The last one must be sliced onions. Spread butter on top, in small bits. Take the meat to the oven and bake at 180°C/350°F/Gas 4 for at least 3 hours, unless the meat is very tender. Turn it occasionally. You may need to add a bit more water, but do it carefully. In the Azores this dish is served with a dense local bread, but mashed potato or plain rice would be suitable.

VARIATION The same amount of meat, leaving it whole, no bacon, 2 large cloves of garlic instead of onion, and the addition of a dusting of paprika and chillies (piri-piri) to taste. In this dish a marinade is made with the pounded spices and the wine, leaving the meat in it for half a day, cooking it afterwards in the same liquid and covering with equal parts of olive oil and butter (2 tablespoons each). This dish is served with quartered potatoes that have been parboiled and then sautéed, before adding to the gravy around the meat.

NOTE In Madeira roast beef is prepared almost the same way, including the allspice, but adding stoned black olives to the finished dish, before taking it to the table. The wine used here is Madeira wine. The meat can also be cooked slowly in a pot with a well-fitted lid, over the stove. New potatoes parboiled and then sautéed in a little olive oil until golden, are the accompaniment.

STEWS

BOILED MEAT AND VEGETABLES, PORTUGUESE STYLE
Cozido à Portuguesa
TRÁS-OS-MONTES PROVINCE, BUT USED COUNTRYWIDE • Serves 6 to 8

This is one of the most typical of Portuguese dishes, enjoying great popularity all over the country, even though it originated in the Trás-os-Montes province, where it is standard fare during the Carnival. It is widely regarded as one of the finest Portuguese specialities, notwithstanding its simplicity. This is peasant food at its best, consisting of a variety of meats and smoked sausages (the more the better) boiled with potatoes and vegetables, with a side dish of rice, cooked in the same broth. It is worth preparing more *cozido* than will be necessary, as any meat and vegetables left over can be used for other dishes or reheated and eaten as they are the following day. The broth is ideal for soups.

450 g/1 lb leg of beef	1 pig's ear (optional)
450 g/1 lb chicken	1 large cabbage (heart)
350 g/12 oz spare ribs (pork) or a piece of smoked bacon or salted pork	8 medium carrots
	8 medium potatoes
110-140 g/4-5 oz *morcela* (p. 00)	4 medium turnips
140 g/5 oz *chouriço* (p. 25)	280 g/10 oz rice
2 *farinheiras* – flour-sausages (if you cannot obtain these, add more bacon)	salt

If using salted meat, soak it first for a few hours, to desalt a little. As to the *chouriço* (p.25) and other cured meats, I must say they are really essential for the proper *cozido* flavour.

In a very roomy saucepan cook the meat in enough water to cover and add a little salt. Skim the surface of the liquid. Check from time to time, to remove any meat whose cooking time is less than the others, until they are all done. Keep the meat aside and in the same liquor cook all the vegetables at the same time. Cut them in big chunks and boil until tender (about 25 minutes to half an hour). Remove from the pan enough stock (you may have added a little more water, in the meantime) to boil the rice (2½ times its volume). When everything is cooked, return the meat and vegetables to the stock, to reheat thoroughly. While you are doing this, dry the rice in the oven (190°C/375°F/Gas 5) for 3-5 minutes. Check seasoning throughout cooking.

TO SERVE make a mound of the rice in a separate dish, and surround it with the *morcela* and other sausages, in thick slices. Put the meat and vegetables in a tureen or deep serving dish, with a little of the stock, to keep them moist. Serve at once.

VARIATIONS According to availability or season, add a few very tender green beans and chickpeas (previously soaked). If using the chickpeas (200-225 g/7-8 oz), remember they take some time to cook, so put them together with the meat, at the beginning.

NOTE: The most famous of Azorean dishes is a *cozido*, with very similar ingredients to the above, but cooked for several hours inside one of the many natural holes (geysers) formed by hot springs (*furnas*) dotting a particular area of S. Miguel Island, near the lakes. A large pot, with a well-secured lid and protected by a sac all around, is lowered carefully into one of these holes. A large wooden lid is placed on top to seal it, and some earth is spread on top. Five hours later the hole is uncovered and the pot taken up, with the meal ready.

Cozido is also prepared in Madeira, but here sweet potatoes are used instead of the usual potatoes, and pork meat substituted for beef.

BEEF STEW
Carne Guisada
Serves 4 to 6

This homely dish is often prepared without the addition of wine, but even if it is just a little, wine will improve the dish enormously.

560 g/1¼ lb stewing beef, cubed	2 medium tomatoes, peeled and chopped
675 g/1½ lb potatoes, peeled and cubed	1 bay leaf
1 large carrot, sliced	3 sprigs parsley, chopped
2 medium onions, sliced	3 tablespoons olive oil
1 large clove garlic, sliced	1 tablespoon lard
6 tablespoons red wine	salt and pepper

Prepare a marinade with the wine, bay leaf, garlic, salt, pepper and parsley. Steep the meat in this and leave overnight. The following day strain the meat and fry it in the oil and lard, together with the onion. Turn, to seal all round. Add the carrot. After a little while add the strained marinade. Cover and cook over gentle heat until the meat is almost tender. Test now and then to see if you need to add a little water or stock to the pan. Taste for salt and add the potatoes. Cover again and cook for a further 30 minutes, when everything should be tender. Check the liquid and seasoning. Serve at once.

GOAT STEW, BAIRRADA STYLE
Chanfana da Bairrada
BEIRA LITORAL PROVINCE • Serves 4

This festive stew used to be prepared in the baker's oven and still is, when possible. There is no reason, however, why one could not prepare it at home. The proper container is a large black earthenware casserole from the same region, but you could use any roomy, fireproof dish with a lid.

Weddings and christening feasts are whole-day affairs in the country, with food and wine brought to the large tables at regular intervals. This stew is but one of the succulent celebration dishes of the Bairrada region, which rates among the richest and most inventive in the culinary field.

Goat meat is the classic choice, but lamb can also be used. Quantities here are given for 4 people, as in most dishes in the book, but obviously these could be doubled or trebled, as needed.

This stew is normally prepared a day or so in advance, and then reheated.

1 kg/2 lb tender goat or lamb, boned and cut into biggish pieces
90 g/3 oz fatty bacon, in small cubes
3 tablespoons olive oil
30 g/1 oz lard
1 teaspoon paprika
3 sprigs parsley, chopped
½ coffeespoon pepper

1 large onion, chopped
1 bay leaf
2 large cloves garlic, chopped
450 ml/¾ pint red wine from the Bairrada region, if possible
¼ coffeespoon nutmeg
salt

Put all the seasonings in the casserole, mix, taste for salt and add the meat. Now pour on some of the wine, so the meat is almost covered. Put the lid on the casserole and bring to the oven, which must be very hot (232°C/450°F/Gas 8). Bake for an hour at this temperature, then check the amount of liquid in the casserole. Add the remaining wine now. Keep the oven at the above temperature for 30 minutes longer, then reduce to 180°C/350°F/Gas 4 until the end of cooking (another 1-1½ hours). Remove from the oven, test for salt and liquid (it should be swimming in gravy) and keep for a day or so, until needed. Then place it in the oven again until really hot. Serve accompanied by boiled potatoes.

BEAN STEW, PORTUGUESE STYLE
Feijoada à Portuguesa
Serves 4

A marvellous stand-by of the Portuguese kitchen. Each region may have its own variations, but basically *feijoada* is a rich bean stew with pork and sausages.

450 g/1 lb dried beans (butterbeans or red kidney)
175 g/6 oz *chouriço*
175 g/6 oz streaky bacon (in cubes)
90 g/3 oz *morcela*
1 medium tomato (peeled and seeded)
2 cloves garlic, chopped
2 medium onions, chopped

2 tablespoons olive oil
2 tablespoons lard
3 sprigs of parsley
1 bay leaf
1 clove (optional)
salt and pepper

Soak the beans in plenty of cold water, overnight. Place the beans in cold water, seasoned with half the olive oil, half the lard and salt. Add one of the onions (with the clove stuck in it, to discard later). Bring to the boil and cook until tender. The cooking time depends on the type of beans. Check now and then, also for liquid, as it should not dry out. Do not overcook the beans, nevertheless. When tender, drain the beans and set aside, keeping the liquor.

Take some of this to another pan to cook the cured meats, boiling until almost tender (15-20 minutes). Meantime fry the other onion in the remaining fat and oil, together with the chopped tomato and the other ingredients, for 3-4 minutes, over low heat. Add the meat (cut into pieces), boil

for a further 2-3 minutes, add the beans, boil again and of course mix in the pan any liquor still left, for a moist consistency, but do not add an excessive amount. Taste for seasoning and serve at once. If you have any left-over liquor, this can be used later for a soup.

In some northern provinces this dish is further 'reinforced' by an accompaniment of *Arroz no Forno* (p.108).

VARIATION The stew can also be served with slices of fried bread, which will then be soaked in the gravy. A larger amount or variety of pork meat can also be added, such as a knuckle, pig's ear, piece of belly and so on, to taste. These can be cooked with the beans.

NOTE FOR VEGETARIANS *Feijoada* is a very good dish even without the meat. Use a little more onion and other seasonings, if desired, for a rich flavour.

KID

ROAST KID
Cabrito Assado
BEIRA BAIXA PROVINCE • Serves 6

> Quite so. Horace would have dedicated an ode to that roast kid. And with the trout, and Melchior's wine, and the *cabidela* – prepared by the sublime squinting dwarf with an inspiration not of this earth – and the sweetness of that June night, showing its dark velvet mantle through the open window, I felt so comfortably lazy and contented that, as the coffee awaited us in the sitting-room, I just collapsed in one of the wicker chairs – the largest, with the best cushions – and shouted in pure delight.
>
> Eça de Queiroz, *A Cidade e as Serras* (*The City and the Mountains*)

The idea is to have extremely tender and delicate meat, so the animal should be as young as possible. In Portugal it is usually only about a month old. The skin is allowed to get nicely browned all over.

1 kid (or a small lamb) whole (if it is a small kid, otherwise use half – about 2.5 kg/5 lb)
150 g/5 oz lard
2 tablespoons olive oil
2 cloves garlic, minced

1 bay leaf, cut into little pieces
4 sprigs parsley, chopped
60 g/2 oz lean bacon, minced
8 tablespoons white wine
salt

Open the kid, empty and clean it inside, wash thoroughly and allow to drain, preferably overnight. Wash the offal and keep it refrigerated until the following day as well.

Prepare all the seasonings, mixing them with the oil and 90 g/3 oz lard into a paste. Brush the kid inside and out with this. Mix any remaining paste with the offal (cleaned and cut into small pieces) and stuff the kid with it. Sew up the opening. Let the meat rest for a couple of hours, then spread the extra 60 g/2 oz lard all over it and bake in a preheated oven (190°C/375°F/Gas 5), allowing about 25 minutes per 450 g/1 lb meat, plus 30 minutes. Baste, and turn 2 or 3 times, to brown evenly. Serve with roast potatoes.

NOTE You can, of course, omit the offal.

KID BEIRA ALTA STYLE
Cabrito à Moda da Beira
Serves 4

Kid or lamb can be used for this dish. In the mountains the free-ranging herds get a good diet of wild herbs, and their meat is deliciously aromatic. This recipe enhances that fragrance, and the result is a mouthwatering dish.

1-1.25 kg/2-2½ lb kid or lamb, cut into convenient-
   sized pieces
300 ml/½ pint red wine
1 kg/2 lb potatoes
2 medium carrots, sliced
2 medium onions, chopped

2 cloves garlic, chopped
6 tablespoons olive oil
2 tablespoons lard
1 heaped tablespoon mixed herbs (to taste)
2 stalks parsley, chopped
salt and pepper

First half-cook the meat on top of the stove by the following method: put the oil, carrots, onions, garlic, herbs, salt, pepper and meat into a saucepan, to fry gently until golden all over (8-10 minutes). Add half the wine and 2-3 tablespoons water (or chicken stock). Cover and simmer for 20-25 minutes. Check the liquid. Meanwhile parboil the quartered potatoes in salted water, drain and set aside. Keep warm. Grease a deep oven-to-table dish (an earthenware one is used in peasant cooking) and transfer the meat, vegetables and liquor to it. Surround with the potatoes, dotted with lard. Bake for 50-60 minutes, basting now and then, until golden brown (oven 190°C/375°F/Gas 5).

OTHER MEAT DISHES

VEAL BARROSÃ FASHION
Vitela à Barrosã
ALTO DOURO PROVINCE • Serves 4

675 g/1½ lb very tender fillet of veal
90 g/3 oz butter
30 g/1 oz lard
1 teaspoon cornflour

1 large clove garlic, well crushed with salt
juice of ½ medium lemon
salt and pepper

Clean the meat of all tendons etc and cut it into thickish strips. Season with salt and pepper, the crushed garlic and lemon juice. Leave in this marinade for 3-4 hours, turning the meat now and then, to absorb all the flavours thoroughly. Then melt the fats in a deep frying pan and sauté the meat over a low heat until done (12-15 minutes). Drain the meat and keep warm. Thicken the sauce with the cornflour, mixed into a paste with a little water or stock. Boil for 2 minutes. Taste for salt and pour over the veal. Serve with any suitable accompaniment, such as mashed potatoes, plain rice or spaghetti.

SPIT-ROAST VEAL
Vitela no Espeto
NORTHERN PROVINCES • Serves 4 to 6

To prepare a spit-roast or barbecue-style dish, one should really use an open fire, since the traditional recipe is always cooked that way. Modern barbecues will suffice, provided the meat is turned regularly.

1 kg/2 lb veal (tender fillet from the tap of leg, or loin, off the bone)	1 bay leaf, cut in small pieces
	½ teaspoon chilli powder
4 tablespoons olive oil	2 cloves garlic, minced
1 tablespoon wine vinegar	salt

Clean the meat and remove any tendons, fat, skin etc. Sprinkle with salt. Place on the spit or barbecue. Using a kitchen brush, paint the meat all over with a paste made with all the seasonings. The meat should be cooked in 45 minutes but pierce it with a skewer first to test – no blood should come out. Do not overlook basting with the seasoning and turning the meat now and then. Serve with roast potatoes.

VARIATION   From the same provinces a version of plain spit-roast veal.

1 kg/2 lb boned top of leg	coarse salt
2 medium onions, very thinly sliced	

Wet the meat slightly, so it holds a good sprinkling of salt, all round. Place it on the open barbecue and roast for 35-40 minutes, turning occasionally. When ready, put the meat in a covered dish for a few minutes, to make it sweat and give out some of the juices. Serve covered with the slices of raw onion and a side dish of boiled potatoes or chips.

TRIPE, OPORTO STYLE
Tripas à Moda do Porto
Serves 4 to 6

It may sound a bit strange to some, but in many countries tripe makes extremely succulent, tasty and nourishing meals. In Portugal the Oporto region specializes in tripe dishes, and the city itself is renowned for its classic tripe recipe.

Oporto's partiality to tripe seems to have stemmed from necessity – or at least this is the generally accepted explanation. When the Portuguese were engaged in the conquest of certain North African towns (for example, Ceuta was taken in 1415), Oporto contributed large amounts of provisions to keep the men going. From the cattle slaughtered for this purpose, only the tripe was retained, so that there was no option for the people but to eat it as best they could. Hence the name *tripeiros* (tripe-eaters) given to the people of Oporto, a name which is still used and which, incidentally, makes them proud, given the reason for it.

It may not always be easy to find tripe on sale, and it may be necessary to order it in advance. In Portugal it is sold all over the country, and it is generally already scraped and bleached but barely cooked, so one has to start practically from scratch, which means longer cooking time. But even when it is bought already half-cooked, it will still need quite a lot of boiling at home to make it tender and extract all the jelly and juice still trapped inside. When properly cooked, tripe is surprisingly tender, well worth trying.

Veal tripe is generally chosen in the Oporto region, for its gelatinous quality, and various other types of meat are added, so this is not the 'poor man's recipe' the historical explanation might have us believe, but of course it is perfectly acceptable to use the tripe on its own, if so desired (or perhaps with just a spicy sausage or bacon, as an enrichment). The grand recipe set out below is used nowadays at restaurants in the ancient and historic city of Oporto.

675 g/1½ lb white tripe (veal, for preference) – honeycomb, flat tripe and thick seam	2 large onions, chopped
	2 medium carrots, sliced
½ medium-sized chicken	1 tablespoon lard
110 g/4 oz streaky bacon	2 sprigs parsley
110 g/4 oz *chouriço*	1 bay leaf
110 g/4 oz *presunto*	450 g/1 lb butter beans
1 calf's foot (optional)	½ coffeespoon cumin seed (optional)
1 pig's ear (optional)	salt, freshly ground pepper

Wash the tripe thoroughly, both outside and in and rub well with lemon and salt to clean still further. Wash again, under the tap. Boil in salted water until tender. It is difficult to predict how long it will take, because much depends on how the tripe dresser has prepared it. The best policy is to cook the tripe well in advance and test it now and then, keeping it waiting later on, if necessary, as it is essential that it is tender. In a separate pot, boil the other meat (remember that the cured meat contains salt already), together with the trotter and/or pig's ear. (You should at least use one or the other, for a richer dish.) Add to this pan the onions, carrots, chopped parsley, bay leaf and lard. When everything is cooked, set aside.

Using enough of the cooking liquor, bring the beans (soaking since the previous day) to the boil, and cook until tender. When all is done, drain the meat and vegetables, cut the tripe and all the other meat in conveniently-sized pieces and mix with the beans. Add some of the liquor to this and boil it all together for 10-15 minutes over low flame, to combine the flavours and thicken a little. Taste for seasoning, add some freshly ground pepper and serve, sprinkled with a few cumin seeds (optional) and/or some chopped parsley. The classic accompaniment for this dish is rice.

NOTE Do not discard the cooking liquor left over. You can transform it into a chowder with all the bits and pieces not used up and with the addition of cabbage and other vegetables, as needed.

RICE IN THE OVEN
Arroz no Forno
MINHO AND DOURO PROVINCES • Serves 4 to 6

In some northern regions, especially the Minho province, rice is an obligatory part of the meal, served as an accompaniment to almost anything. But of course rice is also used there for main courses, if cooked with meat. There is no limit to the amount or variety of meat one can include, depending only on how much one wants or what flavour must predominate. These rice dishes are finished in the oven, which gives them a more lavish flavour and appearance, with the top delectably crisp and the whole texture of the rice much improved.

450 g/1 lb rice
200 g/7 oz braising beef
110 g/4 oz leg of pork
1 leg of chicken
90 g/3 oz *chouriço*
110 g/4 oz smoked ham

1 medium onion, chopped
1 tablespoon olive oil
½ teaspoon saffron (optional)
3 sprigs parsley, chopped
salt and pepper

Boil the meat in enough water to cover and cook until tender. Remove from the heat, strain the meat and leave aside. Measure some of the stock (2½ times the volume of rice) and set aside. Fry the onion in the oil until golden, add the parsley and saffron diluted in a little water and add to the measured liquid. Bring to the boil, add the rice and cook for 12-15 minutes. Transfer to a buttered fireproof dish and finish cooking in the oven (180°C/350°F/Gas 4) for 15-20 minutes. Serve piping hot, with the meat reheated in a little of the stock and served in a separate dish.

VARIATION   A simpler version of rice in the oven uses left-over broth and/or gravy from roast lamb. Serves 4 to 6.

450 g/1 lb rice
90 g/3 oz cooked smoked ham or lean bacon
90 g/3 oz cooked *chouriço)*
1 large onion, chopped
3 tablespoons olive oil

½ teaspoon saffron (optional)
salt and pepper
chicken broth/meat gravy (as available – 2½ times
    the volume of rice)

Fry the onion in the oil until golden, add the chosen liquid and cooked meat (of which the above are only examples) and bring to the boil. Strain the meat, keep warm. Add the saffron (if using) and the rice, cook and serve as before.

PORK

The pig contributes in great measure to the sustenance of Portuguese people. In the Alentejo, a local breed of pigs, leaner and with a more elongated body, roam freely like sheep in places where large oak trees grow, producing the tasty acorns which they feed on.

Especially pleasing to the countryman's tastebuds are the series of succulent feasts that follow the annual pig's slaughter. Relatives are invited to help with the many chores associated with it and to share the special meals when all the bits and pieces that must be consumed while fresh are transformed into gargantuan banquets. These meals more than compensate for the toil involved in the cutting, salting and separating of meat and fat, the making of sausages and preparation of cured hams – which will be eaten raw many months later, cut into thin slivers as the tastiest of snacks or used in various recipes. Long tables are laden with fried liver, roast loin and big platters of *sarrabulho* (pig meat and offal cooked with the blood of the animal) to be washed down with the help of splendid local wines, served from big earthenware jugs. No *caldo verde*, no sardines, no salt cod, on those days! These are winter months, when the comforting warmth of pork dishes is more than welcome, filling the kitchen with appetizing smells.

Suckling pig is a highly recommended regional dish and extremely popular all over Portugal, although none is as good as the Bairrada style. In its province of origin it becomes almost an obsession. Generally it is considered too much trouble to prepare at home, so scores of restaurants, specializing solely in it, are spread throughout the region. Suckling pig is a mouthwatering delicacy, and those who have never tried it before surrender completely to the fine taste and succulence of its meat and to the characteristic crackling texture of the skin, after it is roasted to perfection.

The suckling pig must be really small, no more than a month old, so it does not have too much fat, and it must have been fed only on its mother's milk. It will weigh something like 6-10 lb (3-5 kg) after cleaning. It should not be too difficult to purchase a suckling pig answering to this description, even if you are far removed from a farm. Have a word with the butcher and he may be able to oblige.

The good point about roasting a very young animal (apart from its greater tenderness) is that it should fit into any decent-sized oven without having to cut it. In the Bairrada region an old-fashioned baker's oven is used, the animal being supported by a long stick, which is turned now and then to allow even cooking. Underneath, a large tray collects the precious juices and holds potatoes, which are thus roasted at the same time. At home one has to adapt these things as best one can. Should you find it difficult to fit the whole pig inside the oven, or if the tin is not large enough to hold it lengthwise, cut the pig in half and cook the two halves side by side, or in two consecutive sessions (you can always reheat the half baked first, before serving). If you adopt this method, do not forget to join both halves when serving, disguising the cut with some garnishing.

PORK, ALENTEJO STYLE (CATAPLANA)
Porco à Alentejana
Serves 4 to 6

This dish has become widely known all over the country. The clams and pork make an unusual but rich and exciting combination, and foreign visitors to Portugal find it extremely appetizing. The shellfish should be bought still alive, being opened in the prepared sauce. Keep the shells, as they give the dish its exotic appearance. (See references to clams in the shellfish chapter.)

450 g/1 lb loin of pork, cut into 2.5 cm/1 inch
   cubes
450 g/1 lb leg of pork, cut the same way
1 large onion, finely chopped
300 ml/½ pint white wine
3 cloves garlic, finely chopped
2 sprigs parsley, chopped
1 teaspoon paprika

1 teaspoon concentrated tomato paste
110 g/4 oz lard
2 tablespoons olive oil
675 g/1½ lb clams
1 clove
1 bay leaf
salt and pepper

Prepare a marinade with the wine, garlic, paprika, salt, pepper, bay leaf and clove. Stand the meat in this for 4-5 hours. Drain the meat and fry gently in the melted lard, until golden brown all over. Strain the marinade and add to the pan. Cover and boil with the meat until it is very tender and the sauce reduced by half. Meantime, make another sauce with the tomato concentrate, oil, onion, parsley, salt and pepper, simmering it all for 6-8 minutes. Place the clams in this over low heat. The clams should open in 6-7 minutes. (Remove those which do not, and discard.) Shake the pan and transfer its contents to the top of the meat. Cover. Boil gently for 2 minutes and serve in the same pan, with diced fried potatoes.

NOTE This is the dish usually known as *Carne de Porco na Cataplana* (Pork in a Cataplana Vessel) – *cataplana* being a typical pot used both in Alentejo and Algarve, and consisting of two concave halves, looking like a double wok. They are generally made of copper but can also be made of aluminium. They have handles which interlock and seal the pot. This keeps all steam inside, which enhances the flavour of the dish.

VARIATION (SEE SHELLFISH DISHES) In the Algarve *Cataplana* as a dish signifies also clams with meat, which normally consists of *chouriço*, with the clams. The procedure is similar. The vessel, *cataplana*, is of course suitable also for any stew. The food is taken to the table inside it, always a talking point, for its originality.

SUCKLING PIG, BAIRRADA STYLE

Leitão à Bairrada

BEIRA LITORAL PROVINCE • Serves 8

In order to keep the skin really crisp (a must, in this recipe), the pig should not be placed directly on the bottom of the roasting tin, or it would become soggy. In the absence of a big trivet, use a few wooden sticks, to rest the side of the pig. Do not forget that you will have to turn it, so as to cook and crisp it all over.

1 really small suckling pig	3 cloves garlic
300 ml/½ pint white wine (preferably from the same region)	2 tablespoons salt
	1 teaspoon pepper
60 g/2 oz bacon fat	2 sprigs parsley
60 g/2 oz lard	1 bay leaf

Ask the butcher to prepare the pig, leaving on the head (with the eyes, ears, tongue and teeth) and tail.

Prepare a paste with all the dry seasonings. Use a food processor, if you can. Add a little wine to moisten, if you find the paste too thick. Spread this paste all over the pig including inside, and place in the oven (see previous page) preheated to 210°/425°F/Gas 7, keeping to this temperature for the first 20 minutes of cooking, then reduce to 190°C/375°F/Gas 5 towards the end of cooking (about 2-2¼ hours). There are a few jobs to do during this time: basting the pig, at least every 20 minutes, with its own juices and some of the wine (reserve a quarter of it for later), turning the pig half way through and protecting the parts that may have become too dry (for instance, the ears) with a little foil. Remember that the skin is meant for eating, so it should be golden brown but not burnt.

After the given time (or before, if you think it is done), take the pig out and, using a big spoon or ladle, extract the juices in its belly cavity, as well as the liquid accumulated in the tin. Add all this to the reserved wine and bring to the boil, to reduce and thicken a little. Taste for seasoning and keep warm, to serve afterwards in a sauce-boat. Before you prepare the gravy, put the pig back in the oven (without any liquid) for about 10 minutes, to enhance the crackling quality of the skin. After that put the pig on a very large platter or tray and serve, placing an orange in its mouth. Garnish with lettuce leaves and potatoes, for a most lavish meal.

The left-overs are excellent cold.

SUCCULENT PORK VIANA STYLE

Rojões à Moda de Viana do Castelo

MINHO PROVINCE • Serves 4

This is a dish traditionally prepared during the pig-slaughtering season but it can be had at any time. *Rojões* really come from Minho and the Douro Litoral, but you find variations in other provinces as well. It is an extremely tasty dish and easy to prepare, despite the seemingly long list of ingredients.

1 kg/2 lb loin of pork
110 g/4 oz lard
300 ml/½ pint white wine
1 tablespoon wine vinegar
3 cloves of garlic, finely chopped
1 teaspoon paprika

1 bay leaf
1 tablespoon olive oil
½ coffeespoon cumin seed
100 g/3½ oz streaky bacon, cut small
salt and pepper

Prepare a marinade with the wine, vinegar, paprika, bay leaf, garlic, salt and pepper. Mix well and add the meat, cut into strips about 5 cm/2 inches in length and 2.5 cm/1 inch wide. Leave for 10-12 hours. Keep it, covered, in the fridge. Then melt the lard, oil and bacon, and add the cumin seeds, meat and marinade. Cook over medium heat until the meat is golden and the liquid reduced to a rich, fragrant sauce. Serve with plain boiled potatoes, with the sauce poured over them.

SUCCULENT PORK TRÁS-OS-MONTES STYLE
Rojões à Moda de Trás-os-Montes
Serves 4

This version of *rojões* has an important new item: chestnuts. These can, however, be omitted when not in season.

1 kg/2 lb loin of pork, cut as before
300 ml/½ pint white wine
100 g/3½ oz lard
2 cloves of garlic, finely chopped
1 bay leaf

1 coffeespoon paprika
2 sprigs parsley, chopped
1 small clove
boiled potatoes and chestnuts (boiled and peeled)

Prepare a marinade with the wine, garlic, bay leaf, clove, salt, pepper and half the parsley. Leave the meat in this for at least a day, but preferably 2 days. Keep it, covered, in the fridge. Bring to simmering point until the meat is tender. Remove the meat from the liquid and place in a pan with half the lard. Fry until golden. In the meantime reduce the marinade by a third, to use as a sauce. In a separate pan fry the potatoes and chestnuts (enough for 4 people) in the remaining lard. Serve the meat, potatoes and chestnuts with all the juices and sauces poured over them. Sprinkle with a little parsley.

LIVER WITH THEM (POTATOES)
Iscas com Elas
LISBON AREA • Serves 4

The title of the recipe refers to the fact that this is such a traditional dish that nothing except potatoes would do.

Not long ago there used to be various Lisbon restaurants renowned for their *iscas*. At present *iscas com elas* are less prominent on Lisbon's menus, though they still enjoy great popularity. It is a wholesome, economical and truly delicious dish, provided the liver is not overcooked (which hardens it). A small portion of the animal's spleen is included as well, to thicken the gravy – you should be able to get this from the butcher.

400 g/14 oz pig's liver thinly sliced	1 tablespoon wine vinegar
90 g/3 oz spleen-melts (well scrapped, using only the pulp)	6 tablespoons white wine
	1 bay leaf
2 cloves garlic chopped	salt and pepper
60 g/2 oz lard	boiled potatoes

Make a marinade with the vinegar, wine, garlic, bay leaf, salt and pepper and immerse the liver in it for 4-5 hours. In a large frying pan melt the lard and cook the slices of liver with a little marinade. Cook on both sides over low heat until the liver darkens, but not longer than 4-5 minutes. Remove the liver from the pan, set aside and keep warm. If available, mix the melts pulp in the juices left in the pan and add the strained remaining marinade. Cook gently for 8 minutes, to thicken. Add the liver again, simmer for 2 minutes, taste for seasonings and serve with the boiled potatoes.

EGGS AND SMOKED SAUSAGE
Ovos com Chouriço
ESTREMADURA PROVINCE, BUT USED COUNTRYWIDE

Eça de Queiroz (one of the best Portuguese writers of all time) must have been quite partial to eggs cooked with the smoked sausage so loved by the Portuguese, *chouriço*. In several of his bestsellers he mentions this popular dish as the delight of his heroes. Thus, in *The Remarkable House of Ramires*: 'Gonçalo ... started off by having a plateful of eggs with *chouriço* . . .' In *The Capital* we read again of this special combination: 'Rabeca ordered Mariquitas ... to prepare a lovely fry-up of eggs and *chouriço*. . .' And in *The City and the Mountains*: 'Jacinto had dined on eggs and *chouriço*. Really sublime.'

This is a rich-tasting but very simple omelette.

2 eggs per person	salt
about 5 cm/2 inches *chouriço* per person	oil (or butter) for frying

Make sure you buy *chouriço* that is the 'eating raw' kind. Put the fat in the frying pan and add the *chouriço*, finely sliced and free from the outer skin. Fry for 1-2 minutes. Add the beaten eggs and combine the lot. Make the omelette flat, turning it carefully with a spatula, or fold it, according to your preference.

VARIATION Fried eggs and *chouriço* can be made also. In this case you do not beat the eggs but add them whole to the pan, frying them in pairs with their share of *chouriço* until they are all done.

PEAS WITH SMOKED SAUSAGE
Paio com Ervilhas
Serves 4

> 'What a nuisance! I arrived from Paris with this voracious appetite and forgot to ask for a big platter of peas and *paio* for dinner!'
>
> Eça de Queiroz, *Os Maias (The Maias)*

This is a quick and flavoursome dish, prepared simply with tender peas and smoked loin of pork.

400 g/14 oz shelled peas
280 g/10 oz good *paio*, sliced – cooked smoked ham or bacon can be substituted
1 tablespoon butter
90 g/3 oz lard

1 medium onion, chopped
2 stalks parsley, chopped
4 poached eggs
salt and pepper

Fry the onion gently in the lard until transparent. Add 150 ml/¼ pint boiling water, the peas and parsley. Cover the pan and simmer. Add more water if needed. When the peas are half cooked, add the butter and the meat. Boil until the peas finish cooking. If, however, there is too much liquid in the pan, boil over a high flame for 1-2 minutes to reduce it. Serve with a poached egg per person.

VARIATIONS This dish can be scaled down to the simpler versions which are common in most Portuguese households during the pea season. Try these:

1 Same portions as above, substituting 60 g/2 oz *chouriço* or smoked bacon for the more expensive *paio*.
2   For vegetarians, omit the meat altogether and add a medium tomato (skinned and seeded) to the stew, from the start and/or increase the number of poached eggs.

PIG'S HAGGIS

Haggis is the stomach of the pig (or sheep) filled with an aromatic and rich meat stuffing. It is typical country fare, tasty and warming in winter.

Before you start cooking it, the stomach must be thoroughly scrubbed, inside and out (turn it over, for a complete job). Do this with a kitchen brush. Leave the stomach soaking in salted water for a few hours or until the following day. Alternatively scald it with boiling water, after scrubbing, and discard any loose skin and fat attached to it, then wash in plenty of running water.

There are many variations of haggis, some of which involve smoking it for a few days, at the end of cooking. This turns it into a sausage-like preparation. Usually, it is either roasted or boiled, securely sewn up to keep the stuffing inside.

PIG'S HAGGIS

Bucho de Porco Recheado

TRÁS-OS-MONTES PROVINCE • Serves 6 to 8

1 pig's stomach
4 thick slices bread
450 g/1 lb loin of pork, cubed
450 g/1 lb meaty bacon, cubed
6 eggs, beaten

450 ml/¾ pint meat stock
2 sprigs parsley, chopped
pinch powdered cloves
salt and pepper

Soak the bread in the stock and mash. Mix with the meat and all other ingredients. Taste for seasoning. Pack this filling into the prepared stomach and sew it up firmly. Wrap with muslin and tie up without squeezing it. Do not worry if the stomach does not seem completely full, as the stuffing expands during cooking. Prick the haggis in various places with a thick needle. Boil it in a large pan of salted water, for about 3-3¼ hours. Strain and allow to cool before removing the muslin and cutting into slices.

PIG'S HAGGIS BEIRA BAIXA STYLE

Bucho de Porco Recheado da Beira Baixa

Serves 6 to 8

1 prepared pig's stomach (see above)
560 g/1¼ lb tender pork meat with some fat
300 ml/½ pint white wine
3 sprigs parsley, chopped
3 cloves garlic, chopped
2 medium onions, chopped
2 tablespoons lard

1 tablespoon butter
4 beaten eggs
280 g/10 oz fresh white breadcrumbs
8 peppercorns
juice ½ lemon
1 clove
salt

Divide the wine, garlic and parsley into two. Use one half to marinate the stomach (already cleaned as indicated above) for a few hours, or overnight. Use the other half of the mixture, together with an onion, butter and a tablespoon of lard (seasoned with salt) to cook the meat, over low heat. When tender, mix 200 g/7 oz of the breadcrumbs with lemon juice and eggs. Taste for seasoning. Stuff the stomach. Sew it and tie up with the muslin. Prick with the needle as before. Bring the marinade to the boil together with the remaining onion, peppercorns and clove, adding enough water to cover the stuffed haggis. Simmer for 1-1½ hours. Then unwrap and brush with the remaining lard, roll in 90 g/3 oz dried breadcrumbs and bring to the oven (190°C/375°F/Gas 5) for 15 minutes, or until browned.

POULTRY AND GAME

STUFFED TURKEY FOR CHRISTMAS
Peru Recheado de Natal
Serves 8 to 10

Although the Iberian peninsula was very rich in game and poultry in the Middle Ages, turkeys appeared on the table only in the sixteenth century, after the explorers brought them back from South America. After that, turkey became increasingly popular and a part of Portugal's Christmas fare, as in many countries.

1 medium-sized turkey
150 ml/¼ pint white wine
1 large orange, very finely sliced
1 medium lemon, very finely sliced
2 tablespoons butter

2 tablespoons lard
1 teaspoon paprika
110 g/4 oz fatty bacon, minced
salt and pepper

STUFFING
(FOR THE BREAST-END)
200 g/7 oz lean meat (pork and veal), minced
60 g/2 oz lean bacon, minced
1 large slice white bread
1 small onion, finely chopped
1 tablespoon butter

1 tablespoon lard
2 sprigs parsley, chopped
zest ½ lemon
salt and pepper

(FOR THE TAIL-END)
1 medium onion, chopped
450 g/1 lb floury potatoes
1 tablespoon butter
1 tablespoon lard
the turkey giblets

2 medium eggs
2 sprigs parsley, chopped
8-10 black olives, stoned
pinch nutmeg
salt and pepper

Turkey meat is considered a little dry and bland in taste, so in Portugal it is generally steeped in a special marinade, the day before cooking, to improve it. Prepare the turkey, then put it in a large basin with some cold water to half cover it, salt, wine and the sliced citrus fruits. Turn the turkey around now and then. The following day take the turkey out of the marinade and put it somewhere to drain while you prepare the stuffing.

For the breast-end stuffing, fry the onion in the fats, until transparent, add to the minced meat, mix in the fresh breadcrumbs, and then the other ingredients. Combine this mixture, season and stuff the breast-end of the bird. Secure the skin with a needle and thread, if necessary.

Now prepare the tail-end stuffing. Fry the onion in the fats and add the giblets, well cleaned and cut into quite small pieces. Add a little stock and allow to cook gently, until tender. Reduce the gravy, if too liquid. Meanwhile cook and mash the potatoes and combine with the eggs, olives and parsley. When the giblets are ready, mix them with the potato, check for seasoning and stuff the cavity, again securing the skin with thread.

Make a paste with the lard, butter, bacon, paprika and seasoning and spread all over the turkey. Bring it to the oven (163°C/325°F/Gas 3) for about 3½-3¾ hours for a 10 lb (approx. 4.5 kg) turkey, basting now and then with the wine and its own juices. After that time, see if it is done (piercing one leg with a skewer and observing if blood still comes out). Leave it for a little longer (perhaps increasing the temperature to 191°C/375°F/Gas 5) if it needs browning, but do not allow the turkey to stay too long in the oven, to avoid drying the flesh too much. Baste again and serve with any accompaniments to taste and a large side salad.

NOTE To prevent burning the more exposed parts of the turkey, you may like to cover them with a little foil half way through roasting.

JUGGED CHICKEN OR CHICKEN IN A DEEP POT
Frango na Púcara
ESTREMADURA PROVINCE

This dish has been made quite popular in some restaurants of the Lisbon area. Traditionally it is prepared in a very deep earthenware pot with a tight-fitting lid. Though it will not taste exactly the same, it can, however, be made in any deep fireproof dish with a lid.

1 tender chicken (enough for 4 people)	2 tablespoons lard
8 small onions, whole	½ tablespoon mild made-mustard
3 medium tomatoes (peeled, seeded and chopped)	2 tablespoons port or Madeira wine
	2 tablespoons brandy or equivalent
60 g/2 oz smoked ham or lean bacon in small cubes	4 tablespoons white wine
	2 cloves garlic, finely chopped
1 tablespoon butter	1 tablespoon sultanas or raisins (without seeds)

Grease the chosen container. Place the cleaned chicken in it surrounded by the onions and pour over it a mixture of all the seasonings. Cover and bake at 200°C/400°F/Gas 6 for an hour or until the chicken is tender. Uncover the container, baste the chicken and continue baking for a short while, to allow the chicken to go golden on top. Serve at once with chips, salad and chunks of fresh bread, to dip into the gravy.

NOTE Some people prepare this dish on top of the stove. When the chicken is tender, it is placed (without the lid) under the grill, to brown the top slightly.

CHICKEN FRICASSÉE
Galinha de Fricassé
TRÁS-OS-MONTES AND ALTO DOURO PROVINCES

This is one of the dishes especially prepared for Christmas Eve supper, though it is also used (mainly in the Lisbon area) as an everyday dish in the home. It is delicately flavoured, quick and easy to prepare.

1 chicken, enough for 4 people
1 medium onion, chopped
1 tablespoon lard
1 tablespoon butter
1 tablespoon olive oil

1 sprig parsley, chopped
3 egg yolks
1 dessertspoon lemon juice
salt and pepper

Cut up the chicken and fry in the fat and oil, with the onion, until golden all over. Add a little water, salt and pepper and simmer, until tender. Beat the egg yolks with the lemon juice, add a little of the chicken liquor and mix well. Add this mixture to the pan, over a very low heat, and boil just for a minute, to cook the yolks without curdling them. Serve at once with the chopped parsley on top. It goes very well with plain rice or mashed potato.

CHICKEN RICE, PORTUGUESE STYLE
Arroz de Galinha à Portuguesa
Serves 4 to 6

1 medium-sized chicken, cleaned and quartered
90 g/3 oz *chouriço* (p.25)
90 g/3 oz fatty bacon
400 g/14 oz rice
2 tablespoons olive oil

1 tablespoon wine vinegar
1 large onion, chopped
2 sprigs parsley, chopped
salt and pepper

Fry the onion with the oil until golden, then add the chopped bacon and the chicken and sauté for 5 minutes, turning. Add 150 ml/¼ pint water, the vinegar, parsley, salt and pepper and cook gently until half done. Taste for seasoning and add the rice and enough boiling water or chicken stock to cook it (2½ times the volume of rice, roughly). About 5 minutes before the end of cooking, add the sliced *chouriço*. The rice must be slightly wet and therefore you may need to add more liquid at the end. Serve immediately.

DUCK WITH RICE

Pato com Arroz
MINHO PROVINCE • Serves 4 to 6

This is a dish suitable for a special meal.

1 medium duck, cleaned and cut into large pieces
280 g/10 oz smoked ham, cubed
90 g/3 oz *chouriço* thickly sliced
1 pig's ear, cleaned and cut

400 g/14 oz rice
2 tablespoons butter
juice of ½ lemon
salt and pepper

Cook all the meat together in enough water seasoned with a little salt. Drain off the liquid and measure enough to cook the rice (2½ times its volume). Add the lemon juice, a little pepper and salt (if needed). Bring to the boil. Add the rice. When half cooked (12-15 minutes), transfer the rice to a fireproof dish, dot it with the butter and finish cooking in the oven, for 15-20 minutes (190°C/375°F/Gas 5) until golden and crisp. Garnish with the duck, ham and sausage, return to the oven to reheat them (5 minutes) and serve immediately.

An optional sauce can be made with the remaining liquor and a little cornflour, to thicken. Serve in a sauce-boat.

DUCK WITH RICE AND ORANGE, BRAGA STYLE

Pato com Arroz e Laranja, de Braga
Serves 4 to 6

1 medium duck (whole)
175-225 g/6-8 oz smoked ham
60 g/2 oz bacon
90 g/3 oz *chouriço*
juice of ½ lemon
3 sprigs parsley

2 tablespoons butter
1 clove
salt and pepper
450 g/1 lb rice
1 large or 2 medium oranges sliced

Place the whole duck and the other meat in a roomy pot with enough boiling water to cover. Add the spices and seasoning. Cook until tender, skimming the top now and then. Take care not to overcook the duck. When done, drain the meat and allow the stock to cool down. At this point the fat will have gathered on top, and it will be easy to discard some of it, with a spoon. Cook the rice in the stock (2½ times its volume) as for the previous recipe putting a tablespoon of butter on it when you place it in the oven. When the rice is done, put the duck on top of it and brush the bird with the remaining butter. Bring to the oven again or put under the grill, to crisp up the skin of the duck. Reheat the other meat in the left-over liquid and serve together with the duck and the rice. Garnish with the orange slices.

VARIATION   A simpler version of Duck with Rice can be made using duck legs (which should be available at your supermarket). Personally I favour this simplified method, when preparing smaller amounts. I also cook the duck the previous day, leaving the pan in the fridge overnight, which allows plenty of time for the duck fat to solidify. Serves 4

4 duckling legs
200 g/7 oz Prosciutto
90 g/3 oz pancetta lardons
2 cloves
4 sprigs of parsley

400 g/14 oz long grain rice
2 medium cloves of garlic, finely sliced
1 tablespoon of butter
salt and pepper
1 orange, peeled and quartered

Place the meats in a large pan, cover with boiling water and season with the cloves, half the parsley, a little pepper and some salt. Boil gently until tender (test first, but it should be done in about 45 minutes or so). It is important that the meats are cooked but not too much. Remove them to a bowl, cover and, when cool, place in the fridge, for the next day. Pass the stock through a sieve and keep also in the fridge, when cool.

To prepare the dish, skim all the solidified fat from the stock, and place in a bowl for later use, keeping the rest afterwards in a jar (perhaps in the freezer) to use in other dishes (duck fat is quite precious).

Preheat your oven to 200°C/400°F/gas 6. Transfer enough stock to a roomy pan (2½ times the volume of the rice) and bring to the boil. Add the rice, bring to the boil again and then cook gently until almost tender. Taste. Place half the rice in an ovenproof dish, add the pieces of Prosciutto and pancetta, cover with the remaining rice. Dot with 2 or 3 spoonfuls of duck fat all over and place in the centre of the oven for about 12-15 minutes, then move the dish to the top for 5 minutes to crisp up the rice a little.

Meantime, melt the butter in a frying pan, add the garlic and parsley and the duck legs, and allow to crisp up on both sides, turning them. Add a spoonful of duck fat, turn again and serve on top of the rice, surrounded by the orange slices and covered with the juices from the frying pan.

NOTE Do not allow the garlic to burn, or it will become bitter.

RABBIT WITH WINE
Coelho em Vinho à moda do Alentejo
Serves 4

Rabbit meat (wild or tame) is especially suited to cook with wine. This really improves the meat enormously – the same applies, of course, to chicken and to other game, all of which can be cooked following the recipe below:

1 medium rabbit, cleaned and quartered
150 ml/¼ pint white wine
1 tablespoon port or Madeira – if available,
    otherwise use 1 tablespoon more white wine
2 medium onions, chopped
2 tablespoons olive oil

1 tablespoon lard
1 tablespoon butter
2 large cloves garlic, minced
salt and pepper
4 thin slices of fried bread

Grease a fireproof dish with lid. Place the fried slices of bread on the bottom. Add the pieces of rabbit, sprinkle with salt and pepper and distribute over it the fat, oil and seasoning. Bring to the oven (190°C/375°F/Gas 5) for about an hour until the meat is almost done. Remove the lid, add the wines and continue baking until golden (another 15 minutes). Serve with rice or potatoes, plain or mashed.

HUNTER'S RABBIT
Coelho à Caçadora
ESTREMADURA REGION

A tempting rabbit stew (see opposite), very easy to prepare. Experiment substituting with chicken.

1 rabbit (enough for 4 people), cleaned and quartered	2 medium onions, chopped
110 g/4 oz bacon (medium fat), chopped	2 stalks parsley, chopped
2 tablespoons lard	8 tablespoons red wine
4 medium tomatoes, peeled, seeded and chopped	1 tablespoon wine vinegar
2 large cloves garlic, finely chopped	1 bay leaf
	salt and pepper

If the rabbit is killed at home, keep its blood in a cup, mixed with the vinegar (which will prevent coagulation). Place half the melted lard in a large earthenware pot (if you have one, otherwise use any good saucepan) and layer all the ingredients, starting with the onions and finishing with the bay leaf, parsley and remaining melted lard. Sprinkle a little salt between layers. Pour the wine on top, cover and simmer over the stove until tender (about an hour). Add the blood mixture, if you kept it, and boil for 4-5 minutes. Serve at once with boiled potatoes (or mash) or plain rice.

PARTRIDGE IN VINEGAR SAUCE (TO SERVE COLD)
Perdiz de Escabeche
INLAND PROVINCES

On the table the supper was laid – consisting of cheese, apples, walnuts, chestnuts, two tureens full of escabeche, his speciality, and a bottle of port wine with a promising topaz colour.
Júlio Diniz (1839-71), *A Morgadinha dos Canaviais* (*The Lady of the Reeds*)

4 small partridges (1 per person) or 2 bigger ones	2 bay leaves
2 medium onions, thinly sliced	4 cloves garlic, thinly sliced
7 tablespoons olive oil	8 peppercorns
5 tablespoons wine vinegar	4 sprigs parsley, chopped
4 cloves	salt

Prepare the partridges, tie them with string, to keep their shape, and parboil in enough water to cover them. Season with salt. Remove the partridges (keeping the stock for later) and fry them in a roomy pan, using the olive oil. Turn the birds until golden. Then add all the seasonings and enough cooking liquor to cover them. (Reserve any left-over liquor for a game soup.) Bring to simmering point, cover and cook until tender, adding a little more liquid if needed and turning the birds once or twice for even cooking. Leave in the same pot with the liquor until the following day. Serve cold, with chips.

The dish will keep for several days.

COLD PARTRIDGE
Perdiz Fria
COIMBRA REGION

Although the name implies that this is a cold dish, it can be eaten whilst it is hot. It is very succulent either way. Partridge may not be as plentiful as it used to be, but it remains one of the most popular game birds in Portugal.

4 partridges (allow 1 small bird per person)	2 cloves garlic, thinly sliced
8 tablespoons olive oil	2 cloves
8 tablespoons white wine	8 peppercorns
2 tablespoons wine vinegar or cider vinegar	salt
3 medium onions, thinly sliced	

Clean the birds and tie them with string, to keep the shape. Marinate them for a few hours in the wine, vinegar, salt and oil, turning now and then, to tenderize the meat. Put the partridges, marinade and all other ingredients in a roomy pot with a tight lid, and bring to the boil. Reduce to simmering point, cover and cook until tender, adding some water (or chicken stock) as necessary. Remove the partridges to a deep serving dish, pour the strained liquor over them and serve hot or cold with crisps and salad.

CHICKEN PIES ALENTEJO STYLE
Empadas de Galinha
Makes about 12 pies

These are small, individual pies, made in patty tins, which over the years have become exceedingly popular and which are now sold in pastry-shops all over the country but especially in Lisbon. They are much favoured for light lunches and snacks, during office breaks, for picnics and parties. They are eaten cold, but should ideally be baked on the same day.

PASTRY

350 g/12 oz flour	1 teaspoon salt
140 g/5 oz butter (soft but not melted)	4 egg yolks

FILLING

(to be prepared beforehand)	3 sprigs parsley, chopped
450 g/1 lb chicken meat, without skin or bones	1 clove
1 medium onion, chopped	60 g/2 oz lean bacon, cut into small pieces
60 g/2 oz lard	dusting of nutmeg
1 tablespoon wine vinegar	salt
2 tablespoons white wine	

Cut the chicken into small pieces and fry in the lard, together with the bacon. When golden, add all the seasonings, including the wine and some water almost to cover it. Cook gently until very tender. Reduce the liquid but leave the mixture moist. Taste for seasoning. Set aside, to cool completely.

To start the dough, mix all the ingredients in a bowl, adding just enough water to make it pliable. Knead it very lightly. It should not be sticky. If it is, add a dusting of flour, to remedy this. Roll out to 3 mm/⅛ inch and cut out rounds slightly larger than the patty tins. Set aside half the rounds, to use as lids. Line the tins, pressing the pastry against the sides, and fill them to three-quarters with the chicken stew, which will be almost solid by then and therefore easy to divide. Moisten the edges of the pastry with water and place the lids on top, pressing the edges together and turning them upwards. Brush with milk or a mixture of milk and egg yolk. Bake in an oven preheated to 200°C/400°F/Gas 6 for about 20 minutes or until the pies are a rich golden colour.

NOTE The chicken pies sold at patisseries do vary a little in that the pastry used is generally puff pastry or similar, while this recipe is the original one, from the Alentejo.

VEAL PIES CASTELO BRANCO FASHION
Empadas de Vitela de Castelo Branco
BEIRA BAIXA PROVINCE • Makes about 10 pies

These veal pies are a splendid speciality, which, like chicken pies, above, have transcended the limits of their place of origin to become very popular all over the country.

PASTRY

225 g/8 oz flour	scant 30 g/1 oz lard, melted
1 egg	salt
2 tablespoons olive oil, slightly warm	egg for brushing

FILLING

310 g/11 oz boned cooked veal	1 bay leaf
2 tablespoons white wine	½ teaspoon marjoram
1 medium onion, chopped	sprinkling nutmeg
2 tablespoons olive oil	salt and pepper
1 clove garlic, chopped	

Prepare the pastry first. Mix the flour, oil, lard, egg, salt and some tepid water, to make a medium soft dough. Knead for a moment, cover with a cloth and put aside for an hour.

Meanwhile, put all the ingredients for the filling (except the meat) in a pot and cook gently until the onion is soft. Add the meat cut into small pieces. Cover and simmer for a few minutes, adding a little stock if necessary. Taste for seasonings and leave to cool.

Roll out the pastry to 3 mm/⅛ inch thickness and cut rounds somewhat larger than the diameter of your patty tins (which must be well greased). Cut out another lot of rounds for the lids. Line the tins, fill with the cold meat mixture, place the pastry lids on top, fold up the edges while pressing them, to seal (moisten with a little water, to make it easier) and twist a bit to form a kind of crown. Brush with the beaten egg. Bake at 200°C/400°F/Gas 6 for 20-25 minutes or until the pies are a golden brown.

VARIATION A mixture of veal and pork can be used, instead of veal alone.

CELEBRATION CHICKEN PASTIES
Fogaças
Makes about 10

Many women bring olive oil for the convent's oil-lamps, offerings of bread and chicken *fogaças* [pasties].

> Fialho de Almeida, *Os Contos* (Short Stories)

Fogaças taste like pasties, wholesome and decorative, equally good hot or cold and ideal for picnics. In Portugal they are made especially for religious festivities, as part of traditional offerings to the Church (to be distributed afterwards among the needy, together with bread). But the word *fogaças* also came to be applied to the ornamental tall frames, looking rather like elongated crowns, that hold these offerings, which are carried solemnly on girls' heads.

These contraptions are gaily ornamented with paper flowers and ears of wheat, while the bread and the pasties (and any other offerings) are skilfully displayed all the way up the frames, which are almost as tall as the girls who carry them. The girls bear these *fogaças* with great dignity and poise, balancing them perfectly with the help of one hand only, while the other hand rests on the waist.

Fogaças are also called *tabuleiros* in some places, hence the Tabuleiros Festival in Tomar (Ribatejo province), which is renowned throughout the country and considered one of the best of these magnificent country celebrations. Such festivities are carefully prepared, with the involvement of the entire community, and afford a very good excuse to interrupt the hard routine of peasant life.

Fogaças can be savoury, like these, or sweet.

DOUGH
400 g/14 oz flour
1 sachet (7 g) dried yeast
60 g/2 oz lard
1 tablespoon olive oil
3 large eggs, at room temperature
about 5 tablespoons tepid water
salt

FILLING

450 g/1 lb boiled chicken
90 g/3 oz smoked ham (or lean bacon)
1 medium onion, chopped
4 tablespoons white wine
6 tablespoons chicken broth
30 g/1 oz lard
1 bay leaf
3 sprigs parsley, chopped
salt and pepper

For the filling, fry the onion in the lard until soft, add the parsley, bay leaf, salt and pepper, ham or bacon (cut into small cubes), broth, wine and chicken (boned, skinned and cut into very small pieces). Cook gently for a little while until it is all mixed and the liquid reduced to almost nothing. Taste for salt. Set aside to cool. Discard the bay leaf.

While the filling is resting, prepare a dough, mixing the flour, salt and yeast (crumbling this first). Make a well in the centre and add the warm water, 2 of the eggs and the melted fat and oil (still warm but not boiling). Mix well and knead as for a bread dough. Cover and leave to rise in a warm place for about an hour. Roll out the dough (to 3 mm/⅛ inch) on a floured board and cut half of it into 10 cm/4 inch squares and the other half into rounds 7.5 cm/3 inches in diameter. Divide the cold filling between the squares, placing it well in the centre and covering with the round lids. Fold up the corners of the squares over the round lids. Place the *fogaças* in greased baking trays and leave to rest in a warm place for about 30 minutes. Preheat the oven to 190°C/375°F/Gas 5 and brush the pasties liberally with the remaining egg, well beaten. Bake for 25-30 minutes or until golden.

NOTE: Try this appetizing filling for vol-au-vents or pies.

SAUCES

PIRI-PIRI SAUCE

So now to piri-piri sauce, or, if you are familiar with the South African expression, which has become popular in many places, peri-peri sauce.

Piri-piri is the smallest of the pepper family and fiercely hot. The Portuguese took chillies and all sorts of peppers, as well as numerous other Central and South American products to wherever they went, during the maritime era (15th and 16th centuries). As an example, from not having chillies at all, India is now the largest producer of these 'incadescent' beauties, which enhance many dishes all over the world.

There are, of course, many commercial hot sauces of this kind, following secret recipes, but real piri-piri sauce that you can make at home yourself is something else... The method was given to me by a Portuguese man who had returned from Africa, after decolonization of such places as Mozambique and Angola. I have made this sauce many times for appreciative friends and they do come back for more. The use of whisky guarantees that it lasts for a really long time, although it is better to store it in the fridge, in small, sterilized jam jars.

Use a small portion to dab on chicken quarters (very tender chicken legs are best), or large prawns, for a couple of hours, before grilling. Turn, as necessary, and serve with a salad and a glass or two of really cold beer.

You can, of course, try using a SMALL amount of piri-piri sauce in other dishes, to your discretion. For example, small squid or mackerel fillets. Just remember it is HOT! To use directly at the table, just bring out your sauce jar, with a very small coffee spoon to serve, and allow your guests to use just one or two drops of sauce onto their plates, to season all kinds of roasts, pork, liver and game – for example. Make sure you have this book at hand, because you're bound to be asked for the recipe.

NOTE Please remember to wash your hands repeatedly (or even wear kitchen gloves) when handling this kind of chilli. Especially avoid touching your eyes, even after you think it is safe to do so!

½ medium sized head of garlic
½ medium sized onion (yellow)
12 to 14 chillies (fresh)
50 ml/2 fl oz white wine or cider vinegar
50 ml/2 fl oz very good olive oil

½ medium sized lemon (grated peel and juice)
100 ml/4 fl oz whisky
1 tablespoon sugar
1 tablespoon runny honey
1 tablespoon sea salt

Separate the cloves of garlic, peel, cut and set aside. Grate or finely chop the onion. Wash the chillies, open them and place (with the seeds) in a saucepan with all other ingredients. Mix well and take to a very gentle boil for a little over 1 hour, when everything will be nice and soft. Set aside until almost cold and then blend until you obtain a completely smooth sauce. Transfer to the jars and store when cold.

TOMATO SAUCE, PORTUGUESE STYLE
Molho de Tomate à Portuguesa – or *Tomatada*
Makes about 600ml/1 pint

Whenever you see a menu indicating a dish 'Portuguese Style' it usually means that there is a tomato sauce or some kind of tomato mixture in it. Tomatoes are widely used in Portuguese cookery, so dishes deserve that label.

Tomatoes did not appear in Europe until the Portuguese and Spanish explorers brought them in the sixteenth century from South America, where they were considered solely as a decorative plant with poisonous fruits (belonging, so it was said, to the 'nightshade' family). It was only later that the fruits tempted some people – who probably did not realize they might be poisonous, and having found out that they tasted good and did not do any harm, they started cultivating them as food. In nineteenth-century Britain they were still regarded as poisonous. Known as 'love-apples', they were hawked by itinerant pedlars as curiosities. Portugal is now the third largest tomato producer – after Spain and Italy.

Tomato sauce 'Portuguese Style' is one in which onion is also quite prominent.

450 g/1 lb fleshy ripe tomatoes, peeled, seeded
  and chopped
225 g/8 oz onions, finely chopped
1 bay leaf
2 sprigs parsley, finely chopped

2 large cloves garlic, finely chopped
4 tablespoons olive oil
1 tablespoon lard
salt and pepper
1 teaspoon sugar

Cook everything gently together until tender (at least 45 minutes), reduce any excess liquid, taste for seasoning and use for fish, meat or vegetable dishes. If you prefer a smooth sauce, blend or sieve it, discarding the bay leaf first.

VARIATION You may prefer using half the onions for some dishes.

VILLAIN SAUCE
Molho Vilão
Makes about 300 ml/½ pint

To liven up 'Hake with Everything' (p. 83) some people serve it with this sauce – although mainly that dish is served with just olive oil and a little vinegar. Villain Sauce is also used with other dishes, such as partridge and poached fish apart from the hake. It is especially good with poached mackerel.

150 ml/¼ pint olive oil
1 small onion, finely chopped or grated
2 tablespoons wine vinegar
1 large egg, hard-boiled
1 medium clove of garlic, very finely chopped
2 sprigs parsley, chopped
1 sprig fresh coriander, chopped
salt and pepper

Chop up and sieve the hard-boiled egg. Mix the resulting paste with the grated onion, garlic, parsley and coriander (the latter gives a fresh, aromatic taste to the sauce and it is a good idea to include it). Beat the mixture with the liquid ingredients, taste for salt, dust with pepper and serve in a sauce-boat. If a completely smooth sauce is preferred, liquidize it. It should then look like a mayonnaise-type sauce.

VINEGAR SAUCE FROM THE ALGARVE
Molho de Escabeche
Makes 300 ml/½ pint

This sauce, poured over fried fish, is made with the oil in which the fish was fried. Nice as an appetizer or first course.

150 ml/¼ pint oil (kept from the frying pan)
1 large tomato, peeled and seeded
2 sprigs parsley, chopped
1 medium onion, chopped
3 tablespoons wine vinegar
1 small clove garlic, chopped
½ small green pimento (pepper), seeded
salt and pepper

Cook everything except the vinegar over a low heat until soft. Remove from heat, add the vinegar, bring to the boil again, taste for seasoning and then allow to cool. Serve cold, poured over cold left-over fried fish. This sauce preserves the fish, which can be kept in it for a few days – if the weather is not too hot. Really nice, once you become accustomed to the highly seasoned taste.

VINEGAR SAUCE
Escabeche
Makes about 300 ml/½ pint

This *escabeche* (vinegar) sauce differs from the Algarve version in that it is used for game (especially partridge) and boiled beef, in addition to being good with cold fried fish.

150 ml/¼ pint olive oil
2 tablespoons wine vinegar
2 tablespoons white wine
1 medium onion, finely chopped
1 clove garlic, finely chopped

1 coffeespoon paprika
2 sprigs parsley, chopped
1 bay leaf
1 clove
salt and pepper

Mix all ingredients except wine, vinegar and paprika, and simmer until soft. Remove from heat, discard bay leaf and clove and allow to cool. Then stir in the paprika, vinegar and wine, and taste for seasoning.

PORT WINE SAUCE
Makes 300 ml/½ pint

For this delicious sauce one can use either port or madeira (in their dry version). This is a rich, thick sauce, ideal for special occasions. Use it for livening up cooked meat, such as roast beef or pork, game and duck.

300 ml/½ pint meat or chicken stock (can be made
    with a good cube)
1 small onion, chopped
1 medium carrot, chopped
2 sprigs parsley, chopped
1 bay leaf

30 g/1 oz butter
1 tablespoon flour
1 tablespoon tomato concentrate
3 tablespoons white wine
4 tablespoons port or Madeira (dry)
salt and pepper

Sweat the onion, parsley and carrot in the butter for 5 minutes. Stir in the flour and add the white wine and bay leaf. Mix well and bring to simmering point again. Gradually mix in the stock and tomato concentrate. Allow to cook gently for 30-35 minutes. Sieve and taste for seasoning. Bring to the boil again and add the port or madeira. Serve hot. If the sauce is too thick, add a little more stock, before mixing in the port or Madeira.

HOMEMADE MAYONNAISE

This homemade sauce is much nicer than the bought variety, and it is not as difficult to make as most people think.

For each egg yolk use 150 ml/¼ pint very good olive oil and ½ teaspoon wine vinegar, seasoning with a little salt and ½ teaspoon made-mustard (the mild French type). In a deep bowl beat the egg yolks, then add the oil very gradually with one hand, whilst with the other you go on beating the sauce, always in the same clockwise movement. When thick, add a little salt, the vinegar and mustard and taste for seasoning. It can be kept in the refrigerator for several days.

NOTE You may like to add a little more vinegar and/or mustard, but do this only after tasting and then add just small amounts at a time, until it tastes right. If you like, use a little less oil than indicated. 2 egg yolks should be enough for a sauce serving 4 people.

BEIRÃO STYLE SAUCE
Molho Beirão
BEIRA ALTA PROVINCE • Makes about 450 ml/¾ pint

This sauce can be used in place of mayonnaise.

300 ml/½ pint olive oil
3 hard-boiled eggs, very finely chopped
3 tablespoons wine vinegar

1 medium onion, finely chopped
3 sprigs parsley, finely chopped
salt and pepper

Combine all hard ingredients and stir in the oil. Beat well. Add the vinegar and beat again. Season and beat again. Serve cold. You can liquidize the sauce, if a completely smooth texture is preferred.

VEGETABLES AND ACCOMPANIMENTS

LITTLE FISH FROM THE KITCHEN GARDEN
Peixinhos da Horta
FROM THE CENTRE OF PORTUGAL BUT USED COUNTRYWIDE • Serves 4

This is a curious name for a humble but nonetheless very tasty accompaniment for a meat dish as it does not, in fact, contain any fish. It is prepared with green beans in a batter, and so resembles small fish. *Peixinhos da Horta* are common fare in Portugal, while beans are in season, being served mainly at home, although some restaurants also have them.

400 g/14 oz tender green beans, cooked and cut into equal lengths

For the Batter

120 g/4 oz white plain flour	salt
water	oil for frying
2 eggs	

In a deep plate or roomy bowl mix the flour with enough water to make a paste with the consistency of thick cream. When the flour is well mixed and free from lumps, add the beaten eggs and a little salt, and beat well. Use this batter for coating the green beans, frying them (in twos or threes) over medium heat until golden. Absorb excess fat on kitchen paper as you take the 'fishes' out of the frying pan.

They are good hot or cold. Although they are generally intended to go with any meat dish, you can serve them alone, with a tomato sauce or perhaps with a salad for a self-contained starter dish.

NOTE Some people use milk instead of water for the batter, in which case they do not use eggs. White wine can also be substituted for the water.

THE TEMPURA CONNECTION

A propos of the previous recipe (and also Fish in Batter – p.83), it is interesting mentioning here the story of how 'Tempura' came into being. Following their maritime voyages, launched at the beginning of the fifteenth century – all along the African coast, India and so on – the Portuguese eventually reached China and Japan in 1543 (the first Europeans to do so). It took many years and numerous expeditions, but they did manage to establish the very first global Empire.

Many of the places where they settled in became just trading posts (mainly for spices – the real 'raison d'être' for those voyages), others were taken as colonies. In all of them, however, one of the aims was the spread of Christianity. When they arrived in Japan, the idea was to 'conquer souls' and develop a commercial out-post. Curiously, this would turn out to be quite useful locally, because both the Chinese and the Japanese needed a mediator for the exchange of goods between themselves. They weren't on good terms, politically, yet they wished very much to buy and sell their respective products.

The Portuguese 'go-between' situation was facilitated when they were allowed to settle in Macau (1557), and, a little later (1570) when they bought a splendid port from the Japanese where they founded the city of Nagasaki.

The missionaries accompanying the sailors and merchants kept strict rules of abstinence from meat on Fridays and various other days, called TEMPORAS (Ember Days). On such occasions, one of the things they ate was fried fish in batter – something never seen before in that land. So the Japanese decided to try it. They liked it... And, being Japanese, not only adopted but also adapted it. Lo and behold, 'Tempura' was born!

However, the Portuguese were expelled from Japan in 1641, a century after arriving there, due to their religious activities. But 'Tempura' remained, together with cakes (of course), as well as many words of Portuguese origin, the first Western-type hospital, the first translations of Japanese works, and more.

When the Dutch came, they were told, in no uncertain terms, not to try converting anyone and to confine themselves to the artificial little island of Decima – just a kind of platform. The Dutch accepted the conditions. Their own aim was purely commerce.

Here is an example of a recipe for Tempura Batter (it is possible now to buy packets of ready-mix in specialist shops):

2 egg yolks	1 tsp cornflour
350 ml/12 fl oz iced water	175 g/6 oz self-raising flour

Loosely follow the method for Little Fish from the Kitchen Garden, opposite.

But don't worry about leaving a few lumps, as it doesn't spoil the end result.

BLACK-EYED BEANS SALAD
Salada de Feijão Frade
Serves 4

Black-eyed beans are quite popular in Portugal. They are much quicker to cook than ordinary beans, and their characteristic flavour makes them suitable for tasty hot or cold salads or as a starter dish. If served hot, they will be good with poached salt cod and hard-boiled eggs. If cold, they go well with canned sardines (in tomato or oil), canned tuna fish or the well-loved salt cod cakes (*pasteis de bacalhau*, p.72). They are also very good on their own or with slices of hard-boiled egg, but either way black-eyed beans (hot or cold) must always be laced with some oil and a little vinegar, grated or finely cut raw onion and a good sprinkling of fresh parsley, to bring out their flavour (see opposite).

225 g/8 oz black-eyed beans
1 small onion, very finely chopped
3 tablespoons olive oil

1 teaspoon wine vinegar
2 sprigs of parsley, chopped

Wash the beans, and sort out any debris. Soak overnight or at least for half a day. Cook in twice their depth of water. Add some salt towards the end of cooking. These beans get tender surprisingly quickly, but do not leave them undercooked. After simmering for about 35-40 minutes, they should be ready, but test them before taking the pan off the flame and allow the beans to boil a little longer, if needed. When tender, drain and discard the water, and use the beans as required, following either of the suggestions above, after seasoning them with the onion, oil and vinegar, well mixed. Sprinkle with plenty of chopped parsley.

VARIATION A very good lunch dish is a mixture of cooked black-eyed beans, as above, with the addition of canned tuna and boiled eggs (with raw onion and parsley seasoning).

STEWED GREEN BEANS, PORTUGUESE STYLE
Feijão Verde Guisado à Portuguesa
Serves 4 to 6

As mentioned before, in any recipe named 'Portuguese style', you may expect to have some tomatoes among the ingredients. Stewed green beans make a good accompaniment for eggs and fried food. Choose very tender beans for a perfect result.

450 g/1 lb tender green beans
2 medium tomatoes, peeled, seeded and chopped
1 medium onion, chopped
1 tablespoon olive oil
1 tablespoon lard

1 small clove garlic, chopped
1 bay leaf
1 sprig parsley, chopped
salt and pepper

Wash and cut the green beans lengthwise and then again in 5 cm/2 inch lengths. Melt the fat and oil,

add the onion, tomatoes and seasonings and cook as a *refogado* (p.22) for 5-6 minutes, over a low flame. Add just a little boiling water and the green beans. Cook gently until tender, adding more water if it becomes dry. Taste for salt and serve very hot.

GREEN MOUSSE
Esparregado
Serves 4

This vegetable accompaniment is very common in Portugal. It can be prepared either with tender turnip-tops or with spinach. It is good with meat or fish.

450 g/1 lb cleaned turnip-tops or spinach (only leaves) – see Ingredients, p.28
1 tablespoon flour
2 tablespoons olive oil

few drops lemon juice or scant teaspoon wine vinegar
1 clove garlic (whole)
salt

Cook the greens until tender. Drain and cut them to a pulp or liquidize. Fry the garlic in the oil over a low flame, until the garlic is golden, then discard it (the objective is to flavour the oil). Add the flour, mix to a paste, combine the green pulp and boil gently for a few minutes, to cook the flour and thicken the mousse. Season with a few drops of lemon juice and more salt if needed.

VARIATION   A less 'rural' *esparregado* can be prepared substituting the olive oil with butter, omitting the lemon juice or vinegar and adding a little milk to the flour-and-butter paste, to form a thick white sauce. Mix the green pulp, cook for 1-2 minutes and serve.

STEWED WILD MUSHROOMS
Cogumelos Guisados
TRÁS-OS-MONTES PROVINCE • Serves 4

People in the northern inland provinces immensely value the wild mushrooms that grow in the region, for their protein content, and use them in tasty recipes when in season. Wild mushrooms have a much richer flavour than the rather bland cultivated ones. The amounts given here are for a main-course dish. If used only as an accompaniment, the quantities can be reduced.

1 kg/2 lb wild mushrooms (or cultivated ones)
90-110 g/3-4 oz smoked ham or lean bacon (in small cubes)
4 medium slices of bread

1 clove garlic, finely chopped
4 tablespoons olive oil
1 medium onion, finely chopped
salt and pepper

Wipe the mushrooms and cut off the end bit of the stalks. Cut the mushrooms into small pieces, or slice them to your taste. Set aside. Cook the bacon and the onion very gently in the oil. Add the mushrooms, shake the pan and season with the other ingredients. Cover and cook over low heat for 8-10 minutes. Do not add water, as the mushrooms create their own juices. Serve on top of slices of bread, which can be toasted or fried.

VARIATION The same recipe can be prepared omitting the bacon and adding a little nutmeg.

MASHED POTATOES
Puré de Batata

This accompaniment is very traditional and popular and is served with many fish and meat dishes. But nobody in Portugal would dare serving you mashed potato with lumps in it...

It is essential to use old, floury potatoes – they are fluffier and produce a smooth mash, which is what you're after.

For each serving, calculate a couple of medium sized potatoes. Boil, with a little salt (cut in half or quarters) in enough water to cover, until tender. Drain them really well in a colander. Transfer to the pot and mash with a potato masher or, better still, with a potato ricer. Have some warm milk by the side, add a little, beat it in, mix with a tablespoon of butter and sprinkle lightly with white pepper and ground nutmeg. Taste for salt. You may need a little more milk, but go easy on this. Take to the heat, to warm up again, beating with a fork to keep the mash light and fluffy. Serve at once.

Really traditional households will add an extra layer of richness to the mash, beating an egg yolk as well (1 egg yolk for each 4 servings).

BROAD BEANS

He [Jacinto] cautiously tried a mouthful – and again his eyes, clouded by his chronic pessimism, lit up and caught mine. Another mouthful, deliberately slow, followed, like a friar savouring his food with delight. And finally the unrestrained exclamation: 'Marvellous! These broad beans are different! What broad beans! What a wondrous thing!'

Eça de Queiroz, *A Cidade e as Serras* (*The City and the Mountains*)

Broad beans (fava beans) are extremely popular in Portugal. An old morning cry in Lisbon used to be '*Fava rica!*' ('*Rich broad beans*'). Women carrying the prepared dish, in large quantities, on their heads, would stop and sell a portion to the housewives who had come to their doors. This cry is now part of the past (not a very distant one, though), but broad beans are still consumed in great amounts all over the country, in a wide variety of splendid regional dishes, of which I include some of the best-known recipes.

There is an old saying referring to broad beans: '*Vai à fava!*' ('Go to broad beans!' literally, but meaning 'Go to Hell!') which is really an insult, though not a very strong one and used sometimes in a jocular way. As dried broad beans are commonly fed to donkeys in Portugal it is also the same as calling someone an ass.

RICH BROAD BEANS
Fava Rica
LISBON • Serves 4

Being made with dried broad beans, this dish used to be prepared all the year round and was a most popular dish, sold in the streets of Lisbon. Alas, it has disappeared in modern times, but *fava rica* is easy enough to prepare at home.

450 g/1 lb dried broad beans	1 coffeespoon wine vinegar
3 cloves garlic, chopped	salt and pepper
4 tablespoons olive oil	

Soak the broad beans for 12-15 hours at least, in plenty of cold water. Drain and cook in fresh salted water until really tender. Drain and keep warm. Cook the garlic slowly in the oil, until golden. Toss the broad beans in the flavoured oil, add the vinegar, taste for seasoning and mash a few broad beans to thicken the sauce. Boil again for 2-3 minutes and serve piping hot.

BROAD BEANS WITH CORIANDER (CILANTRO)
Favas com Coentros
THE ALENTEJO • Serves 4 to 6

Coriander is a herb very widely used in Portugal, especially in the Alentejo provinces. Broad beans acquire a beautiful fragrance when cooked with it, as in this regional dish (see opposite), meant as an accompaniment to local pork dishes but also apt to be served on its own (in which case the amounts should be doubled).

1.2 kg/2½ lb broad beans (unshelled)	1 tablespoon wine vinegar
2 spring onions (scallions), chopped	4 tablespoons olive oil
6 sprigs coriander (cilantro), chopped	2 large cloves garlic, finely chopped
3 sprigs parsley, chopped	

Shell the broad beans and cook until tender in salted boiling water, adding just a third of the coriander and a spring onion. Drain and season with all other ingredients (raw), the oil and vinegar. Toss and serve.

BROAD BEANS LISBON FASHION
Favas à Moda de Lisboa

1.5 kg/3 lb broad beans (unshelled)	3 large sprigs coriander, chopped
110 g/4 oz fatty bacon, in cubes	1 large onion, chopped
110 g/4 oz *chouriço* (p.25), thickly sliced	salt and pepper
1 tablespoon lard	
1 tablespoon butter	

Cook the meats with the seasonings (do not add much salt in the beginning) for 4-5 minutes, until golden. Add the shelled broad beans, toss, cover and cook gently for 20-30 minutes or until the beans are tender. Add enough water to prevent sticking and keep moist at all times. Shake the pan occasionally. Taste for seasoning and serve with lettuce salad. An earthenware pot is ideal for cooking this dish.

BROAD BEANS RIBATEJO FASHION
Favas à Moda do Ribatejo
Serves 4 to 6

1.5 kg (3 lb) tender broad beans (unshelled)	2 tablespoons lard
280 g/10 oz lean pork, cut into small pieces	1 clove garlic, chopped
140 g/5 oz lean bacon, cut into small cubes	2-3 spring onions (scallions), chopped
140 g/5 oz chouriço (p.25), thickly sliced	4-6 sprigs coriander, chopped
140 g/5 oz morcela, whole	salt and pepper
2 tablespoons olive oil	pinch of sugar

Shell the broad beans, wash and set aside. Fry the pork in the fat and oil over low heat, until golden. Add the other meat. Fry again. Mix the garlic, coriander, spring onions, pinch of sugar and broad beans. Toss around then reduce the heat and cover. The idea is to cook the broad beans with the steam generated inside the pan, but you will also need to add small amounts of water, gradually. Shake the pan now and then. Taste for salt (do not add the salt at the beginning, as some of the meat contains a certain amount of salt). Serve with lettuce salad, the classic accompaniment for most broad bean dishes.

BROAD BEANS WITH YELLOW SAUCE, BAIRRADA STYLE
Favas com Molho Amarelo
BEIRA LITORAL PROVINCE • Serves 4 to 6

A very traditional recipe of the Bairrada region, prepared as an accompaniment to meat dishes but excellent for vegetarians if served with a salad instead of meat. Its special aroma is imparted by the use of savory.

1.2 kg/2½ lb broad beans (unshelled)	2 egg yolks
2 sprigs parsley, chopped	2 tablespoons flour
2 sprigs savory, chopped	salt and pepper
2 tablespoons butter	

Shell the broad beans and boil with a sprig of savory in salted water until tender (20-25 minutes). Drain and set aside but keep some of the liquor. Make a thick sauce with the butter, flour and part of the cooking liquor. Add the chopped parsley and remaining chopped savory and boil again. Taste for seasoning and add the egg yolks. Beat well over a very low heat, add the cooked broad beans, reheat and serve at once.

BROAD BEANS WITH OLIVE OIL
Favas com Azeite
RIBATEJO PROVINCE • Serves 4

1.5 kg/3 lb broad beans (unshelled)
2 spring onions (scallions), chopped
1 large clove garlic, chopped

4 tablespoons olive oil
salt
4 thin slices corn bread (p. 51) or wholemeal bread

Shell and wash the broad beans and add to a pan containing oil and seasoning already sweated. Toss it all together, cover and cook over a low heat, shaking now and then and adding a drop of water if needed, to prevent sticking and to create a thickish sauce. Serve immediately in individual plates, over the corn bread. Have the classic lettuce salad as a side dish.

TOMATO RICE
Arroz de Tomate
Serves 4

This is especially good with fried fish, salt cod cakes and omelettes.

225 g/8 oz long-grain rice
1 medium onion, finely chopped
2 medium tomatoes, peeled, seeded and chopped
2 tablespoons olive oil

water – 2½ times the volume of rice
1 sprig parsley, chopped
salt

Fry the onion in the oil, for a good *refogado* (p. 22), then add the tomatoes and parsley and cook again for 5 minutes. Add the water, bring to the boil and then add the rice and some salt. Simmer until tender (about 25 minutes) and taste for salt before serving. This rice should not be too dry. When left more on the wet side, rice is sometimes called *malandrinho* (naughty). This suggests just how succulent and tasty it is when made in this fashion, either in its simple version with tomato and onion, or made with fish, salt cod, seafood or meat.

VARIATIONS

1   Pea Rice/*Arroz de Ervilhas* is another countrywide accompaniment worth trying. Use only half the tomatoes and add a handful of peas, which will cook with the rice. If the peas are very tender, add them only later. Good with meat dishes.

2   Chickpea Rice/*Arroz de Grão* is countrywide also. Omit the tomatoes and add a handful of cooked chickpeas. Nice with any kind of fried food.

3   Bean and Coriander Rice/*Arroz Malandrinho* is an accompaniment served in Lisbon restaurants. A generous handful of cooked butter or kidney beans together with a tablespoon of chopped fresh coriander is added five minutes before the end of cooking to the rice. It is delicious with fried food. Vegetarians would, of course, enjoy these recipes with salads and vegetable rissoles or pasties.

SWEET THINGS

The sweet-toothed Portuguese cannot face the day without cakes and desserts. Each town or village seems to have its own specialities, and so the variety and richness of sweets, all over the country, is quite impressive. The liking for very sweet things is probably a result of the Arab influence in Portugal.

To facilitate browsing through the recipes, I have grouped them (cakes, desserts, sweets and so on), hoping that in this way you will not be lost in the maze of the different kinds of 'sweet things'.

PUDDINGS

RICE PUDDING
Arroz Doce
FROM THE MINHO PROVINCE, BUT ADOPTED COUNTRYWIDE • Serves 8 to 10

> Vicencia brought in the rice pudding, and we said grace.
>
> Eça de Queiroz, *A Relíquia* (The Relic)

This is an absolute must at the Portuguese table for any celebration, be it Christmas, birthdays, weddings, parties, special days of all kinds. It is so widely appreciated that any day, in fact, is 'rice-pudding day', and restaurants, snackbars and other eating places always have it at hand.

Rice pudding Portuguese style is made on top of the stove and is meant to be creamy but not very wet (it can in fact be taken out of the mould when cold). Whether served in individual dishes or on a large platter, Portuguese rice pudding must always be adorned with embroidery-like motifs made with cinnamon: heart shapes, initials (if it is intended for someone's birthday), flowers, lattice designs. This is done by pinching a little cinnamon between one's thumb and the first finger and skilfully letting it drop over the rice. The operation may take a little while, depending on the amount of decoration needed and on

the dexterity of the decorator! The children of the house soon get interested and quite adept at this pleasant occupation and normally share it among themselves, comparing results afterwards – and, more often than not, boasting if they think their work was the best!

It is worth making more rice pudding than the amount needed for one sitting, because it keeps well from one day to another (or even for a couple of days), and although it dries out, it will certainly be very good to the end.

450 g/1 lb short-grain rice	½ coffeespoon salt
200 g/7 oz granulated sugar	piece of lemon rind (zest)
1.2 L/2 pints whole milk	cinnamon
3 egg yolks	1 vanilla pod

Wash the rice and cook it for 25 minutes (until tender) in 2½ times its volume of boiling water, with the salt and lemon rind. When cooked, remove the lemon rind and add the boiling milk and vanilla pod, mixing well with a wooden spoon. Simmer until the liquid is reduced and the rice is really soft and creamy (20-30 minutes). Stir now and then. Add the sugar and boil again for 3-4 minutes. Remove from the heat and mix in the egg yolks. Bring to the boil (without allowing further boiling) just to cook the yolks. Taste for sugar (remember that it tastes sweeter when hot than after it has cooled down) and add a little more if liked. Pour into individual bowls or onto a large platter. Decorate, Portuguese style, as indicated above.

Do not be alarmed if some rice sticks to the bottom of the pan. This always happens, and care has to be taken not to allow it to burn, by stirring with the wooden spoon but without attempting to bring up the stuck layer, which would ruin the appearance of the rice. That layer can be scraped at the end and eaten by the cook as a special reward (it is the best part). Serve at room temperature.

EGG CUSTARD

Leite-Creme

BEIRA PROVINCES, BUT USED COUNTRYWIDE • Serves 4 to 6

Egg custard, with more or fewer egg yolks, according to how rich one wants it, is a delectable and wholesome pudding with which to finish a meal, and although it may now be considered old-fashioned, it continues to be a good stand-by, always appreciated in Portugal. Indeed, a good *leite-creme* is the pride of many a housewife.

This custard is not baked but simply made on top of the stove and eaten when cold.

600 ml/1 pint whole milk	1 piece lemon peel or vanilla pod
3-4 egg yolks (depending on size of the eggs)	cinnamon for sprinkling or a little sugar, if a burnt
1 tablespoon plain white flour	top is preferred
140 g/5 oz granulated sugar	

Take 3 tablespoons of the milk to mix with the flour until it is smooth. Keep 2 tablespoons of milk aside to mix with the egg yolks. Warm up the remainder of the milk over low heat, together with the sugar and lemon peel or vanilla pod. Before it starts boiling, mix in the flour paste carefully, with a wooden spoon, and bring gently to the boil, stirring all the time. Let it cook for about 4 minutes. Remove from the heat and very gradually add the egg-yolk mixture. Bring back to the heat, always stirring, to cook the yolks (for about a minute). Remove the vanilla pod or lemon peel and pour the cream into a pyrex dish, sprinkle with some sugar and place under the grill for a very short while, until the sugar caramelizes on top. Alternatively, sprinkle the surface of the pudding with a little cinnamon. It can also be served in individual glass bowls. It gets thicker after cooling, so do not worry if it looks a little thin when pouring.

VARIATIONS

1 A richer version of egg custard can be made with 6 egg yolks instead of the 3-4 indicated above.

2 Another method of preparing this pudding is to mix the yolks with the sugar until really smooth and almost white in colour. Then add 2 tablespoons of milk to make the mixture more fluid and combine with the flour, beating very thoroughly again. Pour this into the remaining milk, beating well and bring to the heat, stirring, allowing it to simmer for a few minutes as above, until creamy. It thickens further after cooling down.

3 A more homely version is the following:

450 ml/¾ pint whole milk
90 g/3 oz granulated sugar
2 egg yolks

1 heaped teaspoon cornflour
flavouring, as above

Mix the flour with a little milk and then add the sugar and egg yolks. Beat well. In the meantime have the milk heated to boiling point. Pour it over the prepared mixture, beat thoroughly and bring back to the heat. Keep stirring. Once it reaches boiling point, remove the pan from the heat, then bring it back again. Do this several times, until the custard is creamy.

4 From the Beira Litoral province comes this luscious egg custard:

450 ml/¾ pint whole milk
250 g/9 oz granulated sugar
5 egg yolks

1½ tablespoons flour
flavourings, as above

Beat the yolks with the sugar, until smooth and almost white. Add the flour and a little milk. Beat again. Combine gradually the remaining milk. Bring slowly to the boil and then simmer, stirring all the time. Allow it to thicken (about 5 minutes). Pour into a serving dish, sprinkle with sugar and place under the grill, to form a golden-brown crust.

NOTE The real secret of these variations is to keep stirring the sweet while cooking.

CRÊME CARAMEL

Pudim Flan

ESTREMADURA PROVINCE • Serves 6

A popular pudding, anywhere. At restaurants, little individual puddings are served (see opposite), but they are troublesome to prepare at home, so you may want to use one large mould.

450 ml/¾ pint whole milk
4 large eggs, well beaten

200 g/7 oz granulated sugar

Prepare the caramel first: bring 110 g/4 oz of the sugar to the boil with 2 tablespoons of water, in a saucepan. Allow it to turn into a liquid caramel and pour immediately into the mould, turning it around, to coat evenly. A spoon may be helpful, to cover the interior of the mould. This operation must be done at great speed, as the caramel dries very quickly. Any lumps left around the mould will melt later, so do not worry much about them. Leave the mould aside. Warm up the milk to blood temperature and beat in the eggs and the rest of the sugar. Combine really well and pour into the prepared mould, 15-18 cm/6-7 inches in diameter. Bake in a bain-marie (placing the mould inside a tin containing boiling water) in the oven (180°C/350°F/ Gas 4) until set (35-40 minutes).

NOTE I save a lot of time and trouble by cooking this pudding in the pressurecooker, using the trivet. 10-12 minutes are enough for the cooking under pressure. Be sure to cover the mould with a tight lid or foil, to avoid water coming into the pudding. Take out of the mould when cold.

CHOCOLATE MOUSSE

Mousse de Chocolate

Serves 4 to 6

The Portuguese are terribly fond of chocolate mousse, which appears on menus everywhere, and housewives like to boast about their particular mousse. To make a good mousse, one must use excellent chocolate and several eggs. This is a superb pudding, and one might as well be generous with the ingredients.

200 g/7 oz plain or bitter chocolate
4 large eggs, separated
6 tablespoons fine sugar (or more if you prefer the

mousse sweeter)
2 tablespoons butter
a little dusting of powdered vanilla (optional)

Beat the egg whites until really hard. Set aside. Break the chocolate into small pieces and put it in a pan inside a bigger one containing boiling water, to melt. Mix in the sugar, vanilla, butter and beaten egg yolks. Keep the mixture in the bain-marie, all the while stirring it carefully. When you have a perfectly homogenous paste, remove the pan from the heat and add the stiffly beaten egg whites. Fold them over and over until well mixed. Note that all this must be done without delay, or the chocolate mixture will harden too much and it will be impossible to mix it evenly with the egg whites. Put the prepared

mousse in a serving bowl and leave in the refrigerator until needed. It should be slightly cool but not iced. Serve it without any additions, which might detract from the wonderful taste and texture. The mousse can also be used as a filling or topping for cakes.

SOFT EGGS
Ovos Moles

AVEIRO, BEIRA LITORAL PROVINCE • Serves 4

This is one of the best-loved and most renowned Portuguese puddings, and in Aveiro it is sold in little wooden barrels, gaily decorated, to be eaten by the spoonful, or as a filling for white shell-like cases (made commercially in Aveiro and sold all over the country). *Ovos moles* are used for all kinds of confectionery: as a topping and/or filling for sponge cakes and tarts, as a thick sauce for puddings, as a decoration for small cakes, and so on. *Ovos moles* are also served as a dessert, combined with a handful of walnuts or roast almonds, roughly ground, sprinkled with just a dusting of cinnamon, or simply on their own.

Ovos moles are easy to make and, although expensive, due to the use of many egg yolks, they can be 'stretched' by adding rice flour or mashed boiled rice. Variations like these are fine to use as fillings, but the basic recipe is much richer, obviously, when intended to be eaten by the spoonful.

250 g/9 oz granulated sugar
8 egg yolks

150 ml/¼ pint water

Bring the water and sugar to the boil over a low flame, until it reaches the 'pearl stage' (p. 32). Allow to cool a little and mix with the beaten yolks, dropping the sugar syrup over them slowly and beating vigorously all the time. Bring to a gentle boil again, stirring, until it resembles a thick custard. Divide the sweet between small glass serving bowls or pour into a larger bowl.

VARIATIONS
1 With boiled rice. Same amounts as before, regarding sugar and water, plus 6 egg yolks (instead of 8) and 60 g/2 oz pudding-type rice, boiled until very soft and made into a pap with fork or liquidizer. Make the syrup, add the rice purée, simmer for 2 minutes while stirring, and then add to the yolks, beating the whole mixture very well. Bring to the heat, stirring, to cook the yolks and thicken. Suitable for fillings and toppings.
2 With rice flour. Same amount of sugar and water, and only 4 yolks. Add 4 level tablespoons of rice flour, made into a paste with a minimum of water, to the sugar syrup. Boil a little, stirring, to cook the flour. Cool slightly and add to the beaten yolks, boiling gently for a short time, while stirring. This simpler variation is especially suitable for fillings or to sandwich sponge cakes. It gets really thick when cold.

NOTE The pumpkin jam on p.208 can also be used as a cheap version of *ovos moles*, if 2-3 egg yolks are added to about 175-200 g/6-7 oz of jam. This will produce a very good filling for cakes. Just boil the jam very gently with the beaten yolks for a minute or so, to cook them, allow to cool and use.

BACON FROM HEAVEN
Toucinho do Céu

ODIVELAS, LISBON AREA BUT FOUND COUNTRYWIDE • Makes about 8 slices

Although many other places have their own 'Bacon from Heaven' and claim the original recipe, this pudding is said to come traditionally from Odivelas, a Lisbon suburb which was of some importance as far back as the thirteenth century when kings found it convenient for discreet 'love nests' near the capital. Philippa of Lancaster (born in London in 1350), the daughter of John of Gaunt, Duke of Lancaster, who became Queen of Portugal through her marriage to King João I, also liked the place and died (of the plague) in the convent at Odivelas in 1415.

The old convent used to be famous for its poetry sessions (at which well-known poets would be invited to recite their work), followed by drinks accompanied by glacé pumpkin and lemon peel, meringues and little quince-cheese squares, also an Odivelas creation (still available at every good grocer in Portugal). But the most tempting of all the convent's confectionery was the 'Bacon from Heaven', a cross between a cake and a pudding, nowadays eaten as a dessert or with tea. The original convent recipe was extraordinarily rich, with many more eggs and possibly the inclusion of bacon – hence the title – and simpler versions, like the one below, have since evolved. These versions are themselves rich – otherwise there would be no point in saying that it is a sweet from Heaven!

250 g/9 oz ground almonds
310 g/11 oz granulated sugar
7 eggs

2 tablespoons flour
½ teaspoon cinnamon

Beat the sugar, cinnamon and eggs until very fluffy. Add the flour and ground almonds. Beat well again. Bake in a buttered and floured round cake tin 18-20 cm/7-8 inches in diameter, at 163°C/325°F/Gas 3, for 25 minutes or until set and golden on top. Take out of the mould after cooling a little, and scrape off the flour from the sides. Sprinkle a little of confectioner's sugar.

VARIATIONS
1 There are several regional variations to this pudding. One of the simplest is another convent creation, from Beja (Alentejo province) and, although not strictly a 'Bacon from Heaven', this version has the virtue of being cheaper while still a very good pudding in itself.

200 g/7 oz sugar
90 g/3 oz flour
2 tablespoons milk

140 g/5 oz ground almonds
3 eggs, separated, plus 2 egg yolks

Beat the sugar with the egg yolks until foamy. Add the milk and beat well. Mix in the almonds and flour. Beat again. Fold in the stiffly whipped whites. Bake in a buttered round cake tin 18-20 cm/7-8 inches in diameter in an oven preheated to 180°C/350°F/Gas 4 for 25-30 minutes or until golden and well set. Take out of the tin when lukewarm. Sprinkle with sugar and cinnamon or soak with a light syrup made with 5-6 tablespoons granulated sugar and enough water to melt it, boiled for 2-3 minutes over gentle heat.

2 This is a rich version, from Murça (Trás-os-Montes and Alto Douro province) and must be mentioned here as it is considered one of the best and most authoritative recipes for 'Bacon from Heaven'.

200 g/7 oz granulated sugar	4 whole eggs plus 6 yolks, all beaten together
90 g/3 oz ground almonds	1 coffeespoon cinnamon

Make a syrup with the sugar and a little water (just enough to melt it), by boiling it until thick (2-3 minutes) – see p.32 for the 'pearl stage'. Add the almonds and simmer for a couple of minutes, stirring. Remove from the heat. Beat in the cinnamon and eggs. Simmer again, to thicken. Pour into a 18 cm/7 inch round cake tin, well buttered, and bake at 190°C/375°F/Gas 5 until set (about 15 minutes). Do not overcook, to avoid its drying too much. Take out of the tin after cooling a little and sprinkle with sugar.

ORANGE ROLL
Torta de Laranja
Serves 4 to 6

A lavish pudding, very popular and almost always available at Portuguese restaurants, though this homemade version may be better still.

150 ml/¼ pint pure orange juice	200 g/7 oz sugar
5 large eggs	grated rind of 1 orange
1 tablespoon cornflour	

Dissolve the flour in the juice and mix in the sugar, grated rind and beaten eggs. Combine well, without whisking too hard. Prepare a baking tray suitable for Swiss roll, 20.5 x 30.5 cm/8 x 12 inches well greased and lined. The lining paper must also be greased and sprinkled with sugar. Pour the mixture onto this and bake at 180°C/350°F/Gas 4 for 15-20 minutes, until firm and with a rich orange colour. Turn into a slightly damp cloth, sprinkled with sugar. Trim the edges and roll up carefully, with the help of the cloth. Place in a sugared serving dish and again sprinkle with sugar, when cold. Cut into thick slices, which are served on their own, as a pudding.

NUN'S BELLY
Barriga de Freira
BEIRA LITORAL PROVINCE • Serves 4 to 6

During the sixteenth and seventeenth centuries, it became a custom in convents to celebrate the election of a new superior with a music-and-poetry evening, to which artists would be invited and later offered delicious sweets and wine by the nuns. Almeida Garrett (1799-1854), in *A lírica de João Mínimo* (*The Lyrics of João Mínimo*) describes it thus: ' ... music and more sonnets and verses of all kinds, with many delicious sweets offered to us by the nuns. As far as I am concerned, this was not by any means the least pleasing of the events of the evening.' One can imagine that 'nun's belly' would be one of the sweets offered to special guests. Such a title, though – and that of so many other sweets of convent origin – makes one think that medieval nuns considered themselves great temptresses. Anyway, all those sweets are somewhat similar, because they are based mainly on eggs and sugar.

280 g/10 oz granulated sugar
2 small slices white bread (no crust) crumbled
5 egg yolks

small piece of lemon rind
30 g/1 oz butter
1 teaspoon cinnamon

Make a light syrup (see p.32 for the 'smooth stage') with the sugar and enough water to melt it, adding the lemon rind. Remove the rind, then add the breadcrumbs, the butter and finally the lightly beaten yolks. Boil very gently, stirring all the time, for 2-3 minutes, to thicken. Pour into a serving dish and sprinkle with the cinnamon.

SLICES, TOMAR STYLE
Fatias de Tomar
RIBATEJO PROVINCE • Makes about 8 slices

Near Tomar there are interesting Roman remains (the towns of Sallium and Nabancia), but the town itself was founded during the twelfth century, when a castle was built on the margins of the Nabão river. This was to be the Templars' headquarters in Portugal. In 1312 this powerful and rich Order became extinct, and it was replaced in 1321 by the Order of Christ, destined for a special role during the voyages of discovery. Prince Henry 'the Navigator' was nominated its governor, in 1416, and this position enabled him to use some of the Order's resources to finance the voyages (together with his own fortune). In return, the Order acquired the privilege of overseeing the spiritual welfare of the lands discovered.

Tomar has never quite lost its medieval flavour, and many questions still await an answer from those times when the mysterious Templars first dominated it. For example, what is the meaning of the *signum solomonis* on the façade of the main temple, and its orientation in relation to the towers – which, according to old tales, are connected to the castle by a secret tunnel? There is an undeciphered symbolism in the main window, and even in the plan of the old town, with four main streets crossing each other and orientated to the cardinal points. Only those secretive 'soldier-monks' would be able to lift the veil.

Today Tomar is an important market centre for neighbouring farms, and it has many festivities, processions and old traditions regarding food, such as these lovely slices.

350 g/12 oz granulated sugar

10 egg yolks

In Tomar there is a special deep oval mould for this glamorous sweet, but it can be baked in any ordinary pudding mould, providing it has a lid.

Beat the egg yolks on their own for a long time, until very light and foamy. The idea is to introduce as much air into the mixture as possible. An electric mixer will do the job in 8-10 minutes, otherwise you need a strong arm to beat it for the best part of half an hour. Pour the beaten yolks into a liberally greased and deep mould (about 15 cm/6 inches in diameter) and place it in a pan containing boiling water, therefore baking it bain-marie style. You can do this either in the oven or on top of the stove. Do not forget to cover the mould with its lid, or with foil, failing this. Keep the surrounding water boiling (topping it up, as necessary) until the eggs are well set (about 30 minutes). Take it out of the mould very carefully after cooling. When quite cold, cut the pudding evenly with a very sharp knife into 1.5 cm/¾ inch slices and boil them, one by one, for a minute, in a light syrup (see the 'smooth stage', p.32) made with the sugar and a bit more than enough water to melt it – about 300 ml/½ pint. Keep the syrup simmering throughout, but add a little water now and then, when it becomes too thick. When all the slices are ready, cover them with any remaining syrup. Serve cold on a glass platter.

CHRISTMAS GOLDEN SOUP

Sopa Dourada
VIANA DO CASTELO, MINHO PROVINCE • Serves 6

In *The City and the Mountains*, Eça de Queiroz recalls his leaving Paris to return to his native village – for family reasons. What a nuisance. But then he realized that there might be compensations awaiting him: 'I thought how good Aunt Vicencia's golden soup would be. I hadn't savoured it for years, nor the roast suckling pig, nor the rice, made at our home!' He confided afterwards: 'I ate with delight Aunt Vicencia's golden soup ...'

Golden soup is a dessert served usually during the Christmas season in the Minho province and more specifically in Viana do Castelo.

175 g/6 oz sponge cake (it can be stale cake), in thin slices	7 egg yolks
350 g/12 oz granulated sugar	150 ml/¼ pint water
	cinnamon

Mix the sugar with the water and bring to the boil to make a thick syrup (see p.32 or the 'thread stage'). Remove from the heat. Using a slotted spoon, dip each slice of cake into the syrup, and place them in a large serving dish. When they are all soaked in the syrup, beat the egg yolks and mix them with the remaining syrup. Bring to the heat for one moment and stir, to thicken, without allowing the yolks to curdle. Pour this custard over the slices, sprinkle with cinnamon and serve when cold.

VARIATION   In Fafe, also in Minho province, there is another, still richer version of this recipe:

300 ml/½ pint *ovos moles* (see p.150 and choose one of the richer variations)	8 medium slices very slightly stale sponge cake (*pão-de-ló*, p.198)
	30 g/1 oz candied fruit to taste

Spread the cake in a serving dish. Cover with the *ovos moles*, warmed up to facilitate absorption, and leave overnight. Decorate with the candied fruit or simply with cinnamon.

PRISCOS PARISH PRIEST PUDDING

Pudim do Abade de Priscos

ENTRE-DOURO AND MINHO PROVINCES • Serves 6 to 8

This pudding was created by the parish priest of the small town of Priscos, Father Manuel Rebello. He was an extraordinary character, a person of extensive culture in the most diverse subjects. A great-grandniece of his, my good friend, Maria Adosinda, has told me of his ability to know and do almost anything, quite apart from being an excellent, pious and beloved parish priest, to the last days of his very long life (1834-1930). He was a great theatre fan and founded a dramatic society in the town, to the immense delight of his parishioners, and was a splendid photographer – rare hobbies for a priest of his time. His embroidery was perfection itself, and some precious pieces were framed and are still kept by his family. But what brought him fame during his lifetime and immortality now was his culinary talent.

He had a little bag, which he kept well away from curious eyes, where he stored all his secret ingredients, spices and seasonings. Unfortunately it disappeared after his death, and nobody found out what was inside. His art became so well known that he used to be called upon to direct the preparation of great banquets, including some in honour of the Portuguese royal family. On account of his merits he was created Honorary Chaplain of the royal household. This recipe uses fatty bacon, which seems unusual but gives a very special taste to the pudding.

400 g/14 oz granulated sugar
300 ml/½ pint water
12 egg yolks, well beaten
2 tablespoons port wine

45 g/1½ oz bacon fat, without rind, very finely
  sliced
1 stick cinnamon
1 piece lemon rind

Put the bacon slices (which will melt, during cooking), the water, 280 g/10 oz of the sugar, cinnamon stick and lemon rind in a pan and bring to the boil, until a syrup is formed. Remove from the heat, cool a little, discard the cinnamon and lemon rind, then add the egg yolks and wine. Beat well and set aside. Prepare the caramel to coat a deep pudding mould about 15-18 cm/6-7 inches in diameter (see p. 31). Pour the prepared mixture into this and bake in the oven, in a bain-marie, at 246°C/475°F/Gas 9 for nearly an hour or until well set and golden. Allow to cool before taking it out of the mould.

SWEET MIGAS

Migas Doces

BEIRA ALTA • Serves 4

Bread is used in Portugal in the making of puddings as it is almost all over the world. In the recipe below the bread serves merely as a thickener, being completely disguised with the egg-and-sugar mixture.

200 g/7 oz granulated sugar
100 g/3½ oz fresh white breadcrumbs
5 egg yolks

60 g/2 oz ground almonds
150 ml/¼ pint water
1 coffeespoon cinnamon

Boil the water with the sugar for a minute, reduce the heat and add the breadcrumbs. Mash well. Mix the ground almonds, stirring all the time over a low flame, until it is homogeneous. Take off the heat and beat in the yolks. Bring the mixture to the heat again, just to boiling point, while stirring. Divide into individual small dessert bowls and sprinkle with cinnamon.

FLOATING ISLANDS
Farófias
ESTREMADURA PROVINCE • Serves 4 to 6

This is a very old-fashioned recipe, useful to use up whites of eggs which abound in Portuguese kitchens, due to the use of so many yolks. It is a very interesting sweet, consisting of white mounds floating on custard, and lightly dusted with a hint of cinnamon. It is best eaten soon after it has been made (prepare it just before the meal it is intended for), as the whites tend sometimes to flatten a little and thus lose some of their visual appeal – though not the taste, which is delicate and delicious.

3 egg whites, stiffly beaten
90 g/3 oz granulated sugar
600 ml/1 pint milk
1 teaspoon cornflour (or the egg yolks)

1 piece of lemon rind
cinnamon
pinch of salt

After the whites have been beaten really well, until forming peaks, fold in about a third of the sugar. While you are doing this, have the milk over low heat with a small piece of lemon rind and the remaining sugar in it. When it is boiling, reduce the flame and maintain just a gentle bubbling. Discard the lemon rind. Cook large spoonfuls of the egg-white mixture in the boiling milk. They cook very quickly, puffing up like small castles. Remove each mound as they cook, using a slotted spoon. Keep the *farófias* in a large strainer, to drain off any excess milk. When they are all cooked, put them in a serving bowl and set aside.

Now prepare a custard using the cornflour (made into a paste with a little cold milk) or the egg yolks, if wanted, and the milk used for cooking the *farófias*. Add also any milk dropped through the strainer and a pinch of salt. Boil gently, to cook the flour, stirring for 2 minutes, and pour into a large serving bowl. Again using a slotted spoon, place the white 'islands' onto the custard, very carefully. Dust with a little cinnamon and serve. All these operations must be done speedily – the *farófias* may collapse a little, if left for too long.

If using the egg yolks for thickening the sauce instead of the cornflour (which is really a short-cut), mix them carefully in the milk, off the heat, bring back to the flame and stir continuously until it thickens, just simmering, for a moment or two.

CHEESE PUDDING
Pudim de Queijo
AZORES ARCHIPELAGO • Serves 6

The Azores' own cheese, Queijo da Ilha, is used for this recipe. Good Cheddar-type cheese can, however, be substituted.

140 g/5 oz grated cheese
60 g/2 oz butter
280 g/10 oz granulated sugar

4 egg yolks plus 2 whole eggs
a few glacé cherries

Simmer the sugar in a little water, enough to melt it, for 3-4 minutes. Remove from the heat. Beat in the grated cheese and the butter. When cool, add the egg yolks and the whole eggs, beaten. Mix well. Grease and sprinkle with granulated sugar a mould 18-20 cm (7-8 inches) in diameter. Place the cherries around the bottom of the mould and pour in the cheese mixture. Bake for 30-40 minutes in a bain-marie in an oven at 190°C/375°F/Gas 5 until golden and set.

SOFT CHEESE PUDDING
Pudim de Requeijão
ESTRELA MOUNTAIN REGION • Serves 6

This is a rich cheese pudding, including almonds. The original recipe indicates rather a lot of sugar, but I find that reducing it by a third, as indicated below, gives a better result – unless, of course, one is extremely sweet-toothed. We can also make the recipe less expensive by using whole eggs, instead of only yolks. There is no significant loss in flavour or texture by adopting these economical measures.

140 g/5 oz fresh cheese/ricotta (*requeijão*)
110 g/4 oz ground almonds
200 g/7 oz sugar

4 eggs
1 coffeespoon cinnamon

Combine the sugar with the almonds and the cheese, to obtain a soft paste. Add the eggs, gradually, and the cinnamon. Place in a well-buttered cake tin (about 18-20 cm/7-8 inches in diameter) and bake in an oven set to 163°C/325°F/Gas 3 for the first 15 minutes, increasing to 180°C/350°F/Gas 4, until golden (about 30 minutes in all). Take out of the mould only after cooling a little. Serve as a dessert, when cold.

DRY SWEET SOUP

Sopa Seca Doce

MINHO AND DOURO LITORAL PROVINCES • Serves 4 to 6

The custom of including meat (especially chicken) in some puddings is still kept up in some northern areas, even though they are prepared mainly for specific rural festivities (grape-picking and weddings). In the Middle Ages, however, the use of sugar and meat was very widespread. The recipe below is but one variation of several still in use and can be considered a bread pudding rather than a cake.

½ leg of chicken

110-140 g/4-5 oz lean beef

30 g/1 oz fatty bacon

2 tablespoons clear honey

2 sprigs of mint

175-200 g/6-7 oz white bread, sliced (no crust)

1 teaspoon cinnamon plus enough for sprinkling

½ teaspoon salt

granulated sugar to taste

Cook the meat in enough water to cover – at least 600 ml/1 pint – and season with salt and mint. When tender, remove the meat (to be used in some savoury dish) and strain the liquor. Measure about 600 ml/1 pint and sweeten it with the honey and sugar to taste, adding the cinnamon. Mix well. Put the slices of bread in a bowl and pour the sweetened liquid over it. Butter a deep fireproof dish about 18-20 cm/7-8 inches in diameter and sprinkle with sugar and cinnamon. Spoon layers of the soaked bread into the dish, alternating with more cinnamon and sugar between each layer. Sprinkle some on top, when all the bread is used up, and cover the dish with foil or greaseproof paper, to prevent burning. Bake for 10 minutes at 190°C/ 375°F/Gas 5, reducing to 150°C/300°F/Gas 2 for a further 15-20 minutes. Remove the foil or paper for the last 5-8 minutes of baking, to produce a golden top. Serve whilst still warm, in the same dish.

STRAW FROM ABRANTES

Palha de Abrantes

RIBATEJO PROVINCE • Serves 4 to 6

From this interesting Roman-founded town comes a well-known egg-yolk-based pudding which, in spite of the name 'straw', is in fact a rich creation in the best Portuguese tradition.

200 g/7 oz granulated sugar

8 eggs

1 teaspoon cinnamon

Make a portion of 'egg threads' (*fios de ovos*) with half the eggs and the sugar, as explained on p.209. Set aside. Boil the remaining syrup until quite thick (the 'pearl stage', see p.32). Take off the heat and allow to cool a little, before adding the other 4 eggs, very well beaten. Simmer, whilst stirring constantly, until thick. Remove from the heat, beat in the cinnamon and pour the pudding into a glass serving-dish, decorating the top with the egg threads, like straw.

HEAVENLY FOOD

Manjar Celeste

ESTREMOZ, ALENTEJO PROVINCE • Serves 6

Another celestial title for a sweet, giving away its origin. You guessed: It was a convent, this time the one at Estremoz, founded in the thirteenth century. Estremoz is a lovely old walled town, favoured by the first kings. Vasco da Gama, the famous Portuguese sea-captain in charge of the expedition which braved the first voyage from Europe to Asia (embarking at Lisbon in July 1497), used to live there.

200 g/7 oz fresh cheese/ricotta (*requeijão*)
200 g/7 oz granulated sugar

4 egg yolks plus 1 whole egg

Make a light syrup (the 'smooth stage', p.32) with the sugar and a little water (enough to melt it). Add the sieved cheese and beat well by hand or with an electric mixer. Simmer until creamy (5-8 minutes). Remove from heat, cool slightly and add the beaten egg yolks and whole egg. Pour into small earthenware bowls (or small ramekins), previously buttered. Bake at 190°C/375°F/Gas 5 for about 15 minutes or until golden and well set.

FOOD FROM HEAVEN

Manjar Celeste

RIBATEJO PROVINCE • Serves 4 to 6

Although this recipe has the same title as the one from Estremoz, it is in fact a completely different pudding.

90 g/3 oz soft breadcrumbs (no crust)
200 g/7 oz granulated sugar plus 2 tablespoons
60 g/2 oz ground almonds

4 eggs
150 ml/¼ pint 'egg threads' (p.209)

Make a light syrup ('smooth stage', p.32) with the 200 g/7 oz sugar and enough water to melt it. Add the crumbs and almonds and mix into a paste. Simmer for 4-5 minutes, stirring. Take off the heat and mix with the beaten eggs, and the 2 tablespoons of sugar, until very fluffy. Bring to simmering point again and cook for 4-5 minutes or until it thickens. Pour into a serving dish and decorate with a mound of 'egg threads'.

EGG AND CINNAMON PUDDING, ELVAS FASHION

Sericá

ALENTEJO PROVINCE • Serves 6

This unusual speciality comes from Elvas, one of the most interesting walled cities in Portugal. Its Roman-Arabian castle and the fortress command views of the city and surrounding landscape. Among all the remarkable constructions in Elvas the aqueduct stands out as a masterpiece of the fifteenth and seventeenth centuries, reckoned the biggest in the Iberian peninsula and the most beautiful in Europe. Elvas' geographical position, bordering Spain, gave it great importance as a meeting-place for kings and nobles from both countries, and at least two royal weddings, involving both Courts, were celebrated there – that of a Portuguese princess with the King of Castile in 1383 and, perhaps more important, that between the daughter of the Holy Roman Emperor Charles V (himself a King of Spain as well) and a Portuguese prince in 1552. I am sure this pudding would do full honours to the banquets that followed, although the city is renowned for all its cuisine, as well as its plums and juicy olives.

225 g/8 oz granulated sugar
6 eggs, separated
450 ml/¾ pint milk
75 g/2½ oz flour

2 tablespoons cinnamon
zest of ½ lemon
pinch of salt

Mix the flour with the milk, add the egg yolks and sugar and beat well. Bring the mixture to a very gentle simmer, stirring it all the time until it thickens like a cream. Allow to cool. Fold in the stiffly beaten egg whites, add the lemon zest, and spoon into a well-buttered flan mould 20-23 cm/8-9 inches in diameter, criss-crossing the spoonfuls of mixture and sprinkling in between with the cinnamon. Bake at 232°C/450°F/Gas 8 until the surface cracks. Serve lukewarm or cold.

EGG AND ORANGE PUDDING FROM MADEIRA
Pudim de Ovos
MADEIRA • Serves 4 to 6

175 g/6 oz caster sugar
300 ml/½ pint milk

4 eggs, separated
zest of 1 orange

FOR THE CARAMEL
90 g/3 oz granulated sugar

Beat the egg yolks and sugar until fluffy. Warm the milk slightly and add gradually to the egg mixture. Add the orange zest. Fold in the stiffly beaten egg whites. Bake in a bain-marie in a pudding mould (with lid, if possible) lined with the caramel. This is made by boiling the 90 g/3 oz sugar with a teaspoon of water, until it becomes brownish and runny. Tip into the mould and swirl around, to cover as evenly as possible. Keep the bain-marie in the oven for 35-40 minutes (180°C/350°F/Gas 4) or until the pudding is set, adding more boiling water to the outer tin, as necessary. Take out of the mould only when quite cold.

BLANCMANGE
Manjar branco

COIMBRA, BEIRA LITORAL PROVINCE • Serves 6 to 8

This is surely one of the most traditional recipes in the Portuguese repertoire. Medieval books cite it as something very delicious and well known.

300 ml/½ pint milk
½ medium sized chicken breast, cooked until soft
100 ml/3½ fl oz liquor from the chicken
90 g/3 oz rice flour

125 g/4½ oz caster sugar
zest of ½ orange
pinch of salt

Mince and then pound the chicken breast very thoroughly, until smooth. Add to all the other ingredients, beating well. Bring to the heat, stirring, and cook until thick. Spoon 10 cm/4 inch mounds onto buttered trays, and bake at 232°C/450°F/Gas 8 until brown specks appear on top (20-25 minutes).

CHESTNUT AND MILK JAM
Doce de Castanhas

ESTREMADURA PROVINCE • Serves 8 to 10

It may sound unusual, but it is an excellent kind of pudding, resembling *marrons glacés*.

300 ml/½ pint milk
1.2 kg/2½ lb boiled chestnuts

675 g/1½ lb granulated sugar
vanilla pod

Sieve the boiled and peeled chestnuts whilst still warm. You may need to sieve this purée twice to make it really smooth, or you could use a food processor. Add the milk gradually, beating all the time, or again using a mixer. Make a thick syrup (the 'thread stage', p. 32) with the sugar and a little water, adding the vanilla pod. Remove the pod when the syrup is ready. Mix the chestnut purée with the syrup. Beat well again. Bring to the heat, stirring, and allow to come to the boil. Remove from heat and then allow to cool before storing in a jar, under refrigeration. It can also be frozen. This pudding may be served with chocolate flakes, for example, or used as a filling for cakes and tarts. A great winter treat.

NOTE A lot of trouble can be saved if canned, unsweetened chestnut purée is available. This would, however, make the mixture wetter, and therefore a third less milk could be used.

COCONUT PUDDING
Pudim de Coco
LISBON AREA • Serves 6 to 8

Although not strictly a traditional recipe, this luscious pudding has enough roots and enough devotees to warrant its being included here. It can be cooked in small patty tins, producing little puddings or cakes, similar to those sold at many Portuguese cake-shops.

350 g/12 oz granulated sugar
200 g/7 oz desiccated coconut

5 egg yolks and 2 whites, well beaten together

Place the sugar in a pan with a little water to melt it and boil until very thick (the 'pearl stage', p.32). Remove from the heat, beat in the coconut and finally the eggs. Bake in a buttered ring-mould 15 cm/6 inches in diameter, at 180°C/350°F/Gas 4, for 20-25 minutes or until set.

VARIATION   Make individual puddings putting the mixture in well-buttered patty tins. They are wonderful eaten lukewarm or cold, for tea.

PEACHES IN WINE AND OTHER FRUIT SALADS
Pessego com Vinho e Saladas de Fruta

> At dinner, last night, I told her [Ana] how fond of peaches my cousin Gonçalo is, especially when they are steeped in wine, so she decided to send you this basket full of peaches . . .
>
> Eça de Queiroz, *A Ilustre Casa de Ramires*
> (*The Remarkable House of Ramires*)

Peaches steeped in wine and sugar are truly something from Heaven, but the Portuguese make beautiful fruit salads anyway, adding wine (port, generally) or liqueur, for more flavour. When not using wine, citrus juices (lemon, orange, mandarin) are added, for a subtle aroma. In order to bring out the full flavours, the salad must be made a few hours before the meal or even the previous day if kept in the fridge – in which case some of the ingredients, such as sliced bananas, will be added only just before serving.

There are no rules for fruit salad ingredients. They depend on the season and on taste – also on the occasion. A grand dinner may include a fruit salad among the desserts (there will be more than one dessert at a grand dinner), and this salad will itself reflect the care put into that meal, so it will probably include a great variety of fruits, among them pineapple (fresh, of course), peaches, pears and so on.

Choose a glass bowl, mix in it the various fruits of your choice (except any soft fruits, such as strawberries and those which will discolour, such as banana, which are added just prior to serving) and dust generously with sugar. If using wine, mix a few spoonfuls of white wine and a liqueur glass of port or equivalent. Taste for sweetness and leave aside, preferably under refrigeration, until needed. Before serving, add the soft fruits, using some of them as decoration. Dust the top with sugar. For a simpler salad, without wine, add citrus juices of your choice and sugar to taste.

BAKED APPLES
Maçãs Assadas
Serves 4

Baked apples are a common pudding offered at Portuguese homes and restaurants. The apples used are large russets, very fleshy and extremely good. In *The Sin of Father Amaro* Eça de Queiroz refers to baked apples: "'Marvellous!", said the Canon, as Mrs Janeira brought a large platter full of baked apples to the table. "I'll have some of those. I never refuse anything as delectable as baked apples!'"

4 large russet apples (or English Cox's)   4 teaspoons butter
4 heaped tablespoons sugar

Wash well but do not core or peel the apples (the pips actually impart a good flavour). Place them in a buttered baking tin. Melt the butter and brush the apples. Sprinkle with the sugar. Bake at 180°C/350°F/Gas 4 for 35-40 minutes or until tender and brown.

VARIATIONS
1 Sprinkle the apples with 4 teaspoons of port wine, after brushing with butter. Dust with the sugar and bake as above.
2 Mix a little cinnamon and/or powdered cloves with the sugar.

SWEET CORNMEAL PORRIDGE
Papas de Milho Doces
NORTHERN PROVINCES • Serves 4 to 6

This is a really 'heavy' pudding, intended as part of a winter meal for very hungry people. It is served hot. It is also good as a hot cereal for breakfast. Think of it as a kind of porridge – and very nice, too.

175 g/6 oz cornmeal (p.27)   cinnamon (optional)
600 ml/1 pint liquid (only water or half milk/half   ½ coffeespoon salt
    water)   1 teaspoon vegetable oil, if milk is not used
110 g/4 oz granulated sugar

Mix the cornmeal with the chosen liquid (and oil, if used) and bring to the boil, stirring all the time. Cook over a gentle heat for 12-15 minutes. Stir frequently. Add the salt and sugar towards the end. Add more liquid and/or sugar, according to taste. Serve whilst still warm, with a sprinkling of cinnamon, if liked. Instead of sugar, honey or treacle (or a mixture of sugar and one of these) can be used.

SWEETS

MARZIPAN SWEETS, ALGARVE STYLE
Doces de Amendoa
Makes about 24 sweets

Even in the Algarve, where almonds grow in abundance, these sweets tend to be expensive, due to the labour involved in preparing them, but nobody would dare return from a visit there without bringing back a frilled box full of almond sweets. They are quite delicious and beautiful to look at, as they are made in various dainty shapes (fruit, fish, vegetables) and decorated accordingly by hand. They are normally filled with *ovos moles* (p.150) or *fios de ovos* (p.209), producing a mouth-watering soft centre which distinguishes these marzipan sweets from the harder ones made with ordinary almond paste and available in many countries.

200 g/7 oz granulated sugar	150 ml/¼ pint water
200 g/7 oz finely ground almonds	

Boil the sugar and water very gently until thick (see the 'pearl stage', p.32) over a gentle heat. Add the almonds. Mix well and boil, whilst stirring, until quite dry. Let the paste cool completely (overnight, if possible). It should now be hard but pliable enough to allow moulding (with slightly wet fingers). If not, it will have to be boiled again for a little while, to get rid of any excess moisture. Cool once more and mould in your favourite little shapes, about 2.5 cm/1 inch in diameter, introducing some egg filling in the middle, as described above. Leave aside for one day and then paint carefully with vegetable dye and decorate to taste. Place each sweet in a paper case and serve on a platter, as you would serve chocolates, to end a meal.

A very pretty shape to make is a nest, with eggs the size of a pea inside (also moulded with the almond paste). The 'straw' is achieved with some 'egg threads'. A darker nest can be made by adding some powdered chocolate to the paste.

EGG SWEETS FROM VISEU
Bolos de Ovos de Viseu
BEIRA ALTA PROVINCE • Makes about 24 sweets

Egg sweets appear in every corner of Portugal, but Viseu seems to be particularly skilful in making them and has become famous for it. Apart from eating egg sweets, however, Viseu calls for a leisurely visit. Romans, Swabians, Visigoths and Arabs claimed it, and later the Christians walled it, to protect this precious town from neighbouring Castilians, and transformed it into an important cultural centre. But while preserving its interesting past, Viseu is also one of the most forward-looking and well planned of Portugal's northern cities.

| 200 g/7 oz granulated sugar | 14 egg yolks |

Add a little water to the sugar, just to melt it and boil until a thick syrup is formed (see the 'thread stage', p.32). Remove from the heat and add 13 of the egg yolks, previously beaten. Combine vigorously and bring to a gentle simmer, stirring all the time until it thickens. Cool the mixture completely (you can speed this up by leaving it in the fridge for a while). With floured hands, mould small shapes – 2.5 cm/1 inch balls, cylinders, pyramids, etc, and coat them in the remaining egg yolk, well beaten with a drop of water. Place under a hot grill for a minute or two, to burn the tops slightly. Put them in paper cases, after rolling in sugar. Serve two days later, to allow the sweets to dry and firm up a little.

WALNUTS CASCAIS FASHION
Nozes de Cascais
Makes about 18 sweets

Romans and Moors had their eyes on Cascais, and so have many people today. Cascais is an extremely pretty little town near Lisbon, favoured by deposed kings, expatriates, tourists and commuters. Its beaches, gardens, quaint old streets and even the new ones attract them all but, in spite of that, Cascais keeps its serene air of quiet elegance and intimacy. Restaurants with marvellous fish dishes abound, and old patisseries still produce Cascais' main sweet specialities: *areias* ('sand' – small biscuits, see p.193) and these crackling walnut sweets, shiny and delicious, with a coat of caramel, like toffee apples.

90 g/3 oz granulated sugar	9 walnuts, in perfect halves (18)
110 g/4 oz ground almonds	5 egg yolks
4 tablespoons water	

FOR THE CRACKLING CARAMEL COATING

| 110 g/4 oz granulated sugar | 2 drops lemon juice |
| 3 tablespoons water | |

Make a thick syrup with the water and sugar. Remove from the heat and mix in the beaten egg yolks, adding them gradually to the syrup. Then mix in the almonds. Simmer, stirring, until thick. Pour onto a plate and leave for a few hours. Then shape 2.5 cm/1 inch balls with this paste. Place half a walnut on top of each and set them aside.

Make a syrup with the water and sugar allowing it to turn into light-coloured caramel. Watch over this carefully. When reaching this point, take off the heat, add the 2 drops of lemon juice, stir and immediately submerge each walnut cake in it, using a fork. Place the coated cakes on a large oiled platter (to prevent sticking) and leave them until the following day. Pare any excess caramel from the sides (with sharp scissors) and place in paper cases. If the caramel dries up half way through the coating operation, add a drop of water to it and bring again to the heat, to restore its fluidity.

BREEZE FROM THE LIS RIVER
Brisas do Lis
LEIRIA, ESTREMADURA PROVINCE • Makes about 1 dozen

These small cake-like sweets are as delicious as the town they come from. Leiria was, however, the scene of bloody fighting between Christians and Moors until, at the final battle in 1134, the Christians won. Later kings built a splendid palace there, which they used on many occasions.

The typical and appreciated little *brisas* from Leiria, are prepared as follows:

60 g/2 oz ground almonds
200 g/7 oz caster sugar

4 large eggs, beaten

Combine all ingredients and bake in small, well-buttered patty tins, in an oven set to 200°C/400°F/ Gas 6, for 20 minutes or until golden and set. Serve in frilled paper cases, for tea or with liqueurs or port.

ANGEL'S BREASTS
Papos de Anjo
MIRANDELA, TRÁS-OS-MONTES PROVINCE • makes 24 to 30 sweets

Anything called 'angel's breasts' must surely be delectable and sweet. Old convents in the Azores, Beja, Amarante and Viseu have different confections under this name. The recipe below is, however, from a convent in Mirandela, a lovely town which is of Roman origin and has a beautiful Roman bridge, rebuilt during the sixteenth century.

350 g/12 oz granulated sugar
6 eggs plus 4 yolks, all beaten up together

2 tablespoons thick jam, any flavour
1 teaspoon cinnamon

Make a thick syrup (see the 'thread stage', p.32) with the sugar and a little water, to melt it. Remove from the heat and beat in the jam. Boil again over a low flame, to thicken again. Cool it down a little and add the beaten eggs and cinnamon, stirring vigorously. Butter really well small patty tins and half fill them with the mixture (the sweets rise a lot, on baking). Bring them to a preheated oven (200°C/400°F/Gas 6) until set and golden. Dust with icing sugar before serving, when cold.

DOM RODRIGO SWEETS
Bolos de Dom Rodrigo
THE ALGARVE • Makes 8 to 10

These sweets are sold wrapped in foil, with the ends twisted upwards, in the middle, to keep any loose syrup inside. They are delicate and very sweet. One can cope with only one at a time, but what a heavenly thing they are!

egg threads (p.209)
3 egg yolks, slightly beaten
90 g/3 oz ground almonds

110 g/4 oz granulated sugar
cinnamon
sugar

Make the egg threads described on p.209 and keep them wet with a little of the syrup left over. Keep the rest of the syrup for later.

Make more syrup (to the 'thread stage', p.32) with the 110 g/4 oz sugar and a little water to cover it. Mix in the ground almonds and cook gently for 2 minutes. Remove from the heat and add the beaten yolks. Mix well and bring just to the boil, to cook them. Remove from the heat again and sprinkle with a little cinnamon.

Divide the egg threads into 8-10 little mounds, and make a well in the centre of each. Fill each well with the almond-and-egg mixture, and cover this filling with the threads, bringing them over it, so that you have 8-10 balls of filled threads. Bring the left-over syrup to the boil (adding just a little water) and cook the 'balls' in it, a few at a time, for only one moment. Take them out with a slotted spoon. When they are all ready and cool, wrap them in squares of foil, as explained above.

FIG LORD

Morgado de Figo

THE ALGARVE • Makes about 36 small sweets

This is the fig-and-almond paste used in the Algarve for moulding all kinds of small shapes, served as sweets or to be made into a large cake, to cut in small sections only when needed, as it will keep almost indefinitely.

225 g/8 oz very good-quality dried figs
225 g/8 oz granulated sugar
225 g/8 oz ground almonds

1 teaspoon cinnamon
2 teaspoons powdered cocoa
grated rind of 1 large lemon

Cut up the figs (discarding the little stems) into very small pieces, using scissors, which facilitates this tedious work. Set aside. Bring 6 tablespoons of water to the heat, add the sugar, cinnamon, lemon zest and cocoa, and boil until a thick syrup is formed. Add the almonds, mix and allow to boil again for 2-3 minutes. Then add the figs and boil for a further 4-5 minutes, stirring, always over a low flame. Remove from the heat and cool until you can handle the mixture. Place it on a sugared surface and press firmly, using your hands and a spatula, to mould the paste.

If the cake shape is what is wanted, it is now ready for decoration with icing sugar and/or little motifs made of almond paste. Otherwise, break off pieces and mould shapes to your taste, with the help of a little sugar. Place them in paper cases. Keep in boxes, to avoid their drying too much.

SWEET POTATO CAKES
Fartes de Batata Doce
Madeira • Makes about 36 sweets

Sweet potato (*batata doce*) is grown in Madeira (and in the Algarve), so one would expect to find local specialities made with this heavy, floury and quite delicious variety of potato. These exquisite sweets from Madeira are very easy to make.

400 g/14 oz mashed sweet potato, cooled
350 g/12 oz granulated sugar
1 tablespoon flour
2 eggs
30 g/1 oz butter plus 2 tablespoons melted butter

for brushing
90 g/3 oz ground almonds
90 g/3 oz mixed glacé fruit
2 tablespoons orange juice

Mix the sugar with the 30 g/1 oz butter and the eggs. Add the mashed potato, flour, almonds, juice and fruit (previously cut into small pieces). Beat thoroughly. Then bring to the boil over low heat, until all moisture disappears, whilst stirring, to prevent sticking. When very thick, take the mixture off the heat and turn it onto a floured board. Shape into 2.5 cm/1 inch squares and place in greased tins. Brush the tops with melted butter and bake at 190°C/375°F/Gas 5, for 10-15 minutes, or until golden brown. When baked, brush again with melted butter and dredge with sugar.

LITTLE EGG AND BREAD SWEETS, BRAGANÇA FASHION
Bolos de Ovos e Pão de Bragança
TRÁS-OS-MONTES PROVINCE • Makes about 36 sweets

A rich mixture, using bread and lots of eggs yolks, as one would expect in traditional recipes.

200 g/7 oz stale bread, crumbled
200 g/7 oz ground almonds
14 egg yolks

400 g/14 oz granulated sugar
1 teaspoon cinnamon
2 tablespoons orange water

Mix the breadcrumbs and ground almonds. Set aside. Make a syrup with the sugar and a little water. Boil until thick (the 'pearl stage', p.32). Remove from the heat and mix in the bread and almonds. Combine the egg yolks into this and beat very well. Add the cinnamon and orange water (or plain water, failing this) if the mixture is too thick. Bring to the heat and simmer, whilst stirring, for 2-3 minutes, to cook the eggs and acquire a smooth consistency. It must become almost solid, but not dry. Leave until the following day and shape small cakes, rolling them in sugar. Put them in paper cases, to savour later, slowly and in peace, as if you were looking at the vast, tranquil horizons enjoyed from Bragança's belvedere, beside St Bartholomew's Chapel.

LORVÃO SWEETS

Pasteis de Lorvão

BEIRA LITORAL PROVINCE • Makes 24 small sweets

This is one of the recipes dreamed up by nuns or monks, and the fact that in Lorvão there was at least one important monastery, of the Cistercian Order, may have something to do with these traditional sweets.

200 g/7 oz granulated sugar	1 tablespoon flour
60 g/2 oz ground almonds	½ teaspoon cinnamon
6 egg yolks	zest of ½ lemon
1 egg white	150 ml/¼ pint water

Boil the sugar and water until a thick syrup is formed (see the 'thread stage', p.32). Take off the heat, stir the almonds and flour and bring to a gentle boil again, stirring all the time. Cool it down before adding the egg yolks, well beaten, the white of egg and remaining ingredients. Mix well and bake at 163°C/325°F/Gas 3 in patty tins previously buttered and floured, until set and slightly browned on top – about 25 minutes. When baked, dredge the little sweets with sugar and put them in paper cases.

LITTLE ORANGES

Laranjinhas

SETÚBAL REGION, SOUTH OF LISBON • Makes about 24.

These sweets originate from the Setúbal area, where oranges grow. Make the *laranjinhas* a few days before they are to be served, to get firmer (see opposite).

4 large carrots	200 g/7 oz granulated sugar
fresh skin (and pith) of 3 oranges	

Cut the carrots in half – not in small pieces, so they do not absorb too much water. Boil the carrots with the orange peel (with all its pith, to avoid too much bitterness), until tender. Drain very thoroughly and dry again in a clean cloth. Mash and sieve. Bring the sugar to the boil for 2-3 minutes with 2 tablespoons water, until thick (see the 'pearl stage', p.32). Add the purée. Boil again, stirring with a wooden spoon. Allow the mixture to dry, without burning (this needs a really low flame throughout and a very watchful eye). Spread the resulting paste on a plate and leave until completely cold. Shape small balls 2.5 cm/1 inch in diameter. Roll them in sugar and place in paper cases. Leave them untouched to dry, for 2 or 3 days. You can make these little oranges more realistic by sticking a small stem and leaf on top.

POTATO DELIGHTS

Delícias de Batata

BENAVENTE, RIBATEJO PROVINCE • Makes 12 to 16

Mashed potato gives an interesting texture to sweets, as these 'delights' from Roman Benavente show.

90 g/3 oz ground almonds
100 g/3½ oz mashed potato
200 g/7 oz granulated sugar
1 tablespoon cornflour
1 tablespoon butter
2 eggs
3 tablespoons water
icing sugar and cinnamon for sprinkling

Mix the water with the sugar and boil to make a light syrup (see p.32). Add the mashed potato and almonds. Boil until thick, over a low flame, stirring. Set aside until almost cold. Add the eggs and flour and beat well. Bake this mixture in well-buttered patty tins, at 210°C/425°F/Gas 7 for 20 minutes or until golden brown. Take out of the tins carefully, before the *delícias* are completely cold, and dust with a mixture of icing sugar and cinnamon.

CANDIED ORANGE PEEL

Casca de Laranja Cristalizada

SETÚBAL, SOUTH OF LISBON

Setúbal was founded by the Celts and later developed by the Romans, who worked its famous salt-pits which, together with the fishing, fruit-growing and wines of the region, contributed to the continuous development of the city. Nowadays various industries in and near Setúbal also give it prosperity.

Oranges are one of the crops around Setúbal, and the region is renowned for its orange *compôte* and candied orange peel. The latter is not too difficult to make at home, and many Portuguese housewives like to keep some homemade candied peel to use in cakes and to eat as a snack.

orange peel – any amount
the same weight of granulated sugar

When eating oranges, save the peel and ask your family to do the same. Most of the pith must be left, when peeling the

oranges, otherwise the peel is too bitter. It will keep in the fridge for a couple of days. Then soak it for 24 hours, changing the water several times, to get rid of the bitterness. Cut the peel into strips 12 mm (½ inch) wide and place them in a pan containing boiling water. Bring to the boil again and remove at once. Drain and put the parboiled peel in a clean cloth, to absorb all moisture. When it is as dry as you can get it, weigh it. Using the same amount of sugar, make a syrup with just the minimum of water, boiling until thick (see the 'pearl stage', p.32). Add the peel and stir it around, to get well coated with the syrup. Do this over very low heat and being careful not to break the peel. Allow the mixture to become quite dry, but without burning it. Pour on a tray and separate the strips immediately with a knife. Allow to cool overnight.

If the peel is not perfectly dry at this stage, it might go mouldy very quickly, so either boil it again with great care, in order to finish drying, or leave it spread out over a tray or board for a day or so, turning now and then. Store in jars in a cool larder.

CHOCOLATE SALAMI
Salame de Chocolate
LISBON AREA • Serves 4 to 6

This is a very popular sweet in some Portuguese households, not needing baking or cooking. Its appearance and taste make it suitable for birthday parties.

90 g/3 oz drinking chocolate (the powdered variety)
90 g/3 oz butter
90 g/3 oz superfine sugar
140 g/5 oz crumbed biscuits (petit-beurre, digestive or any kind of plain biscuits)
1 egg

Mix the butter with the sugar, then add the chocolate, egg and, finally, crumbed biscuits. This will provide a stiff paste, which you will shape like a very thick sausage (hence the name 'salami'). Wrap it in slightly oiled foil and refrigerate overnight to harden. Cut just before it is needed, slicing it thickly. You can also shape small balls with the paste, roll them in powdered chocolate and put in paper cases.

PASTRIES

CREAM (OR BELÉM) TARTS

Pasteis de Nata or *Pasteis de Belém*

LISBON • Makes 10 to 12 tarts

These cakes were first made popular in a very ancient shop in the Belém district of Lisbon. It is still open, and its many rooms, with walls covered in well-preserved Portuguese tiles, are constantly full of people eating the tarts, with coffee. The shop is not far from the splendid Belém Tower, one of the most famous and lovely of Lisbon landmarks, built in the sixteenth century on the spot from which the caravels used to come and go, during the maritime era. *Pasteis de Nata* (custard tarts with a difference) are nowadays available everywhere in Portugal and are perhaps the most popular of all small pastries. They can be extremely good or simply good, according to who prepares them. In fact, there are few places where one can say they are extremely good. Normally there are no points of reference but I am old enough to know what is what, while agreeing that whatever the case may be, they are a very good cake, anyway... The proper recipe is a closely guarded secret, so people have to make do with tentative formulae. One thing is certain, and that is that no amount of goodwill can come up with VERY good cream tarts at home, simply because they need a very hot oven indeed, the sort that only commercial ovens can deliver. So, the moral of the story is: turn your own oven to its highest setting. To make things a little easier, I am indicating here the use of ready-made puff pastry (the best quality possible). And please do not be put off baking cream tarts. They deserve being included in your repertoire.

1 packet of puff pastry	4 egg yolks
150 ml/¼ pint single cream	75 g/2½ oz sugar

Have at hand 10-12 little patty tins or muffin tins, if you cannot get the proper individual moulds used in Portugal. They must be individual, so that you can line them easily with the pastry.

Prepare the custard filling: beat the egg yolks with the sugar, until thick and whitish, then add the cream gradually, mix well and bring to low heat. Let it simmer, stirring, just for a moment, to thicken a little, then set aside to cool. Turn on the oven to its highest setting now, so it will be really very hot by the time you bake the tarts.

Take the puff pastry out of the fridge (if you had it frozen, it must be defrosted previously and kept in the cold). Open up the sheet of pastry and divide it into two portions. Now roll each one over itself, as if you were rolling a Swiss roll, thus making two sausage-like portions.

Using a sharp knife cut each roll into slices about 2 cm/¾ inch thick. Use each one of these rounds to line the tins, pressing the pastry firmly with both thumbs, all around. Fill with a tablespoon of custard and take to the oven until the custard shows browned spots on top and the pastry is golden (15-20 minutes). The tarts should be eaten the same day but if you have any left over then take them for a few minutes to the oven, to crisp-up the pastry again. You can sprinkle the tarts with cinnamon and confectioners sugar, but they are fine without. Incidentally some people call these tarts *Natas* (outside Portugal), or 'custard tarts'.

CHEESE TARTLETS SINTRA-STYLE
Queijadas de Sintra
Makes 24 to 30

Sintra is a very old town, near Lisbon, its ancient castle perched high on a mountain, bearing striking evidence to the former presence of the Moors. Portuguese kings and queens loved Sintra and built many magnificent palaces in and around the town, which is enveloped in thick woods. Sintra is little changed: delightful and noble, of exquisite and enduring charm. Lord Byron wrote of it, artists surrender to it. *Queijadas* are made exclusively there but are available in the best Lisbon patisseries.

DOUGH
280 g/10 oz flour

1½ tablespoons butter
salt

NOTE For a homely and delicious version of these tartlets use ready-made puff pastry.

FILLING
350 g/12 oz fresh cheese/ricotta (*requeijão*)
60 g/2 oz grated hard cheese, Cheddar type
200 g/7 oz sugar

5 tablespoons flour
3 egg yolks plus 1 whole egg
½ teaspoon cinnamon

The cases in which the cheese filling is cooked are thin and crunchy, rather like very thin water-biscuits. The dough is generally prepared well in advance, preferably the previous day. Put the flour in a basin, make a well in the centre, add the softened butter and a little salt. Mix with the tips of the fingers, and add tepid water very gradually while kneading thoroughly. The dough must be elastic and smooth but rather on the dry side, and should not stick to the basin. Cover with a dry cloth and then with a damp one. Set aside to rest until the following day, or at least for a few hours.

Meanwhile prepare the filling. Sieve the fresh cheese, and mix well with the grated cheese, until a smooth paste is obtained. Add the sugar and then all the other ingredients, little by little, beating between additions.

Roll out the dough really fine (the thickness of 3 sheets of paper, put together) on a floured board. Cut out small rounds, 7.5 cm/3 inches in diameter, and line buttered patty tins with them, cutting 4 snippets to adjust the dough into the tins. Fill with the cheese mixture and bake in a hot oven (210°C/425°F/Gas 7) for about 15 minutes or until brown.

When cold, join the tartlets in pairs, placing a small piece of greaseproof paper between them. Keep in tins, to prevent drying.

BEAN TARTS
Pasteis de Feijão
TORRES VEDRAS, NEAR LISBON • Makes 24 tarts

Torres Vedras was an important copper-mining centre in 2000 BC. Nowadays it is a bustling town, with excellent wine, and particularly interesting for its many historical associations and architectural remains. Nearby, the fortress of St Vincent testifies to the presence of British troops under the Duke of Wellington, when fighting to help the Portuguese repel the Napoleonic invaders, led by General Masséna. The impregnable 'Lines of Torres Vedras' built by Wellington successfully halted the advance of the French troops.

The bean tarts, which are supposedly a Torres Vedras creation and still sold as a local speciality (in boxes of 6), are truly exquisite, and the bean purée gives them a texture all their own.

PASTRY

200 g/7 oz flour	water
3 tablespoons butter (or butter and lard)	salt

FILLING

225 g/8 oz granulated sugar	110 g/4 oz ground almonds
110 g/4 oz puréed haricot beans	5 egg yolks

Mix the pastry ingredients with a little tepid water to form a soft and pliable dough. Set aside, covered, while preparing the filling.

Make a syrup with the sugar and 3 tablespoons of water. Boil until thick (see the 'pearl stage', p.32). Add the sieved bean purée and cook for a couple of minutes. Mix in the almonds and boil again. Set aside, until almost cold. Add the egg yolks and bring again to the boil, then remove from the heat and allow to cool. Roll out the dough quite thinly and line small buttered patty tins. Divide the filling between them. Bake at 218°C/425°F/Gas 7 for about 20 minutes or until a golden crust is formed.

VARIATION Instead of bean purée use chickpea purée. All the other ingredients and the method are the same.

RICE PATTIES FROM THE AZORES
Pasteis de Arroz dos Açores
Makes 24

DOUGH

200 g/7 oz flour	1 tablespoon butter
1 tablespoon sugar	1 egg yolk

FILLING

	5 egg yolks
225 g/8 oz rice	45 g/1½ oz ground almonds
350 g/12 oz granulated sugar	pinch salt

Prepare the filling a day in advance, to allow it to cool and thicken. Cook the rice until mushy in 3 times its volume of water, adding a little salt. Sieve the soft rice and set aside. Prepare a thick syrup with the sugar and enough water to melt it. Add the rice and boil gently for 5 minutes, stirring. Add the ground almonds and cook again for 2-3 minutes. Add the beaten egg yolks, mix over the heat and remove from it at once. Keep this mixture until the following day, when it should be very thick.

For the dough, mix the flour with the other ingredients and a little water to obtain a smooth consistency. Knead. Leave to rest for 20-30 minutes. Roll out quite thinly (little more than the thickness of paper), cut rounds 10 cm/4 inches in diameter and divide the filling among them. Fold in half-moon shapes, pressing the edges. Put in buttered baking tins and bring to the oven (163°C/325°F/Gas 3) for 15 minutes, to dry out without actually getting browned. Dust with icing sugar when ready.

ST CLARA TURNOVERS
Pasteis de Santa Clara
COIMBRA, BEIRA LITORAL PROVINCE • Makes 12 to 16 turnovers

Never missing the opportunity of settling at beautiful spots, at the time when they dominated most of Europe, the Romans founded the town of Aeminium, now Coimbra, on the banks of the Mondego river. There are still important Roman remains in the city, especially at nearby Conimbriga (from which Coimbra derives its present name). Coimbra can also claim one of the oldest universities in Europe (dating from 1308) and to have been the first capital of the country, for over a century, chosen by Afonso Henriques, who became Portugal's first king in 1140. Historically and culturally Coimbra is quite remarkable, and it is still one of the most important and interesting Portuguese cities. From its many monasteries and convents came various original recipes, which have been preserved to this day, like these delicious turnovers.

PASTRY

200 g/7 oz flour

110 g/4 oz chilled butter

1 beaten egg for brushing

FILLING

200 g/7 oz granulated sugar

110 g/4 oz ground almonds

7 well-beaten egg yolks

Use the rubbing-in method (with fingertips) to mix the flour with the chilled butter, adding a little very cold water, until a pliable dough is obtained. Cover and keep in a cool place or fridge while you prepare the filling.

Melt the sugar in a little water and boil until thick. Add the ground almonds and yolks, mix very well and simmer, while stirring, until very thick. Cool.

Roll out the pastry to 3 mm/⅛ inch thickness, cut into rounds of about 7.5 cm/3 inches diameter and divide the filling between them, placing it in the middle of each round. Wet the edges and fold, pressing firmly, to form a half-moon shape. Brush with the beaten egg and bake in greased trays at 200°C/400°F/Gas 6 until golden. When ready, dredge with sugar.

TURNOVERS FROM VILA REAL

Pasteis de Vila Real

TRÁS-OS-MONTES PROVINCE • Makes 12 to 16 turnovers

Vila Real, one of the main inland northern cities, was the birthplace of Diogo Cão, a distinguished sailor who in 1482 began his travels along the African coast and initiated the custom of marking these lands with stone monuments (*padrões*) testifying that the Portuguese had been there: 'Here have arrived the ships of the learned King of Portugal.' The monuments erected beside the Zaire river waterfalls signalled the first European contacts with the Congo.

Closer to our time, in 1895, a hydro-electric power station was built on the beautiful gorges of the Corgo river, near Vila Real, making this city the first in Portugal to be provided with electricity.

The turnovers described below originated, predictably enough, at a convent. They can be fried or baked, and among the various existing versions this one is particularly delicate.

DOUGH

225 g/8 oz flour

1 egg

75 g/2½ oz butter, lard or margarine

½ teaspoon salt

FILLING

175 g/6 oz granulated sugar

3 egg yolks

1 medium apple, grated

60 g/2 oz ground almonds

½ teaspoon cinnamon

1 thin slice fresh white bread (if needed)

To prepare the dough, mix the flour with the fat using the tips of your fingers. Then add the beaten egg, some cold water and salt. Knead well, adding a dusting of flour if it is sticky. It should become very elastic and smooth. Form a ball with this dough and set it aside in a cool place for an hour or so.

Meanwhile, prepare the filling. In a pan bring the sugar to the boil with some water, to melt it, and make a thickish syrup (the 'thread stage', p.32). Add the apple and almonds, mix well and boil until very thick. Cool and add the yolks, one by one, and the cinnamon. Bring to the heat again, stirring, and allow to thicken. Should the mixture be slightly wet, add the fresh breadcrumbs (a slice of bread finely crumbled). Work everything together again. Set aside.

Roll out the pastry on a floured board to a thickness of 3 mm/⅛ inch and cut rounds about 7.5 cm/3 inches in diameter, using a pastry cutter. Share the filling between all the rounds (about 2 teaspoonfuls each), fold in half, press the edges with the help of a fork and bake in greased tins in a moderately hot oven (200°C/400°F/Gas 6) until golden. Dredge with sugar immediately after baking.

You can also fry the turnovers but baking makes them less likely to burst.

CHEESE TARTLETS BEIRA STYLE
Queijadas da Beira
Makes 24 to 30

Most Portuguese regions have their own cheese tartlets, made with fresh *requeijão* or similar fresh cheese.

200 g/7 oz sugar	4 eggs
200 g/7 oz fresh cheese/ricotta (*requeijão*)	60 g/2 oz cornflour

Mix the sieved cheese very thoroughly with the sugar and eggs. Add the flour. Beat well. Divide this paste between some small tartlet moulds or patty tins, which must be well buttered. Bake in a hot oven (200°C/400°F/Gas 6) for about 20 minutes or until golden brown. Take them out carefully after cooling a bit.

CHEESE TARTLETS PEREIRO STYLE
Queijadas do Pereiro
BEIRO PROVINCE • Makes about 24 small tartlets

DOUGH

225 g/8 oz flour	½ coffeespoon salt
1½ tablespoons melted butter	

FILLING

200 g/7 oz fresh cheese/ricotta (*requeijão*)	5 egg yolks
200 g/7 oz sugar	

Make a well in the centre of the flour and add some lukewarm water, the salt and the melted butter. Knead well and add some more water, if needed, to form a smooth dough. Set aside, covered, for 45-60 minutes. In the meantime mix the cheese, egg yolks and sugar to a soft paste. Roll out the dough quite thinly, about 3 mm/⅛ inch and line fluted patty tins, which must have been well buttered. Fill them with the cheese mixture and bake at 200°C/400°F/Gas 6, for 15-20 minutes, or until golden brown. Take them out of the tins when lukewarm. Serve cold, with tea or coffee.

CUSTARD TARTS FROM THE AZORES
Covilhetes de Leite
Makes 24 tarts

PASTRY

200 g/7 oz flour	pinch salt
2 tablespoons butter	water
1 tablespoon lard	

FILLING

600 ml/1 pint milk	1 tablespoon flour
225 g/8 oz granulated sugar	1 teaspoon cinnamon
4 egg yolks plus 2 whole eggs	

Prepare a dough with the flour, making a well in the centre, adding the fats and salt and then enough tepid water to obtain a smooth consistency. Mix very well and set aside, to rest.

Meantime, boil the milk with the sugar for a while, to reduce by a third. Remove from the heat and allow to cool. Add the cinnamon, egg yolks and 2 whole eggs, as well as the flour, mixed with a little milk. Beat well. Roll out the dough quite thinly (3 mm/⅛ inch) and line greased patty tins. Fill with the prepared mixture and bake in a preheated oven to 190°C/375°F/Gas 5 for 20-25 minutes or until golden brown. Serve the tarts when cold.

ALMOND TART
Tarte de Amendoa
ESTREMADURA • Serves 6 to 8

This is a lovely dessert, served sometimes in Portuguese restaurants and at parties.

DOUGH

175 g/6 oz flour	90 g/3 oz caster sugar
90 g/3 oz softened butter	Pinch of salt
1 egg	

FILLING

100 g/3½ oz peeled almonds, cut into pieces lengthwise	4 tablespoons milk
90 g/3 oz sugar	90 g/3 oz butter

Mix the flour with the other ingredients rapidly and spread over the bottom of a buttered tart mould. Bake blind for about 15 minutes at 200°C/400°F/Gas 6 or until golden brown.

In the meantime mix all filling ingredients and bring to the boil, to thicken a little. Pour into the baked base, spread evenly and bake at 210°C/425°F/Gas 7 to dry up the top slightly (about 5 minutes).

APPLE TART WITH CUSTARD
Tarte de Maçã e Creme
LISBON AREA • Serves 6 to 8

This tart is a nice addition to any party table or special meal.

PASTRY

175 g/6 oz flour	pinch of salt
90 g/3 oz butter	

FILLING

450 g/1 lb russet apples (or Cox's)
300 ml/½ pint milk
4 tablespoons sugar

2 eggs
1 tablespoon flour

Prepare the pastry first by swiftly mixing the flour with the butter, salt and enough cold water to make a soft, non-stick dough. Leave in a cool place for half an hour. Meanwhile core and peel the apples (in Portugal this is made with *reinetas*, which are very similar to russets but can be substituted by good Cox's). Cut the apples into very thin slices. Roll out the pastry and cover a buttered flan mould with it. Fill the pastry case with the sliced apples, placing them in neat rows all round. Bake at 180°C/350°F/ Gas 4 for about 25 minutes. Remove from the oven and pour over the apples a mixture made with the eggs, milk, flour and sugar, all beaten up. Return the tart to the oven again and bake for a further 20 minutes or until golden and well set. Serve cold or whilst still warm, with or without cream.

FLUFFY CAKES, FROM FAIAL
Fofas do Faial
AZORES ARCHIPELAGO • Makes 30 to 36

These choux-type pastries can be filled with custard or Chantilly cream but are also very nice just by themselves. They are traditionally made in the Azores for the Carnival season.

350 g/12 oz flour
30 g/1 oz granulated sugar
300 ml/½ pint liquid – half milk, half water
100 g/3½ oz butter

10 eggs
1 coffeespoon salt
2 tablespoons aniseeds (or fennel seeds)

In a large pan bring the liquid to the boil with the butter, sugar, seeds and salt. When boiling, mix in the flour, all at once, reduce the heat and stir until the paste is smooth and no longer sticks to the sides of the pan. Remove from the heat and allow to cool. Then mix in the eggs, one at a time, beating vigorously until all the moisture is absorbed, before adding the next egg. It should have the consistency of a thick meringue paste. If you arrive at this consistency before adding all the eggs, do not add any more. If, on the other hand, it is still too stiff after the last egg has been beaten in, mix in another one – although this should not be necessary. Beat well again and bake in small mounds (the size of a ping-pong ball) in buttered trays, until puffy and golden in an oven preheated to 210°C/425°F/Gas 7. After cooling they can be filled with sweetened whipped double cream, Chantilly or a thick custard.

SMALL CAKES AND BISCUITS

'BOWLFUL' FROM ABRANTES
Tigeladas de Abrantes
RIBATEJO PROVINCE • Makes 24 cakes

Abrantes is no longer famous for its silk production, as it was in the eighteenth and nineteenth centuries but it is renowned for these custard cakes baked in the oven. It is possible to buy them outside Abrantes, in good pastry-shops.

450 ml/¾ pint milk
6 eggs
200 g/7 oz sugar

60 g/2 oz flour
pinch salt

Beat all the ingredients very thoroughly by hand for at least 25 minutes, or use an electric mixer for 8 minutes or so. Whilst you are doing this, prepare the small earthenware bowls in which this should be baked, which are like deep saucers (or use ramekin dishes), warming them in the oven, set to 200°C/400°F/Gas 6. (You do not need to butter the bowls.) Put the bowls inside a large baking tin or on a tray, so that you do not burn yourself when pulling them out to fill with the egg mixture. Use a ladle to do this. Bake for 15 to 20 minutes until solid and with brown specks on top. Take them out of the bowls immediately. Serve cold. The *tigeladas* are eaten as cakes with tea or coffee.

ST GONÇALO CAKES
Bolos de S. Gonçalo
DOURO LITORAL PROVINCE • Makes about 24 cakes

Many popular saints' days are celebrated at times coinciding with ancient fertility rites. St Gonçalo is one such saint, nobody seems to know why. He was an architect who in the thirteenth century built the elegant bridge which bears his name and still stands at Amarante, a delightfully picturesque town founded by the Romans. Both here, at the end of the first week in June and on 11 January, in Gaia (opposite Oporto, and famous for the port wine cellars that line its main streets) Christian-cum-pagan festivals celebrate Gonçalo as a saint who finds husbands for old maids. A pilgrimage, a noisy fair, dancing, singing and eating (of suggestive-looking cakes) are all part of the feasts.

200 g/7 oz sugar
200 g/7 oz flour
175 g/6 oz butter
1 tablespoon of liqueur (or brandy)

5 eggs, separated
1 teaspoon baking powder
pinch of salt

Mix the sugar with the egg yolks, then add the softened butter and the liqueur and beat until fluffy. Add the stiffly beaten egg whites and finally the flour mixed with the baking powder and salt. Bake this paste in well-greased patty tins in an oven preheated to 190°C/375°F/Gas 5, for about 25 minutes or until golden. The real St Gonçalo cakes should have a phallic shape, which would demand elongated tins, but obviously any patty tins will do.

ROTTEN CAKES FOR CHRISTMAS
Bolos Podres do Natal
RIBATEJO PROVINCE • Makes 36 cakes

In Portugal there are various recipes of so-called 'rotten cakes'. Their unglamorous title refers only to their dark and generally heavy texture; they are always rich in spices and as a rule contain olive oil and either honey or dark sugar. This one is a kind of scalded dough, so the resulting consistency is similar to that of a pudding.

450 g/1 lb flour
200 g/7 oz soft brown sugar
225 ml/8 fl oz olive oil
5 tablespoons water

1 teaspoon ground aniseed
1 teaspoon cinnamon
icing sugar for sprinkling

In a pan mix the water, oil and spices. Bring to the boil and pour over the flour, already mixed with the sugar. Mix well and shape little pyramids with a 4 cm/1½ inch base and about 6.5 cm/2½ inches high. Bake in an oven preheated to 210°C/425°F/Gas 7 for 15 minutes. When cold, dust the cakes with sifted icing sugar.

VARIATION   Use the same recipe but adding ½ coffeespoon of ground cloves to the dough and putting a peeled whole almond on top of each pyramid, before baking.

CHRISTMAS CAKES FROM BOMBARRAL
Broas de Bombarral
ESTREMADURA PROVINCE • Makes about 48

Bombarral was founded in the twelfth century and is remarkable for the tiles in its churches and public buildings. *Pão-de-ló* (sponge cake) is one of its specialities, but these *broas* can be claimed as the best cakes in town.

450 g/1 lb maize flour (medium-coarse)
450 g/1 lb granulated sugar
675 g/1½ lb sweet potato purée
1 tablespoon cinnamon

grated rind of 1 lemon
1 tablespoon powdered aniseed
pinch of salt
beaten egg for brushing

Make a thick syrup with the sugar and enough water to dissolve it (see the 'pearl stage', p.32). Mix with sweet potato purée made by boiling sweet potatoes in water then mashing and weighing the amount needed. Boil together, stirring, to thicken. Set aside.

In a basin mix the flour, salt and spices and add the hot mixture. Beat well and cover, leaving it until the following day.

Then with floured hands mould little oval cakes, measuring approximately 2.5 cm/1 inch on the widest part. Flatten to 12 mm/½ inch and pinch the ends, to give the cakes the shape of leaves. Brush with beaten egg. Put in tins brushed with cooking oil (not necessarily olive oil). Bake at 210°C/425°F/ Gas 7 for 15 minutes, or until golden brown.

CASTLE CAKES
Broas Castelares
ESTREMADURA PROVINCE • Makes 16 to 20

These are small oval cakes made for the Christmas period. These delicious *broas* are sold all over Lisbon and Estremadura province, both before and well after the season.

110 g/4 oz ground almonds
110 g/4 oz sugar
200 g/7 oz sweet potato purée
1 large egg
2 tablespoons flour

2 tablespoons fine maize flour
grated rind of 1 small orange
grated rind of 1 small lemon
beaten egg for brushing

Make a sweet potato purée by boiling sweet potatoes in plain water then peeling and mashing, weighing the amount needed. Mix the purée, almonds and sugar. Bring to the heat, stirring, to dry up a little. Remove from the heat, add the remaining ingredients and beat well. Cool the mixture and shape small oval cakes, measuring 2.5 cm/1 inch on the widest part. Pinch ends, to make them look like leaves. Flatten to 12 mm/½ inch. Brush with beaten egg. Bake in a hot oven (210°C/425°F/Gas 7) for 15 minutes or until golden brown.

COCONUT CAKES
Bolos de Coco
Makes about 24 cakes

200 g/7 oz desiccated coconut
200 g/7 oz sugar

1 teaspoon flour
3 large eggs

Mix all the ingredients thoroughly. Shape small round cakes, about 4 cm/1½ inches in diameter. Place in well-buttered and floured baking tins and bake at 210°C/425°F/Gas 7 for 10-12 minutes or until golden.

These cakes can also be baked in little mounds or pyramids, instead of round shapes.

FRIED CAKES

Fried Cakes are mostly chosen for serving at the Christmas table, but a few of these recipes are also popular at other times; such as the really lovely Golden Slices (*Fatias Douradas* or *Rabanadas*) – which, in fact, are very similar to French Toast, but served with sugar and cinnamon. Excellent for a hearty breakfast!

DREAMS
Sonhos
Makes 24

Sonhos are fried cakes like small doughnuts, but much lighter in texture. There are many variations on the same theme all over Portugal. Generally speaking, fried cakes are intended for the Christmas season but, being so good and popular, *Sonhos* are made at other times as well, and some specialist patisseries sell them freshly made on a daily basis. The recipe below is flavoured with orange.

140 g/5 oz flour	1 tablespoon butter
4 eggs	juice of 3 medium oranges
175 g/6 oz granulated sugar	pinch salt
150 ml/¼ pint water	oil for deep frying

Bring the water to the boil, together with the butter and pinch of salt. Add the flour and stir thoroughly with a wooden spoon, to form a ball. Take off the heat and place it in a basin. After cooling a little, beat with a quarter of the orange juice and the eggs, one by one. Continue beating, to air the dough. When ready, deep-fry spoonfuls in hot oil, until golden. Set aside, on kitchen paper. Prepare a syrup with the sugar, the remaining juice and 150 ml/¼ pint water. Boil over *low heat* for 2 minutes. Allow to cool. Serve the *Sonhos* after dipping them in this syrup.

VARIATION   The *Sonhos* can be coated with a mixture of caster sugar and cinnamon, instead of the syrup, just after frying.

PUMPKIN CAKES
Bolinhos de Jerimu de Viana
MINHO AND DOURO LITORAL PROVINCES • Makes 24

Although *abóbora* is the Portuguese for pumpkin, in some northern regions it is also known as *jerimu*. These little cakes are a Christmas speciality and were created in the beautiful city of Viana do Castelo (Minho), a paradise for arts and crafts treasure-hunters. Its gastronomic traditions are as rich as its filigree jewellery, local costumes, embroidery, ceramics and architecture.

280 g/10 oz pumpkin purée	cinnamon stick
450 g/1 lb granulated sugar	½ teaspoon salt
4 eggs	oil for deep frying
1 tablespoon flour	

Cook some peeled pumpkin, drain thoroughly, pat dry with a cloth and purée it, weighing enough for the recipe. You can use any left-over purée in vegetable soups. Mix the pumpkin purée with the flour, salt and eggs and beat very well, until fluffy. With the help of two dessertspoons, shape the cakes and go on placing them in the hot oil. Fry until golden brown, turning once. As they dry, put them aside. When they are all ready, make a syrup with the sugar and a little water to melt it, boiling with the cinnamon for one minute. Remove the cinnamon, place the cakes in the syrup and bring again to simmering point for a minute. Drain the cakes with a slotted spoon and put them in a serving bowl, until cold. If there is any syrup left, pour it over the cakes afterwards, to keep them moist. They are better after a few days, so if you are preparing them for Christmas, make them the week before.

VARIATION   Same as before, but omitting the syrup and sprinkling the cakes very liberally with a mixture of sugar and cinnamon.

SWEET POTATO TURNOVERS
Recheios or *Azevias de Batata Doce*
Makes 30 turnovers

These are delicacies for the Christmas table and, like so much of the food of that season, they are fried. Sweet potato makes a most unusual but glorious filling; it can also be eaten alone as a dessert or be used as a filling for tartlets.

DOUGH
350 g/12 oz flour	½ coffeespoon salt
15 g/½ oz butter	oil for deep frying
30 g/1 oz lard	

FILLING
450 g/1 lb sweet potatoes	1 cinnamon stick
280 g/10 oz granulated sugar	sugar and cinnamon for sprinkling

Prepare the filling first. Cook the sweet potatoes in their jackets, until tender. Drain, peel and sieve. Mix with the sugar. Bring to the boil, with the cinnamon stick. Cook gently, stirring, until really thick. Remove the cinnamon and set aside to cool.

Meanwhile, prepare the dough, a type especially suitable for frying. Combine the fats with the flour with finger-tips. Make a well in the centre and add the salt and enough water to make a smooth dough. Knead thoroughly for 15 minutes. Form a ball and cover with a cloth. Place a damp cloth on top. Allow to rest for 45-60 minutes, before rolling out to 3 mm/⅛ inch. Using a pastry wheel, cut rounds off the dough 10 cm/4 inches in diameter. Place a tablespoon of filling in the middle of each round; fold and press the edges.

When all half-moons are done, deep-fry them, 3 or 4 at a time, according to the size of frying pan, turning once, for an overall golden colour. Place in kitchen paper to absorb excess fat and then sprinkle liberally with a mixture of ⅔ sugar to ⅓ cinnamon.

These turnovers are delicious accompaniments for tea or coffee and, although at their best on the same day, they will still be nice one or two days afterwards – if allowed to be left around that long!

CHICKPEA TURNOVERS FROM ST CLARA CONVENT
Pasteis de Grão do Convento de Santa Clara, Évora
ALENTEJO PROVINCE • Makes 18

Romans, Swabians, Visigoths, Moors and many Portuguese kings have left their mark on Évora. Today, with its old monuments, convents and monasteries, splendid buildings and Roman remains (such as the Temple to Diana), Évora is still one of the most attractive, learned and important of Portuguese cities.

DOUGH

200 g/7 oz flour	pinch salt
1 egg yolk	oil for deep frying
1 tablespoon olive oil	

FILLING

90 g/3 oz ground almonds	60 g/2 oz butter
200 g/7 oz granulated sugar	5 egg yolks
140 g/5 oz chickpea purée	½ teaspoon cinnamon

To prepare the dough, first make a well in the centre of the flour, add the salt, egg yolk, oil and about 3 tablespoons tepid water. Knead until smooth, mixing more water if needed. Cover and allow to rest for 45-60 minutes.

For the filling, make a light syrup (see p.32) with the sugar and just enough water to melt it. Take off the heat and mix in the sieved chickpea purée, ground almonds, butter and cinnamon. Bring to simmering point and cook for 5 minutes, whilst stirring. Remove from the heat and combine the beaten egg yolks. Simmer again for a minute. Stir the mixture all the time. Allow to cool, when ready.

Then roll out the dough thinly (3 mm/⅛ inch) and cut rounds of about 10 cm/4 inches. Divide the filling among them, fold in half and press the edges with a fork, to seal. Lift each turnover carefully and deep-fry, turning once, until golden. Place in kitchen paper to absorb excess fat. Serve lukewarm or cold, sprinkled with sugar, with tea or coffee.

CHRISTMAS FRIED CAKES

Filhós de Natal

Makes about 48

There are scores of fried cake recipes from all over Portugal, especially for the Christmas season. *Filhós* are among the most traditional.

1 kg/2 lb flour
450 g/1 lb pumpkin
4 tablespoons brandy or equivalent
15 g/½ oz fresh yeast
1 teaspoon baking powder

1 coffeespoon cinnamon
grated rind of 1 small lemon
oil for frying
mixture of caster sugar and cinnamon for
    sprinkling (or honey syrup)

Peel the sliced pumpkin and boil until tender (use a minimum of water and do not overcook). Drain. Keep the water. Put the flour in a basin and make a well in the centre. Put the mashed pumpkin in this and mix to a dough, using also some pumpkin water. Add the yeast, baking powder and all other ingredients. Work this dough very thoroughly for at least 30 minutes until it is light and fluffy. You may need to add a little more tepid water to obtain an elastic, smooth consistency. Cover with cloth and blanket and put aside in a warm place, to rise. When it doubles its volume, heat the oil in a deep frying pan. With two spoons shape egg-sized cakes and drop them one by one in the oil. Fry until golden brown. When ready, dust them liberally with the sugar and cinnamon mixture ($^2/_3$ sugar for $^1/_3$ cinnamon). Some people prefer them soaked in a light honey syrup (honey diluted to taste with some water and boiled for a minute).

CHRISTMAS FRIED CAKES, RIBATEJO FASHION

Filhós de Natal do Ribatejo

Makes 36 to 48, according to size

450 g/1 lb flour
280 g/10 oz white bread dough
3 eggs
90 g/3 oz sugar
350 g/12 oz pumpkin

1½ oranges (juice and zest)
2 tablespoons brandy
cinnamon and sugar for sprinkling
oil for frying

Mix the bread dough with the sugar, brandy and puréed pumpkin (see previous recipe). Make a soft dough, adding some of the pumpkin liquor. Add the flour, alternating with the eggs and the other ingredients, until everything is mixed. Add more liquid if necessary, but only very gradually, although this is a softer dough. Beat very hard for 30 minutes at least, until fluffy. Cover with a blanket and keep in a warm place until it doubles in volume. Heat the oil and fry spoonfuls of dough until golden brown. Sprinkle with the sugar/cinnamon mixture.

ABBOT'S EARS
Orelhas de Abade
NORTHERN PROVINCES • Makes 24

Very plain and easy to make, this is typical Christmas fare in the northern provinces of Trás-os-Montes and Alto Douro. Referring to all the delicious fried sweets made there during that season, Ramalho Ortigão mentions in *As Farpas* (*The Arrows*) '. . . the "abbot's ears" had come out of the frying pan and were placed on big platters, forming pyramids.'

200 g/7 oz white bread dough
sugar and cinnamon for sprinkling

oil for frying

Have the bread dough prepared in advance and ready, when you want to fry the ears. Knead it again. Roll out small portions of dough very thinly with the rolling pin, over a floured board. Spread the pieces further, pulling with the fingers. Cut out ear-shaped bits of rolled-out dough and fry in preheated oil to 182°C/360°F, until golden, turning once. Place on kitchen paper to absorb excess fat, then dip each ear in a mixture of ⅔ fine sugar to ⅓ cinnamon. They are best eaten the same day.

FRIED SWEET POTATO
Fritos de Batata Doce
MADEIRA • Makes 18 sweets

A very common sweet, served in Madeira as a snack or dessert. It is equally good hot or cold.

450 g/1 lb cooked sweet potato
150 ml/¼ pint light beer
90 g/3 oz flour
1 large beaten egg

sugar and cinnamon for sprinkling
pinch of salt
oil for frying

Boil or bake the potatoes (in their jackets), until tender. Peel and cut into thick slices. Set aside. Prepare a batter with the flour, beer and egg. Beat until foamy. Mix the slices of potato into this batter. Warm up the oil to 182°C/360°F and fry by the spoonful, until golden, turning once. Place in kitchen paper, to absorb excess fat, and sprinkle with a mixture of sugar and cinnamon, to taste.

GOLDEN SLICES
Fatias Douradas or *Rabanadas*
Serves 8

Golden Slices seem to have originated in the Minho province though they are now prepared and greatly enjoyed all over the country. There are variations, of course. Some are finished just with a good sprinkling of sugar and cinnamon, others are dipped in syrup or honey, and so on. One thing they all have in common is a delicious richness.

On Christmas Eve *Fatias Douradas* form a centrepiece for the array of desserts following the traditional late meal. They are best eaten the day they are made but I still have yet to see any being thrown away, even after they have lost their first appeal.

Júlio Diniz vividly illustrates the importance of *Fatias Douradas* at Christmas in his *Morgadinha dos Canaviais* (*Lady of the Reeds*), in which Henrique, the central male character, wishing to help make the *rabanadas*, approaches the lady who is busy pouring honey over some fresh ones: "'Well,' she said. "Are you not aware that *rabanadas* are the very essence of Christmas supper? How could I entrust them to you?'" How, indeed. Nobody would entrust that work to a mere helper, however willing.

400 g/14 oz day-old thickly sliced white bread (close textured)	pinch salt
	oil for frying
300 ml/½ pint milk	sugar and cinnamon (2 parts of sugar for one of
5-6 eggs	cinnamon), for sprinkling – or syrup, or honey

Never use bread which is too soft or the 'cotton-wool' type, as it would become too mushy and bland. Have one bowl with the milk and another with the beaten eggs, with the salt.

Mix 110-140 g/4-5 oz fine sugar and a tablespoon of cinnamon, to start with, as you can always prepare some more later, if needed. It all depends on how generous you are with the sprinkling, but it is a good idea to be quite generous. Alternatively you can make a light syrup with 200 g/7 oz granulated sugar and twice its volume of water, boiling both for a couple of minutes. Or make a honey syrup by warming up 150 ml/¼ pint clear honey and the same amount of water, mixing both very well over low heat. Set aside whatever sweetener you have decided upon, to be used after the slices have been fried.

Soak each slice of bread in milk, transferring it immediately to the bowl of beaten egg. Allow it to become well coated on both sides and deep fry until golden, turning once. Remove from the oil with a slotted spoon or slice, and place in a platter. Two or three slices can be fried at once, depending on the size of the pan. When ready, and still very warm, sprinkle the slices with the cinnamon mixture or use one of the given syrups, making sure that each slice gets its share of sweetener. Serve soon after they have been made, or when cold.

VARIATIONS

1 An old recipe, still in use in various parts of the country, indicates red wine (450 ml/¾ pint) for the syrup, sweetening it by boiling it with enough sugar and honey to taste, and a little cinnamon. Use as before.

2 A so-called rich version of *rabanadas* uses a light sugar syrup like the one made as a sauce, in the main recipe (flavoured with a cinnamon stick and lemon rind) to cook the egg-coated slices, for 2 minutes each side, instead of frying them in oil. Add a little hot water to the syrup now and then to prevent its thickening too much. Any remaining syrup is poured over the slices, when they are all ready.

S-SHAPED BISCUITS, PENICHE FASHION
SS de Peniche
ESTREMADURA PROVINCE • Makes about 30 biscuits

Perhaps someone in the lovely fishing town of Peniche was thinking of the intricate lace typical of the area and wanted to reproduce its twists and turns in the form of biscuits. Whatever the reason, a long time ago it was decided to call them 'S-shaped biscuits'. They have the advantage of using up left-over egg whites (always something to be considered when cooking Portuguese style, which demands so many yolks), but they are really very tasty and delicate, keep well and are ideal for tea.

280 g/10 oz sugar
280 g/10 oz ground almonds
100 g/3½ oz flour

2 tablespoons butter
5 egg whites, stiffly beaten

Place the sugar, butter, almonds and beaten egg whites, well mixed together, in a pot over a low flame. Stir and allow to come to the boil. Remove from the heat, cool a little and add the flour. Beat well. Bring to the boil once more. Stir and cook gently until stiff but pliable. Cool and shape the biscuits with sugared hands in the form of two Ss together. Bake in buttered and floured tins, in an oven preheated to 190°C/375°F/Gas 5 until golden (approx 10 minutes). Handle with care when removing from the tins, using a spatula.

SAND FROM CASCAIS
Areias de Cascais
Makes 36

These are small biscuits of the shortbread type, typical of the beautiful small town of Cascais, near Lisbon.

310 g/11 oz flour
110 g/4 oz granulated sugar
175 g/6 oz lard

1 tablespoon butter
½ coffeespoon cinnamon
grated rind of ½ small lemon

Work the fats into the flour with the tips of your fingers, then mix in the sugar and flavourings. Shape small biscuits, the size of a walnut, with floured hands. Bake on greased and floured trays at 190°C/375°F/Gas 5 until just golden. When ready (about 10-15 minutes) roll them in caster sugar, to give the impression they are covered with sand. Store in tins, after cooling.

PINE-SEED BISCUITS
Bolos de Pinhões
BEIRA LITORAL PROVINCE • Makes 36 small biscuits

Pine trees grow all over Portugal, and therefore pine-seeds are abundant. These cakes make use of them, although more often than not pine-seeds are eaten by themselves, rather than being used in cooking.

140 g/5 oz fine cornflour or arrowroot flour
90 g/3 oz flour
200 g/7 oz pine-seeds, roughly ground, leaving
   some whole
90 g/3 oz melted butter

140 g/5 oz sugar
4 medium eggs
½ coffeespoon cinnamon
pinch salt

Mix all the ingredients, except a handful of whole seeds. Shape the biscuits between hand and spoon. Place a few whole seeds on top of each and bake 12-15 minutes at 210°C/425°F/Gas 7 in buttered and floured baking tins, until golden brown.

BUNS

BUNS FROM COIMBRA
Arrufadas de Coimbra
BEIRA LITORAL PROVINCE • Makes about 18 buns

No one should go to the old university city of Coimbra without buying its best-known speciality, these lovely buns, eaten all the year round.

675 g/1½ lb flour
15 g/½ oz fresh yeast
90 g/3 oz softened butter
3 large eggs

175 g/6 oz sugar
4 tablespoons tepid milk
1 teaspoon cinnamon
pinch of salt

Mix the flour with the yeast, which must have been dissolved in the tepid milk. Add the sugar, cinnamon, salt and beaten eggs. Knead, add the butter, knead again, very thoroughly. If the dough is too hard, add a little more tepid milk. It should resemble a bread dough. Cover and leave in a warm place until the following day. Prepare baking tins lined with greased greaseproof parchment. Mould round cakes 6.5 cm/2½ inches in diameter. Allow to rest for ½ hour. Then brush with milk and bake in an oven preheated to 210°C/ 425°F/Gas 7, until golden brown.

SWEET BUNS, POMBAL FASHION
Fogaças Doces de Pombal
BEIRA LITORAL PROVINCE • Makes about 18 buns

These buns are made with a yeast dough and keep very well. There are many regional variations under the name of *fogaças*, including savoury versions, but all of them are meant for religious festivals. These sweet *fogaças* come from Pombal (south of Coimbra), a town of remote origin.

The story is told of a rich woman, whose surname was Fogaça, who asked the Holy Virgin to rid the town of a plague of locusts (a confirmed happening in the twelfth century) which was destroying crops. As the locusts disappeared, she prepared cakes as a thanksgiving and offered them to the priest. The recipe later acquired her own name and has been perpetuated ever since. Despite the tradition, it is possible that the word had already been introduced into Portuguese in Roman times, for Italians still have *focaccia*, a kind of flat bread made during the Christmas season.

450 g/1 lb flour	60 g/2 oz sugar
15 g/½ oz fresh yeast	60 g/2 oz lard
3 large eggs	90 g/3 oz butter
150 ml/¼ pint milk	pinch of salt
1 tablespoon powdered aniseed	beaten egg for brushing

Prepare the yeast dough first. Mix a third of the flour with the crumbled yeast and half the milk (lukewarm). Cover and set aside.

Put another third of the flour in a basin, make a well in the centre and add the softened butter and lard, salt, milk, aniseed and sugar. Mix thoroughly. Add the yeast dough. Knead really well for 8-10 minutes. Start adding the eggs, one by one, alternating with the remaining flour and kneading well between additions. The dough should not stick to the sides of the basin, when ready. Form a ball with it, cover with a cloth, then a blanket and leave in a warm place, to rise.

When it is ready, roll it out to a 2.5 cm/1 inch thickness and mould handfuls into rounds and horseshoe shapes. Brush with beaten egg and leave again in a warm place for a while (45-60 minutes) on buttered baking trays. Bake in an oven preheated to 190°C/375°F/Gas 5 for 35-40 minutes or until golden brown.

SWEET BUNS
Regueifas
MINHO PROVINCE • Makes 18 medium-sized buns

A yeast dough, enriched with eggs and the popular cinnamon, means these buns are always found at country festivities, as they keep well for the several days they are needed.

110 g/4 oz sugar	½ coffeespoon saffron
560 g/1¼ lb flour	1 coffeespoon cinnamon
15 g/½ oz fresh yeast	1 coffeespoon baking powder
60 g/2 oz melted butter	pinch of salt
2 whole eggs, plus 3 egg yolks	butter for brushing

Mix the saffron and cinnamon in a little tepid water. Set aside. Crumble the yeast, add tepid water, salt and baking powder and mix with 110 g/4 oz flour. Combine well and leave in a warm place, covered, for 1½ hours. Mix the butter, sugar, eggs and yolks with the spices. Beat well. Put 450 g/1 lb flour in a bowl, make a well in the centre and place the yeast dough in it. Add the egg mixture. Combine well and knead until smooth. Leave in a warm place, covered, to double in size. Then, with floured hands, mould buns in various shapes to your taste. Leave again for a while, to rise. Bake until golden (the time depends on the size of your buns) at 210°C/425°F/Gas 7. Brush the tops with butter, once ready, and whilst still warm.

ALL SAINTS' DAY BUNS
Bolos dos Santos
BEIRA BAIXA PROVINCE • Makes 12 to 18 buns

All Saints' Day (1 November) is celebrated all over Portugal with family gatherings, especially in rural areas, when cakes and chestnuts are eaten. A little sadness creeps in, as on the following day, 2 November, families visit cemeteries and remember the departed.

450 g/1 lb flour
30 g/1 oz fresh yeast
3 eggs
60 g/2 oz melted lard
90 g/3 oz sugar

1 tablespoon cinnamon
1 tablespoon powdered aniseed
pinch of salt
beaten egg for brushing
sugar for topping

Place the flour in a warm basin and make a well in the centre. Pour into this the crumbled yeast, already dissolved in 4 tablespoons of warm water, with a pinch of salt. Mix and add all other ingredients, moistening with more tepid water, if needed, to form a smooth, bread-like dough. Cover and leave in a warm place to rise for 45-60 minutes. Then shape buns 5 cm/2 inches in diameter and place them on buttered baking sheets. Leave to rest in a warm place for 10-15 minutes. Brush with beaten egg, top the centre with a little mound of sugar and bake at 210°C/425°F/Gas 7 for 15-20 minutes or until nicely browned.

ALL SAINTS' DAY BUNS
Bolinhos dos Santos
BEIRA LITORAL PROVINCE • Makes about 30 buns

450 g/1 lb maize flour
225 g/8 oz flour
30 g/1 oz fresh yeast
225 g/8 oz brown sugar
2 eggs
1 kg/2 lb pumpkin
175 g/6 oz dried fruit (mixed nuts, sultanas, etc.,
    to taste)

2 tablespoons olive oil
1 orange (juice and zest)
1 lemon (zest only)
3 tablespoons brandy (or equivalent)
1 tablespoon powdered aniseed
1 tablespoon cinnamon
1 coffeespoon salt

Prepare the yeast with a little of the flour and tepid water. While it rests, cook the pumpkin in just a drop of water; drain and absorb any excess moisture in a cloth. Place the maize flour in a warm basin and add the cooked pumpkin, still hot. Work both together. Add the flour and the yeast dough. Knead well. Add all other ingredients except the dried fruits, and knead again until you have a really elastic, light dough. Mix in the fruit, previously cut into rough pieces, cover the basin and leave in a warm place, to double in size. Butter baking sheets and shape cakes 3.5-5 cm/1½-2 inches in diameter. Allow to rest for 15-20 minutes and bake at 210°C/425°F/ Gas 7 for 15-20 minutes or until golden brown.

EASTER BUNS

Bolos de Páscoa

TRÁS-OS-MONTES PROVINCE • Makes 24 to 30 buns

After the rigours of the Lent period – which, in remote areas, can still be a reality in this day and age – good things to eat are very welcome, when Easter finally arrives.

350 g/12 oz fine sugar	45 g/1½ oz fresh yeast
9 eggs	½ teaspoon baking powder
150 ml/¼ pint olive oil	1 tablespoon brandy (or equivalent)
150 ml/¼ pint milk	1 heaped tablespoon cinnamon
enough flour for the dough	1 coffeespoon salt

Crumble the yeast and mix with a little tepid water. Add the salt, baking powder, milk, brandy, cinnamon and olive oil. Beat well. Set aside for a moment while you beat the eggs with the sugar and heat them to blood temperature, stirring all the time. Combine this with the previous mixture and pour into a large basin. Add flour gradually until a smooth dough is formed (the amount of flour depends on local varieties). The consistency of the dough should be similar to that of bread, and it should not stick to the sides of the basin. After kneading thoroughly, cover the basin with a blanket and leave in a warm place until the following day.

Next day knead again for a little while and mould small balls out of this dough (the size is up to you, but a diameter of 5 cm/2 inches, would be adequate). Place the cakes in buttered baking tins and leave for another hour before baking until golden in an oven set to 180°C/350°F/Gas 4. Brushing them with a mixture of beaten egg and milk before baking will improve their appearance.

LARGE CAKES

SPONGE CAKE
Pão-de-ló
Serves 4 to 6

The best-known versions are from some northern provinces, such as Minho, Douro and Beira Alta, but there are various other recipes of *pão-de-ló* all over the country. This has been, and perhaps will always be, one the best loved cakes, to eat on its own when fresh and, when it becomes hard, as a basis for puddings. In Portuguese patisseries and good grocers *pão-de-ló* is sold in its traditional shape, baked in a ring-mould, and wrapped in strong white paper, which is used to line the mould, when prepared in commercial ovens. Homemade *pão-de-ló* will always be a little different from the bought one, on account of the oven, if not the recipe. Nevertheless, whatever oven is used, this cake is always a good bet for tea. The secret for a good texture lies in the thorough whipping. Sponge cake in Portugal is always made without fat.

5 eggs	140 g/5 oz sugar, free from any lumps
75 g/2½ oz finest white self-raising flour, sifted	pinch of salt

If you are not prepared to whip hard by hand, use an electric mixer. With it you can halve the times indicated here.

Whip the eggs with the sugar for 20 minutes, then add the flour and whip again for another 15 minutes. Bake in a ring-mould 18-20.5 cm/7-8 inches in diameter, lined and greased with butter, in an oven preheated to 190°C/375°F/Gas 5, for about 20 minutes or until golden brown and springy to the touch. Check it with a cake-tester.

VARIATIONS

1   A very light and nicely textured *pão-de-ló* is obtained with the following recipe. Serves 6:

5 eggs, separated	130 g/4½ oz fine rice flour
200 g/7 oz sugar	1 teaspoon baking powder

Beat the yolks with the sugar very hard (at least 10 minutes), until they become whitish. Carefully add half the stiffly beaten egg whites. Then mix in the flour (sifted with the baking powder), trying to achieve a smooth texture without actually beating. Finally fold in the remaining egg whites. Bake as for the previous cake.

2   This recipe is a simpler, homely version – one that I use often with good results. Serves 6:

4 eggs, separated	1 teaspoon baking powder
200 g/7 oz sugar	4 dessertspoons cold water
140 g/5 oz fine plain flour	

Mix the yolks with the sugar as in variation 1. Then add the water, little by little, beating well between additions. Mix in the flour (sifted with the baking powder) and finally fold in the whipped egg whites. Bake as before.

SPONGE ROLL, VIANA FASHION
Torta de Viana do Castelo
MINHO PROVINCE • Serves 4 to 6

This delicious sponge roll is but one of the many specialities typical of Viana do Castelo. 'The Princess of the Lima', as Viana is called, stands at the mouth of that river and offers superb views from St Luzia hill and its interesting basilica. A few miles away is Ponte do Lima, another lovely old-world town on the banks of the river.

200 g/7 oz sugar	3 large eggs, separated
90 g/3 oz flour	Filling – any good jam or *ovos moles* (p.150)

Grease a swiss roll-type baking tin, about 23 x 31 cm/9 x 13 inches and line it with buttered greaseproof paper. Beat the egg yolks with the sugar, then the whites until stiff and add to the yolks, folding and alternating with the sifted flour. Do not beat the mixture. Bring to the oven in the prepared tin and bake at 232°C/450°F/Gas 8 until just golden (only 7-10 minutes). Do not overcook, or it will dry and break when rolling. Turn it into a sugared tea-towel, spread the filling swiftly and roll up carefully, with the help of the tea-towel. Trim the edges and cool on a cake-rack.

FRUIT CAKE
Bolo de Frutas
MADEIRA • Serves 6 to 8

Like the dark (almost black) and richly spiced Molasses Cake on p.200, this one is a Christmas treat in Madeira, containing all the traditional dried fruits and nuts common to so many recipes for that season, the world over.

200 g/7 oz flour	90 g/3 oz raisins (free from seeds) or sultanas
200 g/7 oz sugar	60 g/2 oz candied mixed peel
150 ml/¼ pint milk	60 g/2 oz almonds (flaked)
110 g/4 oz butter	60 g/2 oz dried plums
90 g/3 oz lard	3 tablespoons sweet Madeira (or port)
3 large eggs	grated rind of 1 small lemon
1 tablespoon cinnamon	½ coffeespoon nutmeg
2 tablespoons runny honey	1 tablespoon baking powder

Mix well all the nuts and spices, rind and dried fruits with the flour, baking powder, sugar and wine. Add the milk and beaten eggs. Melt the fats and honey and beat in the mixture. Bake in a buttered round cake tin about 20 cm/8 inches in diameter in an oven preheated to 180°C/350°F/Gas 4 for 40-45 minutes or until firm and golden brown. Try with the cake-tester.

This cake keeps well but in Madeira it is generally eaten within one or two days of baking

RICH MOLASSES CAKE

Bolo Rico de Mel

MADEIRA • Serves 10 to 12

Although it is commonly known as 'honey cake', it should really be called 'molasses cake', as the 'honey' used comes from the cane, not the hive. This is a very old recipe, evolved from the times when spices and sugar cane first came to Madeira, following the navigators' loaded caravels from the East and Africa. Madeira itself started cane-sugar production from its early days as Portuguese territory. Molasses cake is the most traditional and irresistible of Madeira's sweet specialities. It is intended as a Christmas treat, though it is eaten all the year round and now exported to Lisbon, where it is sold in great quantities. Molasses cake keeps well for at least a year, and even when dried up and old it is still pure delight, with its rich and spicy flavours lingering in the mouth.

450 g/1 lb flour
225 g/8 oz crushed walnuts
90 g/3 oz lard
200 g/7 oz butter
225 g/8 oz sugar (the darker, the better)
60 g/2 oz candied peel
110 g/4 oz stoned prunes
225 ml/8 fl oz molasses
grated rind and juice of 1 medium-sized orange
grated rind of 1 medium lemon
140 g/5 oz ground almonds
1 teaspoon each of powdered aniseed, mixed spices,
    clove, nutmeg
1 tablespoon cinnamon
1 teaspoon salt
1 sachet (7 g) dried yeast and 110 g/4 oz flour to mix it with
1 teaspoon baking powder
1 handful of whole peeled almonds, for decoration

To prepare the yeast dough, first make a well in the centre of the 110 g/4 oz flour, add the yeast and enough tepid water to form a soft dough. Sprinkle with flour and leave to rise in a warm place, covered with a cloth, for 2 hours. In a large basin place the flour, mixed with the sugar and baking powder, and make a well in the centre. Add the yeast dough

and mix. Gradually add the warmed molasses and the melted fats, the juice and grated rind of the orange, the lemon rind, crushed walnuts, ground almonds, cut-up prunes and spices, alternating the various ingredients while combining and kneading everything very thoroughly, until it no longer sticks to the basin. Cover with a cloth, then a blanket, and leave to rise in a warm place with a constant temperature for two days.

Preheat the oven to 190°C/375°F/Gas 5. In the meantime divide the dough into four portions and grease generously round baking tins 18 cm/7 inches in diameter. The cakes do not rise much while baking and their thickness can be gauged when distributing the dough: about 4 cm/1½ inches. Flatten the top of the cakes and decorate with almonds, in a circle. Bake for 40-45 minutes or until a cake-tester comes out dry. To ensure that the cakes are completely cold before storing, leave until the following day. Then wrap in greaseproof paper or foil and keep in tins.

CHRISTMAS CAKE
Bolo de Natal
AZORES ARCHIPELAGO • Serves 12

In spite of its name, this cake is also used for celebrations other than Christmas, such as birthdays and weddings, decorated accordingly. It keeps well and should in fact be made two or three weeks in advance.

400 g/14 oz flour
2 teaspoons baking powder
200 g/7 oz butter
310 g/11 oz sugar
3 tablespoons molasses
4 large eggs, separated
400 g/14 oz glacé fruits and candied peel
grated rind of 1 lemon (or orange)
2 tablespoons brandy (or equivalent)
2 tablespoons port wine (or equivalent)
90 g/3 oz walnuts

Sprinkle some flour onto the fruit, to prevent it sinking, and set aside. Cream the butter with the sugar and egg yolks, and add the flour gradually (previously mixed with the baking powder) alternating with the molasses, wine, brandy and grated rind. Fold in the stiffly beaten egg whites and finally the fruits. Bake in a large mould, 20-23 cm/8-9 inches in diameter, at 180°C/350°F/Gas 4 until a cake-tester comes out clean (45-50 minutes). Decorate only when completely cold, or leave it as it is.

ROTTEN CAKE
Bolo Podre
ALENTEJO PROVINCE • Serves 8

The so-called 'rotten' cake owes its name to its dark, rough appearance. It is one of those tasty and homely cakes that makes people come back for more.

350 g/12 oz wholemeal flour	3 tablespoons brandy (or equivalent)
1½ teaspoons baking powder	½ coffeespoon ground cloves
300 ml/½ pint olive oil	1 tablespoon cinnamon
300 ml/½ pint dark honey	handful of whole peeled almonds, for decoration
4 eggs	

Mix all ingredients except the flour and the almonds, and beat until it thickens. Using an electric mixer saves effort. Gradually add the flour and baking powder. Beat again. Leave to rest until the following day.

Pour the mixture into a large, well-buttered cake tin 20-25.5 cm/ 8-10 inches in diameter or use two smaller tins. Decorate the top with the almonds and bake at 180°C/350°F/Gas 4 for 45 minutes or until a cake-tester comes out clean.

HONEY CAKE
Bolo de Mel
RIBATEJO PROVINCE • Serves 6

A simple cake for any occasion. The flavourings can be varied, to give it different guises (try mixed spices and grated orange rind).

200 g/7 oz flour	150 ml/¼ pint dark honey
1 teaspoon baking powder	60 g/2 oz dark sugar
6 eggs, separated	2 teaspoons cinnamon
2 tablespoons softened butter	1 teaspoon powdered aniseed
4 tablespoons olive oil	pinch of salt

Mix very well the egg yolks with the sugar and the butter. Add the oil, honey and spices. Mix in the flour with the baking powder, gradually. Fold in the stiffly beaten egg whites. Bake in a well-greased tin 20 cm/8 inches in diameter at 190°C/375°F/Gas 5 until a cake-tester comes out clean (about 40 minutes).

KING'S CAKE

Bolo Rei

ESTREMADURA PROVINCE • Serves 10 to 12

Ever present in enormous quantities, in all patisseries and good grocers, from the start of December well into January and sometimes at other occasions, too (increasingly, during the Easter celebrations). As the name implies, though, it really belongs to Twelfth Night (Epiphany), a day which, until recently, was a Bank holiday in Portugal and which is still very much a part of the Christmas celebrations. Generally, it contains a small prize inside (a little heart, an owl or something, wrapped up in paper) and also a dried broad bean. The person who eats the slice where the broad bean or the prize is, soon finds out. When the prize is found, a great cheer is given, but whoever gets the broad bean is meant to buy the King's Cake the following year.

675 g/1½ lb flour	3 large eggs
2x7 g sachets easy-blend yeast	6 tablespoons port wine (or equivalent)
140 g/5 oz sugar	grated rind of 1 lemon and 1 orange
140 g/5 oz butter	1 teaspoon salt
140 g/5 oz mixed nuts and dried fruit	1 beaten egg, for brushing
140 g/5 oz mixed glacé fruit and candied peel	1 dried broad bean and 1 small souvenir (optional)

Steep the dried fruits in the wine, to swell up. Mix the yeast with a little warm water (enough to dissolve it) and add it to about 110 g/4 oz of the given flour. Mix well and set aside for 20 minutes in a warm place, to rise.

Beat the eggs with the sugar, the softened butter, salt and grated rind. Mix in the yeast dough and then the flour, gradually. Knead really well, until it becomes elastic and smooth. Mix in the fruit with the wine and knead again. Gather the dough into a ball and sprinkle with flour. Cover and keep in a warm place for 5-6 hours, to double in volume. With floured hands, shape one large or two smaller King's Cakes into a ring. Brush the cake or cakes with the beaten egg and stick the glacé fruits and candied peel on top, all round. Bake at 210°C/425°F/Gas 7 for 20-25 minutes or until golden brown. After cooling, put the cakes in tins or wrap in foil, to keep them moist.

FANCY BREAD

PLAIN CAKE

Boleima

ALENTEJO PROVINCE • Serves 8 to 10

This plain cake is a variety of 'fancy bread', and it does help if one has already some bread dough prepared. Weigh it and add the other ingredients in the proportions indicated below.

450 g/1 lb white bread dough	110 g/4 oz lard
1 teaspoon baking powder	2 tablespoons butter

280 g/10 oz sugar

3 eggs

2 tablespoons brandy (or equivalent)

grated rind of 1 orange (or lemon)

1 teaspoon cinnamon mixed with 2 tablespoons sugar

Add all the ingredients except the cinnamon mixture to the bread dough and mix very well. Put into a well-buttered baking tray (20 x 30 cm/8 x 12 inches) and sprinkle with the sugar/cinnamon mixture. Bake at 190°C/375°F/Gas 5 for 20-25 minutes or until golden brown.

NOTE For a simple bread dough see recipe in the Bread and Bread Dishes Chapter.

FANCY BREAD FOR EASTER

Folar de Páscoa

ESTREMADURA PROVINCE BUT USED COUNTRYWIDE IN SIMILAR FORM • Serves 8 to 10

Fancy breads eaten during the Easter period are very attractive loaves with one or two boiled eggs stuck on top, as decoration, secured by a trellis made of dough. They remain excellent to the very end, and the traditional flavourings of aniseed and cinnamon make them a most welcome companion for tea or coffee.

Folares can also be eaten at other times apart from Easter.

400 g/14 oz white bread flour

1 sachet (7 g) easy-blend yeast

90 g/3 oz sugar

90 g/3 oz butter

1 large egg

300 ml/½ pint milk

1 teaspoon powdered aniseed

1 teaspoon cinnamon

½ teaspoon salt

FOR DECORATION

2 hard-boiled eggs, unshelled

1 beaten egg for brushing

In a warm bowl combine the yeast with a quarter of the given flour and a third of the milk (which should be warm). Mix in half the sugar. Make a dough with these, then cover and leave in a warm place to rise, for about half an hour. Meanwhile, beat the egg with the remaining milk and sugar, salt and spices. Add the flour gradually and work the dough for a few minutes. Add the softened butter and work again. Mix the yeast dough and knead really well. When ready, it should not stick to the sides of the bowl. Cover and set aside in a warm place, for about three hours, to rise. Then with floured hands shape one big or two smaller loaves (round or slightly egg-shaped) and place the boiled eggs on top, half buried and secured with two strips of dough, crossing each other. Brush the *folar* with beaten egg and bake in a hot oven (210°C/425°F/Gas 7) until nicely brown (about 30 minutes).

JAMS AND JELLIES

LIGHT-COLOURED OR 'WHITE' QUINCE CHEESE
Marmelada Branca

I imagine that the name 'cheese' has been given to this jam, in English, because it becomes so hard after drying that it can be cut with a knife. However, even when one does not manage to achieve this perfection – for which you need strong sunshine – quince jam is always quite thick and suitable to eat either on its own or with bread, biscuits or cheese as the Portuguese do.

1.2 kg/2½ lb quinces (*gamboas* or *marmelos*)	1 kg/2 lb granulated sugar

The secret for keeping quince cheese light in colour is to avoid oxidizing the fruit. Therefore no metal spoons or knives must touch it. To do this, cook them whole, unpeeled (but very thoroughly washed and free from the 'fur' which normally covers part of the skin) in enough boiling water just to half cover them (you can turn them over half way through). They will be tender in 10-12 minutes. Try not to overcook them. Drain very well and peel, after cooling enough to handle. Do not use a knife but your fingers not only to peel the cooked fruit but also to open it and take out the pips. Mash and sieve the flesh (keep the pips and all the bits and pieces you have put aside at this stage, including the skin, if you want to make some jelly). The pulp must be smooth, and if you think it isn't, sieve it again.

Meanwhile, put the sugar in a large pan and add a little water or use some of the liquid in which the fruit has been cooked (keep the remainder also, for the jelly). Use the minimum of liquid, though, otherwise it will take ages to dry up the jam. Boil the sugar and liquid until they make a 'soft ball' syrup (p.32). All you really want is a syrup as thick as possible, before it actually gets too hard.

Add the prepared pulp and stir into the syrup with a wooden spoon. When it is well mixed, bring it to the boil over a gentle heat, stirring, and let the jam dry as much as you can, without burning. (Protect your hand from splashes with a cloth or thick glove.) The longer the jam boils, the more danger there is of its becoming reddish, so the idea is to go through all these operations fairly quickly.

Take the pan off the heat as soon as a 'parting' is formed at the bottom of the pan when you stir with the wooden spoon. Beat it energetically for a little while after finishing cooking, until it cools down. Pour into bowls or trays, to harden.

Traditionally, the *marmelada* is dried in the sun. This is where a warm climate comes in handy. The containers are set outside, in some protected spot, covered with a net to prevent flying insects having a go at them, and allowed to dry until a crust is formed on top. This may take several days, so one takes the *marmelada* out every morning and brings it in again in the afternoon for, say, 4 or 5 days, then it should be ready to store in a damp-free place (a cool larder, for example), covering the surface with cellophane. I find that, in the absence of strong enough sun shining reliably for that length of time over my *marmelada*, it is a good idea to bring it to a cool oven (121-135°C/250-275°F/Gas ¼-½) for several hours. A crust will thus be formed on top. I pour the *marmelada* into fireproof containers, of course. The trouble with this procedure is that the resulting *marmelada* will never be quite as light in colour as was intended. However, I actually prefer the reddish version, which to me looks much richer even though the taste is about the same.

VARIATION For the 'red' version (*Marmelada Vermelha*), use the same amounts of fruit and sugar as before.

The idea, in this case, is to oxidize the quinces as much as one can, so make free use of metal knives and spoons. Peel and cut the quinces before cooking (quartering them and keeping the cores with the pips, and skins, for jelly) and bring to the boil until tender, as before. Drain and follow exactly the same procedure. The remaining water (after cooking the fruit) is used to cook all the bits set aside, for 10-15 minutes. Drain and keep the liquor, which at this stage will be full of wonderful pectin for a fragrant jelly.

QUINCE JELLY
Geleia de Marmelo

This is of course a must, when making *marmelada*, as it would be a great pity to waste the richly flavoured skins and cores of the quinces. It does not really differ from other fruit jellies, so all you do is to use the liquid in which the fruit was cooked, boil it with any skins and cores that have been put aside, so as to extract as much flavour and pectin as possible, then strain it thoroughly and measure the resulting liquor. The general rule is to use the same amount of sugar as of liquid, so you have to calculate this yourself, according to how much you have. Then mix both ingredients and boil (take off scum if necessary but do not stir) until a jelly is obtained 10-12 minutes after you first start boiling it. Test this by putting a teaspoonful of jelly on a cold plate. Push with fingertips – it will wrinkle, if ready. Store in jars.

GRAPE JAM
Doce de Uvas

This is a delightful light jam-cum-jelly with a very delicate taste. It is not made as often now as it used to be (which is a pity) but I remember a dear aunt of mine, from the Ribatejo province, having jars of white grape jam every year, after the gathering of ripe grapes in the vineyard.

1 kg/2 lb cleaned grapes	1 kg/2 lb granulated sugar

Bring the grapes and sugar to the boil. Some of the skins will rise to the surface, and it is easy then to skim them off with a slotted spoon. Place the lot in a sieve, press with a spoon, to extract all the juice and flesh, and return this to the pan. Continue simmering until set – test a drop in a saucer. It should not, however, take too long (12-15 minutes, perhaps). Bottle in prepared jars.

SPAGHETTI SQUASH JAM
Doce de Chila

Spaghetti squash is a gourd which, when cooked, becomes like thin spaghetti – hence the name. The threads are then made into a jam, which is very popular all over Portugal, to eat by the spoonful or to use as a filling for tartlets and cakes. It has a very characteristic texture, at once fleshy and crunchy, different from anything else. Spaghetti squash is not available everywhere, but sometimes it is imported into the countries where it does not grow. It looks like an elongated melon.

450 g/1 lb spaghetti squash (after having cooked it) – buy about twice this amount uncooked

450 g/1 lb granulated sugar

In order to keep the jam very pale in colour, one must not use a knife when cutting the gourd. The classic way of breaking it is to throw it on the floor. The pieces are then picked up, washed and freed from seeds and from the yellow mushy centre, by hand.

Put all these pieces (skin and all) in a roomy pan with boiling water and cook until the skin comes apart. Remove from the heat and place in cold water. Working with your hands, separate the skin from the flesh, and discard any seeds that have emerged during cooking. Then put the clean flesh in a container, making it all into threads, with your fingers. Cover with water and a little salt and leave to soak until the following day.

Then drain the threads and wash them in clean water, using a sieve under the tap. Drain well. Meanwhile make a syrup with the sugar and 300 ml/½ pint water, until thickish. Add the prepared threads and boil again until thick, stirring now and then. This will now look like fine cooked spaghetti, shiny with the sugar. Pour into bowls, to store and cover with cellophane.

This jam can be used for filling cakes as it is or mixed with egg yolks, bringing it just to the boil, to cook the yolks, before using. Add two yolks for each 140 g/5 oz of jam. Try this to fill turnovers either baked or fried, and also in recipes calling for 'egg threads'.

FRIAR JOHN'S DELIGHT

Delícia do Frei João

ALCOBAÇA MONASTERY, NORTH OF ESTREMADURA PROVINCE

Although nuns were known for their inventiveness in regard to sweets, and monks for their wines, this does not mean that monks could not create some sweet concoctions of their own. The one below is a jam made with all (or most) fruits in season (Alcobaça is rich in fruit) mixed with walnuts. The jam is a real speciality of the Benedictine monks.

The monastery was founded in 1178 and inaugurated during the reign of the first Portuguese king. Alcobaça became an important cultural centre, the monks contributing greatly to its splendour, with historical works set on their own printing-press in the sixteenth century. The abbot was a very powerful man, with many titles, including that of 'lord of the water and wind', referring to the wind- and water-mills on the Order's extensive estates. Unfortunately, much of the riches accumulated by the monks over seven centuries (silver and precious books) were pillaged during the Napoleonic invasions and the remainder confiscated at the abolition of the religious orders, in 1834. But Alcobaça's noble ancestry is still much in evidence today.

1 kg/2 lb mixed ripe fruit (half peaches and the remaining weight made up of seeded and peeled muscat grapes, sweet melon, pears, apples, quince, etc.)

675 g/1½ lb granulated sugar
60 g/2 oz very good quality walnuts, roughly crushed

Wash, peel and core the fruit. Cut it into small pieces. Add the sugar and boil gently, in a roomy pan, until a thick jam is formed. Stir the mixture carefully most of the time, and be careful not to let it burn. When a thick consistency is reached, add the walnuts, boil for another minute, remove from the heat and bottle.

PUMPKIN JAM
Doce de Abóbora

This is an excellent jam very useful for filling tarts and cakes or as a dessert, mixed with toasted almonds or crushed walnuts. If mixed with a couple of egg yolks and simmered, it can be used for fillings where *ovos moles* (p.150) are called for.

450 g/1 lb cooked pumpkin   1 teaspoon cinnamon
560 g/1¼ lb granulated sugar

Peel and clean the pumpkin and cook in water until tender, adding just a pinch of salt. Place in a sieve to drain it as much as possible while pressing it lightly to extract the liquid trapped inside. Mash and sieve, to obtain a very smooth purée. Mix with the sugar and boil, stirring with a wooden spoon until it thickens. Take off the heat and stir in the cinnamon. Pour into a glass bowl and sprinkle with just a hint of cinnamon.

NOTE Pumpkin jam is very nice with cheese, as well. For this purpose one can prepare it with less sugar (half of what is indicated above) and use a cinnamon stick instead of powdered cinnamon. Instead of sieving the cooked pumpkin one can just mash it, leaving it slightly lumpy and therefore with a different texture. This lighter jam will have a shorter shelf life but it is possible to keep it in the fridge. It also freezes well.

TOMATO JAM
Doce de Tomate

This jam is made in most Portuguese households whenever there is a tomato glut. Tomatoes make a tasty, thick jam of a rich dark red colour. The flavour is definitely 'different' from that of any other jam.

ripe tomatoes (big, ripe, and pulpy, if possible)   lemon juice
granulated sugar   1 vanilla pod or 1 stick cinnamon

Peel, deseed and cut tomatoes. Drain excess juice. Weigh the pulp and mix with an equal amount of sugar. Boil with the vanilla pod (or cinnamon stick) over a low heat, stirring from time to time with a wooden spoon. When a small amount of jam resembles jelly when dropped in a saucer, the tomato jam is ready. At the last minute add the juice of ½ lemon (for each 1 kg/2 lb) tomatoes. Pour into sterilized jars. Serve with bread and butter or as a filling for cakes.

If you prefer a smoother jam, liquidize the pulp before adding the sugar, but to my way of thinking it is better to find little 'chunks' of tomato when eating this jam by the spoon.

TOMATO JAM
Doce de Tomate

There is a version using unripe tomatoes, less common than the ripe alternative, but useful as a standby and also when you want to use up unripe tomatoes.

1 kg/2 lb unripe tomatoes (still green in colour)
675 g/1½ lb granulated sugar
1 medium lemon

1 vanilla pod or cinnamon stick
1 clove (whole)

Wash the tomatoes and slice them very thinly. Add the lemon, also thinly sliced, the sugar and the spices. Let this mixture stand for 24 hours. Remove the spices and boil over a gentle heat, without a lid, for 1½-2 hours. Bottle as usual. This can be eaten by the spoonful in small amounts or with bread and butter, or can be used as a decoration and filling for cakes.

FILLINGS

EGG THREADS
Fios de Ovos

This is another way of preparing egg yolks and sugar (Portugal's favourite taste) for sweets. Egg threads look rather like mounds of yellow noodles and, like *ovos moles* (p.150) are served as a garnish to cakes and puddings or to fill Algarvean almond cakes.

Most people buy egg threads at sweetshops, when wishing to prepare something special at home. They are a little troublesome to make, and professional cooks have a funnel with various narrow openings to make the egg yolks drop in fine threads over the boiling sugar. Failing a special funnel, one must of course use an ordinary one, but the operation becomes much more precarious, and success does not always ensue. Nevertheless, do not dismay, because any egg yolk dropped unevenly over the syrup will still be edible, though less pretty to look at than the proper yellow noodle-like threads.

200 g/7 oz granulated sugar
1 whole egg plus 4 egg yolks, beaten lightly,
   together

scant 100 ml/3 fl oz water

Boil the sugar and water, until thickish (see the 'thread stage' p.32). Reduce the heat, but keep the syrup at boiling point. Drop half the egg mixture into the syrup through the funnel, rotating it to form the threads and allowing them to cook for a couple of minutes. Remove with a slotted spoon and place on a damp plate. Repeat the procedure with the remaining eggs, after adding a drop of water to the syrup, to prevent it becoming too hard. Separate the cooked threads with the help of two forks, so that they do not remain stuck together. Use the same day. The syrup can be left for some other sweet.

NOTE   See also 'soft eggs', page 150.

CHANTILLY CREAM, PORTUGUESE STYLE

Nowadays Chantilly cream is widely used in Portugal to fill cakes and to decorate all kinds of sweets sold at the many patisseries. It can be bought ready made at good delicatessens in Lisbon and other cities (not so much in small towns), but to ensure freshness it is always better to prepare it at home.

150 ml/¼ pint double cream
1 egg white, stiffly beaten

30 g/1 oz icing sugar (sifted, to avoid lumps)
1 or 2 drops vanilla extract

Whip the cream (do not overdo it, or it will turn to butter), flavour with the vanilla, add the egg white and sweeten with the sugar. Do not, however, add all the sugar at once unless you prefer the cream sweeter. Place in the refrigerator until needed. It will keep for a couple of days.

VARIATIONS
1   I find that the real Portuguese Chantilly taste is achieved quite well using half double cream and half good soured cream. Beat well as before, add sugar to taste and a drop of vanilla. If you want to bulk it up, add the stiffly beaten egg white.
2   Whip double cream as in the recipe above, then add a tablespoon of plain yogurt, vanilla and sugar to taste. Again use the egg white if you want, but you do not need to do so.

CHESTNUT FILLING

300 g/10 oz chestnut purée (made with sieved,
    boiled chestnuts – or use from a tin of
    unsweetened purée)
90 g/3 oz icing sugar

3 tablespoons milk
90 g/3 oz butter
150 ml/¼ pint double cream (whipped)
4 drops vanilla extract

Mix the cold chestnut purée with the sugar, vanilla, softened butter and milk. Beat very hard until smooth. Fold in the whipped cream. Taste for sugar.

This filling can be used for tartlets, topping or filling cakes, but it is also a good dessert by itself, after it has been in the refrigerator for a while. Decorate with cream and/or chocolate vermicelli.

COFFEE CREAM FOR FILLINGS

110 g/4 oz butter at room temperature
icing sugar – to taste
1 egg yolk

1½ tablespoons instant coffee (or very strong real coffee)

Beat the butter until it is soft, add the yolk, the coffee and enough sugar to sweeten. Beat well and use for filling cakes or as a topping.

VARIATION   Add a handful of broken walnuts to the cream.

BUTTER CREAM FOR FILLINGS, PORTUGUESE STYLE

200 g/7 oz butter
2 egg yolks
175 g/6 oz icing sugar, sifted

flavouring (vanilla extract, lemon rind, etc. – to taste)

Mix the sugar with the butter and yolks. Beat well. Add the flavouring. Beat well again. It must be thoroughly creamy. Use as a filling for sponge cakes, as a topping for small or large cakes or to sandwich biscuits.

CUSTARD FOR FILLINGS, PORTUGUESE STYLE

300 ml/½ pint milk
2 large eggs (separated)
1 tablespoon cornflour

90 g/3 oz granulated sugar
flavouring – to taste

Mix the cornflour to a paste with some of the milk. Beat in the yolks, add the remaining milk, the sugar and chosen flavouring. Bring to the boil, stirring all the time and cook very gently until it thickens. Set aside while you beat the egg whites stiffly. Fold them into the custard. Use for filling sponge-type cakes, puff-pastry cases and mille-feuilles. It can also be served as a sauce for puddings and cooked or preserved fruit, in which case you can omit the tablespoon of cornflour.

PORTUGUESE WINES

Nothing filled him with more enthusiasm than the Tormes [Minho region] wine, poured from the green jug – a crisp, light, fragrant wine, with more soul and more soul-giving than many a poem or sacred book.

Eça de Queiroz, *The City and the Mountains*

Maybe palaeontologists are right in saying that the vine existed well before man. Certainly references to wine appear even in the oldest of documents, and it seems that the cultivation of vines and the making of wine were associated with the greatest civilizations of the past. It is generally accepted that when the Phoenicians and Romans established themselves in what would become the Portuguese nation they brought with them a great variety of vines and other plants. Whether or not this initial stock gave rise eventually to the grapes now grown in the country the fact is that there is an incredible variety of grapes in Portugal, some of which do not seem to occur elsewhere. Their quaint names are always guaranteed to amuse foreigners, who, of course, cannot pronounce them. For example, Trajadura, Viozinho, Esgana Cão, Rabo de Ovelha, Donzelinho, Borrado das Moscas, and so on. Dozens and dozens of them. Not surprisingly, Portuguese wines have been promoted with the slogan 'discover the variety'. They are unique and they are varied, because winemakers continue to tap into the natural rich variety of local grapes, though sometimes using also a few foreign ones (newly planted), such as Chardonnay or Merlot. These grapes, blended with indigenous ones, produce yet more varieties, adding to the already long catalogue of wines coming from Portugal.

It is said that it was the Crusaders who encouraged the first wine exports from Portugal. When stopping to help the Portuguese repel the Moors, they were impressed by the quality of the local wines and soon word got around. Nothing like a personal recommendation of this kind! Even Chaucer, the English poet (*c*.1340-1400), had something to say on the subject of Portuguese wines.

By the reign of King Fernando (1367-83), exports were already well established, albeit on an irregular basis. By the fifteenth century it was common practice to send to England wine from around Lisbon and the Minho region, long before the port wine trade as such had even been born.

From the beginning of the sixteenth century Portugal held a monopoly on the sale of spices and other precious merchandise from Brazil and the East. This forced foreign traders to visit Lisbon and Oporto to purchase these products, and consequently Portuguese wines became better known, especially among the English, who were the most assiduous in their commercial dealings with Portugal. This eventually caused English merchants to establish themselves in the Lisbon and Oporto areas and later to concentrate their efforts on the export of wine to England, once the profitable trade in spices had been diversified to countries other than Portugal.

The long Alliance (well over 600 years now) between England and Portugal, particularly through the Treaty of Methuen of 1703, helped consolidate the wine trade (though it had its ups and downs) and to establish the reputation of Portuguese wines and port. It is not within the scope of this book to enlarge on this, but it would be worthwhile reading elsewhere about England's fascinating involvement with Portugal through wines throughout the centuries.

The wine industry is highly regulated with codes of practice and demarcated or regional areas, according to types of wine produced and grapes used. Given the extraordinary number of different labels it would be impossible to mention here all those who deserve it, but I shall attempt to give an overview, among the best.

A few pearls of popular wisdom, regarding wines:
'Cheer up, belly – wine is coming!'
'Better to get drunk than to catch a cold.'
'Those who are old and eat soup with wine become young again.'
But also a word of warning:
'Run away from a bad neighbour and from excess of wine.'
'More men get drowned in a glass than at sea.'
'When drink comes in, wisdom gets out.'

PORT, MADEIRA AND OTHER FORTIFIED WINES

Fortified wines are called *licorosos* or *generosos*, by the Portuguese. Well, *generous* they certainly are, in their fullness, richness, depth and aroma. The country is blessed with a variety of such wines and no 'taste of Portugal' would be complete without their noble presence. First and foremost, Port comes to mind. This, 'The best Portuguese Ambassador', is over three centuries old and it grows along the Douro river, a region that was demarcated by the Marquis of Pombal in 1756 – the first region in the world to be protected in this way.

> 'A wine aged ninety.' . . . 'My grandfather inherited it.' . . . 'Senatorial port! we say. We cannot say that of any other wine. Port is deep-sea deep. It is in its flavour deep; mark the difference. It is like a classic tragedy, organic in conception.' . . . 'Port is our noblest legacy!' . . . 'I will say, that I am consoled for not having lived ninety years back, or at any other period but the present, by this one glass of your ancestral wine.'
>
> George Meredith, *The Egoist* (1879)

The above quote clearly endorses the accepted view that in the past port was considered 'the

Englishman's drink'. Although less so at present *vintage port* is still kept as a valuable heirloom or reserved for special auctions held at the best world market, namely London. Port is tightly regulated by law to prevent adulteration and unlimited production, and only up to half (sometimes less) of the grapes grown in the Douro are permitted for port itself, despite the fact that some vines give only around 1 kilo of grapes. From the tremendously difficult planting process, in stony slopes and terraces up the mountain, to the harvest and production of the wine itself, the whole operation reads like an epic yearly staged by the brave people who dare tame that land. There are around 40 varieties of grapes suitable for port and planted in the area, but in practice only 5 really dominate this wine: *Touriga Nacional, Touriga Francesa, Tinta Roriz, Tinta Barroca* and *Tinto Cão*.

There are various styles of port: the *White*, which can be sweet or dry and must be served cool, sometimes with a twist of lemon. It is good on its own but ideal as an aperitif, perhaps with olives and salty almonds. The *Ruby* is a blend of ports that have matured for 3 years in wood. It is young and spicy, with a lovely ruby colour. Good with cheese.

Then comes the *Vintage Character*, which is a blend of 4-year-old ports, and will improve if left in bottle to mature further. This is a more rounded port than the previous one and excellent with pâtés and other potted meats, or on its own.

The *Tawny* is again a blend that has been kept for longer in wood, acquiring a lighter yet rich colour and a lovely smooth quality. They often have an indication of age: 10, 20, 30 or 40 years old, and these are guaranteed to be excellent. When bottled, they are fully matured and therefore ready to drink. They are nice slightly chilled before or after a meal, or at any time. *Colheita* is another style, made from a single harvest. It is a tawny of high quality kept in wood for a minimum of 7 years. It is smooth and rich, very good with dried fruits and nuts. *Late Bottled Vintage*, or *LBV*, is again port from one single harvest, matured for 5 or 6 years in wood. It is a deep and complex wine and will improve if left in bottle. It may need decanting. A *Single Quinta Vintage* is from one estate only and a single harvest, treated as a vintage, i.e., matured in bottle after 2-3 years in wood. Like the Vintage it should be left for at least 10 years in bottle, to acquire its full potential. It must, therefore, be decanted. The *Vintage* style is port from a single harvest that has been declared as vintage due to its very high standard. It is kept in wood for 2 or 3 years and then bottled, continuing to mature practically forever. As it ages it gets much lighter in colour, with a beautiful amber and wonderful complexity. Leave it in bottle at least 10 years, although it might be better still after 20 or more. It must be decanted. Marvellous on its own, or with walnuts and cheese.

The choice of ports is vast and may cause some confusion when buying, but here are some distinguished producers: *Ferreira, Sandeman, Taylor's, Rozès, Ramos Pinto, Warre/Smith, Woodhouse/Dow's/Graham's (Symington Family), Messias, Real Companhia Velha, Cálem, Burmester, Offley, Quinta do Vale D. Maria, Quinta do Noval, Quinta do Crasto, Niepoort, Kopke, Fonseca, Delaforce/Croft* – among many others.

The next great fortified wine is Madeira, which is also known the world over. It has been produced since the 17th century and the grapes were planted in the island by orders of Prince Henry the Navigator himself, after the island was discovered and the land was prepared for cultivation – not only of vines, but also sugar cane, tropical fruits and flowers and a host of crops. Just as in the Douro, the terrain here is difficult to conquer and man-made terraces had to be carved for the vines. Land for this product is hard to come by and nowadays the island is reviewing its position in this regard.

The process involved in the production of Madeira wine is quite unique, consisting of a controlled fermentation and heating in special vats. This, and the ageing that follows, creates a characteristic wine full of aromas with a rich amber colour. The main grapes used are *verdelho, sercial, boal, malvasia, terrantez, moscatel* and a very prolific and accommodating grape called *negra mole*. There are a few other permitted varieties. Madeira wine is divided into four styles; the *Sercial*, or dry, is lighter in colour, balanced by enough acidity and a nutty taste. It is served chilled as an aperitif with or without light food. When old *Sercial* acquires a richer colour and aroma and is the preferred choice for many drinkers. *Verdelho* is the medium-dry style, a little darker than the previous one and greatly appreciated by Madeira wine lovers. It is smooth, fuller than the dry version and excellent also as an aperitif. Do not chill it. This is generally the wine used for special dishes calling for Madeira. Next on line is the *Boal*, medium-sweet. Many people prefer this to any other Madeira. It is rich and full, round and aromatic, ideal for drinking with friends. *Malvasia*, or *Malmsey*, is the fourth style, the sweetest of them all. It is velvety, highly aromatic, full of fruit. It goes extremely well with cakes, namely the honey cake from Madeira. All these wines are very flexible, due to their special maturation process and they will last for a long time after opening.

As with port, most meat dishes improve with the addition of a little Madeira, as well as sauces, fruit salads, other desserts and chocolate. It is also excellent for accompanying dishes prepared with delicate meats. The British have been involved with the production of Madeira wine from the start, just as happened in the Douro and to this day they still dominate the trade. But it is a small island and there are not too many producers. The ones with the highest profile are: *Blandy's, d'Oliveira's*, the grand *Henriques & Henriques, Barbeito, Cossart Gordon, Borges, Justino's* and *Broadbent*. Some producers are also trying their hand at table wines, at least for local consumption.

Moscatel (lovely with chocolate) from a DOC region in the Setúbal peninsula, south of Lisbon, is a splendid fortified wine quite popular in Portugal and unfortunately not very well known yet abroad. Being made with the grapes of the same name, *moscatel*, or *muscat*, this wine has a lovely amber colour, extraordinary aromas and a mouthful of raisins. Probably the best is the elegant *Alambre* by *José Maria da Fonseca*. Although there are a few more fortified wines in Portugal made in small quantities and more often than not consumed by those who prepare them, there is one kind which deserves to be mentioned. It is the '*vinho abafado licoroso*' of which the one exponent worth the highest praise is the lovely *Quinta da Alorna* made not with the muscat grape as one might think, but with the *Fernão Pires* grape. It is aged in cask for a long time and has a full bouquet of raisins with flavours to match. It is good at any time or to start – or finish – a meal.

The Azores has its own, albeit limited, wine production. There is a local passion for what is called '*vinho de cheiro*' (aromatic wine) which sure enough smells and tastes of ripe strawberries and is drunk with meals and is also widely used for cooking. More serious wines are the white *Terras de Lava* and the red *Basalto*, quite good in their own right, but the star of the Azorean wines is the fortified *verdelho Lajido*, from the *Pico Island* and coming direct in line from the *verdelhos* that used to enchant Russian Tzars, when this wine was also popular in other European countries and America. This is dry, pale amber wine, with a strong aroma and complex overtones, good at any time but especially as an aperitif. This wine is now being revived after years of neglect. *Verdelho* from *Biscoitos*, also in the Azores, is equally excellent.

TABLE WINES

Despite the fact that the world has been literally flooded with wines from everywhere, their character does not always seem to differ that much from each other, as they more or less depend on the characteristics given by a relatively restricted number of grape varieties.

Portugal is lucky on this score: it's small area manages to merge favourable micro-climates and terroir, together with an incredible abundance of very interesting, 'different' native grapes: an irresistible combination. The appeal and uniqueness of Portuguese wines derives mainly from the intriguing character of those grapes, skillfully highlighted by very resourceful, well-schooled winemakers (men and women), who are working wonders up and down the country.

MINHO is the first area to consider. This is *Vinho Verde* region. *Verde* (green) does not imply colour, it simply means that the wines must be drunk while young. Most are white, light and zesty, low in alcohol, having sometimes a hint of fizz. They should be served cool and go well with light food, fish or just by themselves. Depending on the grapes used (Alvarinho and Loureiro are the best) they differ in character – some more lemony, some more floral – but they are all delightful. Some 'espumante' (sparkling) types are now being made here, as well.

The main estates in the lush Minho region are Quinta da Franqueira, Aveleda, Quinta de Ferro, Vila Beatriz, Quinta de Azevedo, Quinta do Soalheiro, Quinta da Lixa, Quinta das Carvalhas, Quinta do Reguengo, Quinta de Paços, Casa de Sezim, Quinta de Simães, Casa de Cello, Quinta de Tapada, Quinta de Melgaço, Quinta da Boavista, Quinta do Ameal, Casa do Paço, Quinta de Santa Maria, Quinta de Covela and a few good Cooperatives (i.e. PROVAM, Monção and Ponte de Lima).

TRÁS-OS-MONTES (meaning 'beyond the Mountains') region embraces part of *Douro* (port wine) and many of its Houses are located there, so they will be included in the next paragraph. The challenging rocky soil in Trás-os-Montes signifies low yields but means also deep, rich red wines, such as those from Casal de Valle Pradinhos and Quinta do Sobreiro de Cima.

DOURO (port 'country' par excellence) is the next region. It goes from near Oporto, all along the River Douro, across the country. Although there were always some worthy exceptions, port producers weren't particularly focused on table wines in the past. However, the last two decades (mostly the last decade) have seen a revolutionary approach towards the potential of their table wines. The *Douro Movement* (as some started to call it) meant a concerted effort to produce table wines as good as their counterparts. The *Douro Movement* (also known as the *New Douro Group*) embraces practically all of the most enthusiastic and dynamic producers, generously sharing ideas and resources, such as the Symington Family (the most extensive estate owners here, as well as in Madeira Island), Quinta do Crasto, Quinta de S. Luiz, Alves de Sousa, Quinta do Portal, Quinta Nova, Quinta de la Rosa, CARM (a great olive oil producer, as well), Rozès, Ramos Pinto, Quinta do Infantado, Quinta da Casa Amarela, Quinta do Cotto, Quinta da Pacheca, Lavradores de Feitoria, Churchill's, Quinta da Gaivosa, Quinta do Roriz, Quinta do Vale Meão, Quinta do Vale Dona Maria, Niepoort, Quinta do Vallado, Quinta das Carvalhas – among others.

Although they all work incredibly hard (as they must, in that spectacular but uniquely difficult region), five of them have become exceptionally involved, literally making the country stand up and listen. They are known as *The Douro Boys*, namely Quinta do Vale Dona Maria (Van Zellers & Co.), Niepoort, Quinta do Vallado, Quinta do Crasto and Quinta do Vale Meão. Dirk Niepoort and Cristiano van Zeller were in fact the main catalysts for the profound Douro transformation – always engaged in endless projects to improve the industry.

BAIRRADA (Beira Litoral) region is where the 'espumantes' (champagne-type) come from, in Portugal (see Sparkling Wines, p.219). Most of these estates make really interesting table wines, as well – many of them white though reds are also top quality (ideal for the local suckling pig). The most prominent name here at present is Luis Pato, with a large portfolio of labels. Others are: Adega Cooperativa de Cantanhede, Quinta do Poço do Lobo, Campolargo, Quinta das Bageiras, Quinta de Baixo, Caves Messias, Casa de Saima, Quinta do Encontro, Caves do Solar de S. Domingos, Caves de São João, Caves Aliança (with estates in various other regions, too).

DÃO is a classic region for wines that are splendid with food. It has risen also to the general call for improved techniques and some of its main producers are: Quinta da Aguieira (Borges), Quinta dos Roques, Co-op UDACA, Casa de Darei, Quinta da Ponte Pedrinha, Quinta dos Carvalhais (Sogrape), Boas Quintas, Quinta de Sães, Quinta das Maias, Quinta do Perdigão, Quinta da Vegia, Quinta da Pellada, Dão Sul, (Quinta de Cabriz, Casa de Santar), Quinta da Bica, Aliança, Casa do Insua.

BEIRA INTERIOR, an inland region just like Dão, offers a good variety of wines, dominated by Cooperatives: Covilhã, Figueira de Castelo Rodrigo, Fundão and Pinhel. Other producers are: Rogenda, Quinta Foz de Arouce, Almeida Garrett (Sabe), Quinta do Cardo, Vinhos Andrade de Almeida, Quinta dos Termos, Murganheira, Mateus & Co., Quinta dos Cozinheiros.

ESTREMADURA region used to be known mainly for its Bucelas, Colares and Carcavelos wines. That area along the coast is too near Lisbon to be able to retain all the necessary land for that purpose, although it still manages some production. However, Estremadura has other horizons away from the coast, so all is well… The main producers (embracing the whole region) are: Quinta da Murta, Quinta da Romeira, Adega Regional de Colares, Adega Co-op Dois Portos, Sociedade do Formigal, Adega Co-op Arruda dos Vinhos, Companhia Agrícola do Sanguinhal, Quinta dos Loridos, Quinta dos Pesos, Quinta do Monte d'Oiro, Quinta do Gradil, Quinta de Pancas, Quinta do Carneiro, Agrovitis, Quinta de Chocapalha (its owners are Sandra Tavares da Silva's parents, winemaker at Quinta do Vale D. Maria, Douro. She makes the wine for her parents, too – a great bonus), Quinta da Cortezia, Palha Canas, Quinta da Abrigada, Quinta de Parrotes, Casa de Santos Lima, Quinta da Folgorosa, Adega Co-op de Torres Vedras.

RIBATEJO is an extensive province, with enough wine areas – some sharing the Tagus river valley with a lot of agriculture and pasture. But Cartaxo, Alpiarça, Almeirim, Tramagal and Benfica do Ribatejo, for example, more than make up for that. Producers from the Ribatejo are among the best: Falua (João Portugal Ramos), Casa Agrícola Dom Luis Margaride, Pinhal da Torre, the impeccable Quinta de Alorna, Quinta do Casal Branco, Encosta do Sobral, Caves Velhas, Quinta da Ribeirinha, Quinta da Lagoalva, Vale d'Algares, Quinta do Cavalinho, Quinta da Fonte Bela (winemaker José Neiva), Quinta Casal de Coelheira, Fiuza, Quinta do Falcão, Casa Cadaval, Casal de Monteiro, Quinta Vale de Fornos and Adega Co-op Benfica do Ribatejo. They all produce whites and reds.

TERRAS DO SADO region is south of Lisbon (taking in Setúbal Peninsula). Despite shrinking land it maintains its hallmark *Moscatel* (see Fortified Wines p.213). The region offers magnificent table wines as well, mainly by Bacalhoa Vinhos de Portugal (of Tinto da Anfora fame), José Maria da Fonseca, Casa Ermelinda Freitas, Romeira, Adega Co-op de Palmela, Sociedade Agrícola de Pegos Claros, Quinta de Camarate and Co-op. Sto. Isidro de Pegões.

Next we come to the vastness of the two ALENTEJOS. Some of the estates are vast, as well – such as Herdade do Esporão, with very good labels and also excellent olive oil. Other producers are: Herdade da Malhadinha Nova, Herdade das Anforas, Encosta do Guadiana, Herdade do Mouchão, João Portugal Ramos (a great name in the country), Fundação Eugénio de Almeida (a Trust, famous for its Pera Manca and Cartuxa labels), Quinta do Carmo, Herdade dos Coelheiros, Herdade dos Grous, Roquevale, Herdade da Vidigueira e Monsaraz, Co-ops (of Borba/Redondo/Portalegre), Quinta do

Centro, Herdade da Mingorra, Cortes de Cima and Herdade do Peso (Sogrape).

ALGARVE is the last region to be mentioned in the context of Portuguese Table Wines. This wasn't a very exciting region up to now, but that is changing and a few names give it good credence, like Quinta dos Correias, Quinta do Morgado da Torre, Quinta de Barranco Longo and Adega do Cantor (*The Singer's Winery*), owned by Sir Cliff Richard and very popular. The climate here favours whites (high in alcohol) but there are some good reds and rosés, as well.

SPARKLING WINES

In the Bairrada region (South of Douro and North of Estremadura), the climate, soil and type of grapes growing there (mainly the so-called *Bical*) are all very propitious for the production of sparkling wines and, although they cannot sport the name of 'champagne' some are actually quite good, in their own right.

They call them *Espumante* (Foamy). In olden times, there used to be only a handful of *Espumante* producers, but at present there are many more, all very keen to improve still further. For example: Caves Aliança, Caves Messias, Quinta das Bageiras, Luis Pato, Caves de S. Domingos, Adega Cooperativa de Cantanhede, Filipa Pato, Caves de São João and Raposeira. Many of them also excel in table wines.

CONTACTS AND OTHER INFORMATION RELATING TO WINES

The main and splendid source is *Viniportugal*. It is an organization sponsored by the producers and the EU, working tirelessly for the improvement of the industry, organizing wine tastings in various countries and maintaining a detailed website with everything the public (and the professionals) may be interested in, such as grape varieties, regions, wine routes, suppliers and so on. *Viniportugal* has two permanent showrooms, as well, in Lisbon and in Oporto. These are called OGIVAL and offer free tastings, as well as a good display of wines (which can be purchased there at a discount).

Website: www.viniportugal.pt/index-en

SALA OGIVAL, Praça do Comércio, Lisbon (opposite the Tagus river) and SALA OGIVAL, Palácio da Bolsa (Old Stock Exchange, Oporto – a most beautiful building in the centre of the city).

Sites with interesting information on grape varieties, tasting notes (by experts) and other details:
www.wineanorak.com/portugal
www.agoodnose.com/index
www.thewinedetective.co.uk/portugal
www.portugal-info.net/wines

www.douroboys.com/dossier (these and other producers will be happy to show their installations and some can provide accommodation – which must be booked. See also USEFUL INFORMATION before the Index, as some of the sites also give details on where to stay).

Note that in Oporto and Gaia (opposite that city) there are various Port Lodges open to visitors.

Boat trips along the river Douro can be arranged through www.douracima.pt and www.douroazul.com

Special train journeys (some quite unique) – Details from the Railway Authority (www.cp.pt) and sites given in Useful Information.

Wine Tours arranged by a company based in the US: La Dolce Vita Tours, Inc. N. York – www.dolcetours.com/ep_port.htm

ONION AND PORT COMFIT
Comfit de Cebola e Porto

This very original recipe was given to me by Joana van Zeller (from Quinta Vale D. Maria). Easy to prepare (you just allow things to boil for a long time), this kind of condiment, with a compôte texture, is good to serve by the spoonful with all sorts of roasts, pâtés, game and of course cold and smoked meats.

10 medium onions, peeled and cut into fine rings	6 tablespoons of olive oil (mild)
1 bottle of Vintage or LBV port	salt and pepper

Use a deep, thick-bottomed pot. Place over the heat. When warm, add the oil. When it starts sizzling add the onion rings, turn them over several times to coat them with the oil, and fry very gently for about two hours, whilst adding the wine, little by little.

Season with salt and pepper and cook until you get a thick jelly-compôte-like dark and perfumed mixture. Taste. Keep in jars, in the fridge, or leave just one jar for use and freeze the rest.

PARTRIDGES WITH PORT AND MUSCAT GRAPES
Perdizes com Porto e Uvas Moscatel
Serves 4

This is a speciality from Quinta Vale D. Maria. They prefer to use wild partridges, but of course you can use farmed ones.

4 partridges, plucked and cleaned

1 bottle of Vintage or LBV port

4 tablespoons each of mild olive oil and butter

1 large mild onion, cut into rings

24 muscat grapes (washed, dried and free from seeds)

Marinate the birds from the previous day in the wine, with some salt and pepper. Turn them once or twice. For cooking, drain them and fill the upper cavity with 6 grapes each. Close with tooth-picks or string. Use a large pot. Fry the onion until transparent in the fats, then set it aside. Fry the partridges in the same fats, all over, until golden. Return the onion to the pot, season a little and add the marinade. Cook really slowly for two hours. You may find that the birds are nice and tender before that – please test. Rectify seasoning and serve with white rice.

MULLED PORT
Porto Quente
OPORTO REGION

This rather grand recipe uses only port and brandy, which may be excused, as this is intended for Christmas Eve supper as well as New Year's Eve. If it is cold outside, this special brew will put life into any wavering soul.

450 ml/¾ pint good sweet port

1 tablespoon brown sugar or good honey

3 tablespoons raisins without seeds (or sultanas)

1 cinnamon stick

2 tablespoons brandy

Soak all the ingredients for half an hour in a saucepan. Then bring to the boil and simmer for 2 minutes, serving immediately in cups, with a ladle.

Apart from mulled port one can also include port in a number of dishes and the Ramos Pinto family has an old 'in house' recipe book which is a little treasure. It recommends adding 1 small glass of port to most meat dishes as well as fruit salads, of course – especially, they say, a melon which is cut in half, cleaned of all seeds, sprinkled with sugar and filled with some port in the centre. It must be served well chilled, a couple of hours after being prepared, to bring out all the aromas. They also add a small glass of port to their crème brûlée, whilst cooking, and do the same to cakes and puddings. This is their recipe for Port-Flip:

1 egg yolk

2 teaspoons of sugar

2 to 3 tablespoons of port

(1 serving)

Beat very well all ingredients in a cup and . . . drink. Heavenly.

MULLED WINE
Vinho Quente
MINHO AND DOURO PROVINCES

'I have already chosen my task,' said the councillor, grabbing a spoon from Christina's hands, while she was preparing the mulled wine, that national punch which it would have been disastrous not to have included in that very special meal [at Christmas].

Júlio Diniz, *A Morgadinha dos Canaviais* (*The Lady of the Reeds*)

300 ml/½ pint port	200 g/7 oz sugar
300 ml/½ pint light red wine	6 eggs
300 ml/½ pint Madeira	900 ml/1½ pints water

Bring the water to the boil in a large pan. Add the Madeira and the light red wine, and allow to reach boiling point. Using a separate container, beat the eggs vigorously with the sugar. Add some of the hot wine to the egg mixture, beat again, then add this to the rest of the hot wine. Bring once more to the boil, stirring, and once this point is reached remove from the heat. Now add the port and mix very well. It should be sweet enough, but you can add more sugar to taste. Strain and put aside until it is time to serve the punch.

To serve, warm it up in a bain-marie. For this, put the pan containing the wine mixture inside a bigger pan which must contain boiling water, put this over a low flame to keep a gentle bubbling until the punch is hot enough. The bain-marie method is necessary to avoid curdling the eggs, but do stir the mixture now and then, while reheating. Pour into cups with a ladle. Some people take this drink with small pieces of bread dipped into it.

Serve to round off Christmas Eve supper, after Midnight Mass.

LIQUEURS AND SPIRITS

Since alcoholic drinks are so important to complement meals, it is customary in Portugal to serve a little something with the coffee, as the perfect finish to a special meal. The ladies may be given a small glass of liqueur, but the men will plump either for *bagaceira* (a white spirit, very much like eau-de-vie) or a good *aguardente* (brandy) aged for a long time. There are various such *aguardentes*, rich and aromatic, with a lovely amber colour. Two of the very best are *Aguardente Velha Reserva* (*José Maria da Fonseca*) and *Adega Velha* (*Avelleda*). Most Portuguese households also make their own liqueurs, with recipes handed down from mother to daughter. It is easy enough in Portugal to obtain alcohol as a base from these liqueurs, using either *bagaceira*, *aguardente* or even *pure alcohol*, available over the counter at chemists. This pure alcohol has no taste at all (perfect for the purpose) and is about 96% proof, which means that it can be diluted a lot. Liqueurs have a strength of between 25% and 40%, more or less, according to taste. If you would like to try some of the recipes that follow and cannot find alcohol, *aguardente* or *bagaceira*, try and substitute these by vodka or brandy. When the recipes indicate clarification it is better to follow the procedure, although this is not always necessary if the ingredients do not cloud the mixture.

CLARIFICATION After the maceration or infusion period has elapsed, pour into the bottle the white and crushed shell of one egg. Shake hard, to mix well, and leave to stand for 2-3 days. By then there will be a lot of sediment in the bottom. Without disturbing the liquid too much filter it into another container using paper filter. Stand again for one or two days. You may need to strain the liqueur again but then you will have a beautifully clear liqueur ready for bottling a tight-fitting decanter or any nice bottle with a good cork. However, most liqueurs will be fine just filtering once or twice.

MORELLO CHERRY LIQUEUR
Ginjinha or *Ginja em Aguardente*

Ginjinha is widely made at home in Portugal, but it is also made commercially and sold at every wine bar and restaurant. '*Ginjinha*' is the popular name for '*Ginja em Aguardente*' – the Portuguese are very fond of using the diminutive for anything they like or which is dainty or homely. *Ginjinha* is perhaps the most traditional Portuguese liqueur, even mentioned in popular songs. If morello cherries are available, it is possible to make ginjinha outside Portugal without any difficulty (using brandy if not *aguardente*, see p.222).

450 g/1 lb very sound morello cherries
200 g/7 oz sugar
1 clove

1 cinnamon stick
enough spirits to cover the fruit, about 450 ml
(¾ pint)

Wash the cherries, dry them and discard the stems but do not stone them. Place the fruit in a liqueur bottle (with a widish mouth), cover with the sugar, the spices and the chosen spirits. Put in a suitably sized cork or the bottle's own stopper, very carefully, to ensure that no air at all gets into the bottle. Put it in a dark place, shaking daily for the first week, then leave to stand. It will be ready in 3 months but it is much better if left for nearly a year. A few cherries are served inside each glass of ginjinha.

NOTE Even if morello cherries are not available you can make this liqueur, using ordinary cherries and a little less sugar.

MILK LIQUEUR
Licor de Leite

This is a rich, thick and spicy liqueur, of which there are two main versions.

600 ml/1 pint spirits (*aguardente* or brandy)
600 ml/1 pint milk (cold)
450 g/1 lb sugar
1 clove

¼ vanilla pod, cut into small pieces
1 medium lemon, thinly sliced (with the rind) –
 wash it first
1 tablespoon ground almonds

Discard any pips from the lemon slices (but use all the juice that may drop while slicing it). Place all the ingredients in a wide-mouthed bottle or jar and cover very tightly. Leave it to macerate for 8 weeks, shaking the bottle twice a week. Clarify and filter as indicated on p.223 before bottling and corking well.

VARIATION

600 ml/1 pint cold milk
600 ml/1 pint spirits, as above
280 g/10 oz sugar

1 vanilla pod, cut in pieces
1 whole nutmeg
1 lemon, cut in pieces

Proceed as above. After 6-8 weeks it will be ready to filter and bottle.

COCOA LIQUEUR
Licor de Cacau

Another popular liqueur made by Portuguese housewives.

300 ml/½ pint spirits (vodka/*aguardente*/brandy)
280 g/10 oz sugar
300 ml/½ pint water

100 g/3½ oz powdered pure cocoa
½ vanilla pod, cut into pieces

Place the sugar, water and vanilla in a pan. Bring to the boil for just a minute. Whilst still warm, add the spirits and the cocoa. Mix well and put in a bottle to macerate for two weeks. Clarify (p.223), filter and bottle.

ANISEED LIQUEUR
Licor de Erva-Doce

This aromatic liqueur is a favourite of mine. My mother used to be a great specialist at it. It improves with age, like most liqueurs, and if well made it is just like any very good bought liqueur.

350 g/12 oz sugar
300 ml/½ pint spirits (vodka/*aguardente*/brandy)

300 ml/½ pint water
½ oz (15 g) aniseed, crushed

Place the spirits in a jar or bottle with the aniseed, cover tightly and leave for 3-4 days, to draw all the flavour. Then prepare a syrup with the water and sugar, until it thickens a little (about 2-3 minutes, over low heat). When the syrup is almost cold, pour it into the bottle, mix well with the spirits and seeds and leave for 3-4 weeks, shaking it during the first 3-4 days only. Clarify (p.223), filter and bottle.

NOTE If you cannot find aniseed, try this liqueur using 3 star anise.

COFFEE LIQUEUR
Licor de Café

Another popular liqueur, at least in more old-fashioned households.

120 ml/4 fl oz water
450 ml/¾ pint spirits (*aguardente* or brandy)
450 g/1 lb sugar

2 tablespoons of very aromatic freshly ground coffee (not the instant variety!)

Place the spirits in a bottle or jar and mix in the coffee, which must have been ground just prior to using. Leave for 2 weeks, shaking the bottle 3 times a week. Prepare a syrup with the water and sugar, boiling just for a minute. Cool and add to the bottle. Shake well. Leave to stand again for 2 or 3 days. Clarify, filter (p.223) and bottle.

TANGERINE LIQUEUR
Licor de Tangerina

Wonderfully fragrant, this liqueur is also excellent for flavouring cakes, puddings and fruit salads, and as an aid to digestion (hence very appropriate to serve after a meal).

600 ml/1 pint spirits (vodka, *aguardente, bagaceira* or brandy)
rind of 5 medium-sized tangerines (or clementines or mandarins)

juice of 3 of the fruits used (strained)
600 ml/1 pint water
350 g/12 oz sugar

Macerate the rind, juice and spirits for 3 weeks. After that add a syrup made with the water and sugar, boiled for 2-3 minutes and cooled. Mix well. Leave to stand for 2-3 days. Filter and bottle.

NOTE When cutting the rind of the chosen fruit, take care to use only the fine, zesty part of it.

USEFUL INFORMATION

Nowadays it should be possible to buy most of the ingredients needed for Portuguese traditional cuisine anywhere in the world. Except those special pork products already mentioned (some of which can be substituted for prosciutto and pancetta, for an approximate taste), and salt cod. The real thing, as well as certain much loved spices like aniseed (grain and powder), and that lovely quince cheese (*marmelada*), apart from various other yummy titbits... can only be obtained at Portuguese shops. If visiting Portugal itself, stock up on all you can, at any good supermarket or even after you check-in at Lisbon's airport where you will find a good selection of fine foods for yourself or as presents. Please bring back some cheeses, for example, but try also less well-known – and unmissable – things like spiced cashew nuts, fried broad-beans (dried), Elvas plums, crystallized fruits, bean tarts (*pastéis de feijão* from Torres Vedras – something to die for...), canned fish.

In Britain, London is the best place for Portuguese shops, although there are a few in towns where there is a large concentration of Portuguese people. These are the main ones, in London:

LISBOA DELI – This is the best and one of the oldest – at 54 Golborne Road, W10 (off the Portobello Road), and opposite, their magical patisserie, with really well-made *pastéis de nata* (those divine 'custard tarts') and many other cakes, as well as good snacks and coffee. They do have various other outlets under the same name, in London.

DELICIAS DE PORTUGAL – Is a good general store and also has various outlets, one of them very handy, at 43 Warwick Way, SW1 (Victoria).

FERREIRA MINI-MARKET – Is small but well stocked and has only one shop, at 40 Delancey St. NW1 (Camden Town).

For bulk buying it is worth consulting www.atlantico.co.uk

In the USA there are some good specialist shops, selling direct or online (or both), such as:

SEABRA's SUPERMARKET – 260 Lafayette St. – Newark, NJ (973)589-8606 and www.seabrasupermarket.com

www.portuguesefood.com (good range – sales online)

LOPES SAUSAGE, 304 Walnut Street – Newark, NJ 07105 (973) 344-3063

POPULAR FISH MARKET – 129 Ferry Street, Newark, NJ 071105 – (973)344-7939

MELLO'S NORTH END – 63 North Court St., Fall River, MA 02720 (800) 673-2320 – also www.melloschourico.com

AMARAL'S – Lisbon Sausage Co.Inc., 433 South Second St., New Bedford, MA 02740 – (800)7257 – also www.amarals.com

OTHER INTERESTING CONTACTS

www.lusoamericano.com

This is a useful online newspaper for the Portuguese community in the USA. It also has a splendid bookshop with books on all subjects relating to Portugal (in English and Portuguese) at 66 Union Street, Newark, New Jersey.

If visiting Portugal, don't forget that the country has much more to offer than just beaches and golf.

In fact, the variety and richness of pursuits available within such a small space is astonishing and the only problem is one of time to see all that may interest you. So, to facilitate your choices and have at hand all the details needed to organize your visit beforehand, here are a few ideas:

For the widest range possible of activities and local general information, such as fishing, horse riding, water sports, flower (and other) trails, Natural Parks and Reserves, railways and narrow gauge railways (Douro), visits to places like the Foz Coa World Heritage Site (dating from the Stone Age), Manor House and other places to stay and much more, consult www.iknowportugal.com

Foz Coa (something exceptionally interesting) also has its own site: www.ipa.min-cultura.pt/pavc (email for booking visits is: visitas.pavc@ipa.min-cultura.pt).

One of the most fascinating places you can visit is Porto (Oporto), the country's second city, (www.gooporto.com), and its environs: (Gaia, Matozinhos, Leça da Palmeira), all with excellent fish restaurants. Porto has metro, tram and buses, as well as river connections and the train taking you up the Douro (S.Bento Station is a gem, with wonderful tiles). There is so much to see... City tours are a good idea: www.en.dianatours.pt

Other sources of information you may want to look into include:

www.taste-portugal.com (on the main products – food and wine, cheese, etc.,), recipes, olive oil, salt, land products. Official site.

www.portugal-info.net – Gives useful general information on most aspects, from history to food and where to stay.

www.visitportugal.com/pturismo is a very good official site giving also general information, complementing similar sites.

www.festivalnacionaldegastronomia.com (Santarem Food Festival)

www.portugal-sport-and-adventure.com concentrates on activities but offers alternatives worth considering.

Also www.portugaltravelguide.com/en and en.lifecooler.com

Anyone interested in the Lusitano horse will want to look up www.lusobreedsociety.co.uk and perhaps read the masterly written '*The Royal Horse of Europe*' – by Sylvia Loch, Pub.J.A.Allen

Specific sites for the Azores and Madeira Islands, are: www.azores.com, www.madeira-tourist.com

If going just to the Lisbon area and city, look up: www.golisbon.com/culture/history and all kinds of other details, like the best central cafés and patisseries.

www.lisbonguide.net/do/culture/museums is a good guide and shows you the way to the museums not to be missed in the capital: The Tile Museum, The Gulbenkian, Ancient Art, Musical Instruments, Chiado, etc. And walk to the very centre (Praça do Comércio, facing the river), to visit the Lisbon Welcome Centre, which has a good information desk plus shops, café, restaurant and gallery.

All of the above cover a lot although not all the places one might like to visit, but should help... Regarding wines and wine routes, please see the wines chapter of this book.

Travellers to Portugal will find very good information in the Eyewitness Travel Guide, The Rough Guide, Lonely Planet and others, as well as the comprehensive Wine and Food Lover's Guide to Portugal (C. Metcalfe & K. McWhirter).

LIST OF VEGETARIAN RECIPES

The following are recipes which are strictly vegetarian:

Soups
Chickpea Soup/*Sopa de Grão and Variation* (p.45)
Bean and Cabbage Soup/*Sopa de Feijão* (p.45)
Vegetable Purée/*Sopa de Legumes* (pp.46-7)
Tomato, Egg and Bread Soup/*Sopa de Tomate com Ovo e Pão* (pp.47-8)
Green Bean Soup with Tomato/*Sopa de Feijão Verde com Tomate* and Variation (p.48)
Dried Chestnut Soup/*Sopa de Castanhas Piladas* (pp.48-9)
Cornmeal Porridge/*Papas de Milho* (p.49)

Bread Dishes
Bread-Pap/*Açorda* (p.52)
Coriander Bread Soup/*Açorda Alentejana* (p.53)
Agorda Madeira Style/*Açorda Madeirense* (p.56)
Migas Ribatejo Style/*Migas do Ribatejo* (p.57)
Migas Beira Litoral Style/*Migas à Moda da Beira Litoral* (pp.57-8)
Garlic Dry Soup/*Sopa Seca de Alho* (p. 61)
Gaspachos (p.62)

Sauces
Tomato Sauce/*Molho de Tomate* (p.129)
Villain Sauce/*Molho de Vilão* (p.130)
Mayonnaise (p.133)
Beirão Style Sauce/*Molho Beirão* (p.133)

Other Dishes
Little Fish from the Garden/*Peixinhos da Horta* (p.134)
Black-eyed Beans Salad/*Salada de Feijão Frade* and Variation (p.136)
Stewed Green Beans/*Feijão Verde Guisado* (pp.136-8)
Green Mousse/*Esparregado* and Variation (p.138)
Tomato Rice/*Arroz de Tomate* and Variations (p.143) *
Rich Broad Beans/*Fava Rica* (p.140)
Broad Beans with Coriander/*Favas com Coentros* (p.140)
Broad Beans with Yellow Sauce/*Favas com Molho Amarelo* (p.142)
Broad Beans with Olive Oil/*Favas com Azeite* (p.143)

All Sweet Things recipes (p.131 to p.201) except:

Priscos Parish Priest Pudding/ *Pudim do Abade de Priscos* (p.155), Dry Sweet Soup/ *Sopa Seca Doce* (p.158) and Blancmange/ *Manjar Branco* (p.161)

These recipes may be successfully adapted to vegetarian dishes as indicated below:

Soups

Green Broth/ *Caldo Verde* and Variations (pp.34-6) – omitting *chouriço* slices
Broad Bean Soup/ *Sopa de Favas* (p.46) – omitting ham
Pea Soup/ *Sopa de Puré de Ervilhas* (p.46) – omitting ham

Bread Dishes

Migas Beira Baixa Style/ *Migas à Beira Baixa* (p.58) – omitting pork meat

Other Dishes

Bean Stew/ *Feijoada* (pp.102-4) – omitting pork meat
Peas with Smoked Sausage/ *Paio com Ervilhas* (p.115) – omitting the pork meat
Stewed Wild Mushrooms/ *Cogumelos Guisados* (pp.138-9) – omitting bacon
Broad Beans Lisbon Fashion/ *Favas à Moda de Lisboa* (pp.140-2) – omitting pork meat

INDEX

ACKNOWLEDGEMENTS

Previous acknowledgements, at the beginning of this book (page 5) are still very much in order. However, after another twelve years, it is only fair that I reiterate my great appreciation for the continuous encouragement given to me by my family and friends, as well as by many others, although, even so, I am acutely aware that there will be omissions – for which I humbly apologise.

Sincere thanks are due to Paul Richardson, who has followed this book from the start and remains touchingly faithful; to David Burnett; to the BBC (whose praise means a lot to me); former journalist colleagues, for their many articles; to the late Alan Davidson for his endorsement (*Oxford Companion to Food*) and lovely review (*Petit Propos Culinaires*); to a long list of writers, who either noted the book in their bibliography or quoted recipes in various articles, such as: Nigel Slater, Hugo Arnold, Brian Glover, Marie-Pierre Moine, Marion Kaplan, Loyd Grossman, Charles Metcalfe, Clarissa Dickson Wright, Philippa Davenport, David Leite (USA), Sophie Grigson, and of course Frances Bissell, whose kind words were very much appreciated.

Many thanks also to various publishers who recommended the book as "essential reading" (i.e. *The Lonely Planet, The Rough Guide, Insight Guide*).

And finally, but not least, my deep gratitude to Grub Street Publishers (Anne Dolamore, John Davies and their kind team), who took on the book in 1995 with great enthusiasm and continue to be its most trusted and steadfast allies.